It is remarkable that recent theoretical developments in narratology have bypassed poetic narrative, concentrating almost exclusively on prose fiction. Clare Kinney's original study aims to redress the balance by exploring the distinctive narrative strategies of fictions which unfold in the artificial and self-conscious schemes of language bound by poetic form. She illuminates the ways in which poetic narratives exploit a simultaneous attraction to both lyric and narrative poles of discourse to complicate their conclusions. Kinney's close reading of three sophisticated poetic narratives, Chaucer's *Troilus and Criseyde*, Book VI of Spenser's *The Faerie Queene*, and Milton's *Paradise Lost*, suggests that these diverse works are united by a common tendency to exploit the alternative patterns of lyric in order to defer undesirable conclusions and offer subversive counterplots. Her final exploration of Eliot's *The Waste Land* as poetic "anti-narrative" leads into a consideration of the ways in which poetic fictions employ their various, inherently double designs – in particular their ability to invoke the resources of lyric – to pre-empt unhappy endings. Emerging from this study is the conclusion that it is a defining characteristic of poetic narrative to redouble the poet's and the reader's vision: to tell at least two stories at once.

STRATEGIES OF POETIC NARRATIVE

STRATEGIES OF POETIC NARRATIVE

Chaucer, Spenser, Milton, Eliot

CLARE REGAN KINNEY

Associate Professor of English, University of Virginia

CAMBRIDGE
UNIVERSITY PRESS

CAMBRIDGE UNIVERSITY PRESS
Cambridge, New York, Melbourne, Madrid, Cape Town, Singapore, São Paulo, Delhi

Cambridge University Press
The Edinburgh Building, Cambridge CB2 8RU, UK

Published in the United States of America by Cambridge University Press, New York

www.cambridge.org
Information on this title: www.cambridge.org/9780521107808

First published 1992
This digitally printed version 2009

A catalogue record for this publication is available from the British Library

Library of Congress Cataloguing in Publication data

Kinney, Clare Regan.
Strategies of poetic narrative: Chaucer, Spenser, Milton, Eliot
Clare Regan Kinney.
p. cm.
Includes bibliographical references and index.
ISBN 0 521 40542 4
1. Narrative poetry, English – History and criticism. 2. Chaucer.
Geoffrey, d. 1400 – Technique. 3. Spenser, Edmund, 1552?–1599
Technique. 4. Milton, John, 1608–1674 – Technique. 5. Eliot, T. S. (Thomas
Stearns), 1888-1965 – Technique. 6. Narration (Rhetoric)
I. Title.
PR509.N3K56 1992
821′.0309–dc20 91-30821 CIP

ISBN 978-0-521-40542-3 hardback
ISBN 978-0-521-110780-8 paperback

For my parents

Contents

Acknowledgments

My interest in poetic narrative was first excited by two of my teachers, John Hollander and Maureen Quilligan. I am indebted to the former for turning my attention to the narrative dynamics of verse fictions, and to the latter for entangling me in the "endlesse traine" of *The Faerie Queene*. The earlier stages of my project profited from the generous criticism and keen ear of Marie Borroff. Margaret Ferguson offered unsparing support and crucial advice at both the beginning and end of my labors. I also owe thanks to Gordon Braden, Lars Engle, Alastair Fowler, John Guillory, Dan Kinney, Holly Laird, Katharine Maus, and R. Allen Shoaf for their helpful comments on various portions (and various avatars) of my manuscript. I am especially grateful to Mark Edmundson, for his encouragement, and to Pat Gill, for her solicitude, her wit, and her friendship.

The final revisions of this book were completed with the help of a Sesquicentennial Fellowship from the University of Virginia. Peggy Gibson and Ida Gordon both assisted me in the later stages of manuscript preparation and Peggy Gartner was indefatigable in checking my references. A portion of chapter 5 was first published in *The Journal of Narrative Technique* 17 (1987); it is reprinted here by kind permission of the editors of that periodical. My concluding thanks go to Kevin Taylor of Cambridge University Press for his advocacy, advice, and editorial acumen.

Abbreviations

ChauR	*The Chaucer Review*
ELH	*English Literary History*
ELR	*English Literary Renaissance*
MLN	*Modern Language Notes*
MP	*Modern Philology*
NLH	*New Literary History*
PMLA	*Publications of the Modern Language Association of America*
PLL	*Papers in Language and Literature*
PQ	*Philological Quarterly*
RES	*Review of English Studies*
SEL	*Studies in English Literature, 1500–1900*
UTQ	*University of Toronto Quarterly*
YES	*Yearbook of English Studies*

CHAPTER I

Introduction: some strategies of poetic narrative

Underlying many studies of fictional narrative is an unspoken assumption that one may safely equate "narrative fiction" with "fiction in prose." Etymologically, this semantic slippage has little justification. To narrate is to tell, and "for writing to be narrative no more and no less than a teller and a tale are required"[1] – although the term "narrative," by extension, may also come to designate the aesthetic object created by the artistic plotting (the *re*telling) of the raw material of story.[2] A fiction (like a poem) is, quite simply, a linguistic "making" of the imagination, and nothing in the original sense of the term prevents narrative verse, or, for that matter, non-narrative prose, from being classified as fiction. In much twentieth-century criticism, however, the term tends not only to become a loose synonym for "narrative," but also to gravitate towards prose works; as William Nelson has remarked, "the category of 'fiction' now seems to exclude poetry, once almost synonymous with it."[3] The reader who picks up a book called *The Rhetoric of Fiction* or *The Language of Fiction*, or who peruses, in a larger study, a chapter entitled "The Nature and Modes of Narrative Fiction," will not be surprised to find in each case an examination of the novel which displays little interest in other forms of narrative.[4]

In the last fifteen years, however, narratologists (particularly those influenced by the French structuralists) have been rather more insistent that the term "narrative" need not necessarily and exclusively signify the novel; their systems and analyses are now derived from and extended to such forms as biography, historiography, or film.[5] This broadening of focus offers encouragement to the critic particularly interested in poetic narrative, and indeed, on the very first page of *Narrative Fiction: Contemporary Poetics*, Shlomith Rimmon-Kenan announces that her investigations will encompass all kinds of narrative fiction "whether novel, short story, or narrative poem."[6] She is not really interested in discussing narrative poems, however: while she makes one or two passing references to Chaucer and Browning, her study offers no extended account of a sophisticated poetic narrative. The question of how (or whether) the poem-as-narrative fits into a theory of narrative, side-stepped by Rimmon-Kenan, is confronted a little more directly in Mieke Bal's *Narratology*. Having identified various constitutive characteristics of the narrative text, Bal remarks:

> The problem, however, remains that there are texts which display all [these] characteristics, but which nevertheless, on the basis of either tradition or intuition, are not regarded as narrative texts. This is true of many poems. *The Waste Land* by T. S. Eliot is one of the numerous examples. A poem such as this may be termed a narrative poem, and its narrative characteristics may also be narratologically described. That this does not often occur can be attributed to the fact that the poem displays other, more salient characteristics, namely poetic characteristics; Eliot's poem remains first a poem, and its narrative characteristics are of but secondary importance.[7]

What is striking here is Bal's draconian separation of the "narrative" and "poetic" aspects of *The Waste Land*: for the purposes of critical discussion, it seems, a work has to be interrogated either as a poem or a narrative and cannot be both poem and narrative.

Despite the invigorating eclecticism of the new generation of narratologists, critics and theorists continue to oversimplify an already artificial opposition between poetry and narrative (fiction)[8] – sometimes further condensing it into the lyric/novel dyad – and ignore the poem-as-narrative altogether.[9] Jonathan Culler's *Structural Poetics*, for example, has chapters on the "Poetics of the Lyric" and the "Poetics of the Novel," but does not venture a "Poetics of the Narrative Poem."[10] A more recent introduction to narrative/linguistic theory by Michael Toolan discusses the oral narratives of schoolchildren and those heard in the courtroom alongside novels and short stories, but makes no mention of any narrative in poetic form.[11] Nobody, I am sure, would deny that such works as *Paradise Lost* and *The Faerie Queene* possess a narrative structure which (to quote a contemporary narrative theorist) "communicates meaning in its own right, over and above the paraphrasable contents of the story."[12] Indeed, passing references to (and on occasion even extended examinations of) poetic narratives find their way into studies of prose fiction – Homer is a particularly favored "honorary novelist," and in *Narrative Discourse: An Essay in Method*, Gérard Genette juxtaposes an analysis of the opening lines of the *Iliad* with a dissection of the first few sentences of a Proust novel.[13] In such instances, however, the poetic narrative is prone to be treated as ontologically indistinguishable from a prose narrative; there is little interest in the possibility that its manner of "telling a story" may be shaped by phenomena peculiar to narrative poems. Completely reversing Ben Jonson's precept (borrowed from Aristotle) that "the fable and fiction is, as it were, the form and soul of any poetical work or poem,"[14] literary critics tend to find the "fable and fiction" of an extended poetic narrative its most detachable and translatable element, the part of its structure least tied to form, genre, historical moment, or conditions of production.

Through an exploration of the intricacies of three long poetic fictions, *Troilus and Criseyde*, Book VI of *The Faerie Queene*[15] and *Paradise Lost*, I will attempt to fill part of the critical vacuum left by the absorption of a whole range of questions about narrative process into the almost exclusive investigation of prose fictions. Readings of these three long works as *narratives*, will form, respectively, the second, third, and fourth chapters of this study. The texts I have chosen offer particularly rich material for a study of poetic storytelling. All three are acutely self-conscious acts of narrative (Spenser even goes so far as to project himself into the Book of Courtesy in the form of his pastoral *alter ego*, Colin Clout). All three present complex relationships between the process of narration and that of interpretation (and as each of their makers strives to satisfy both the aesthetic and didactic "ends" of his poetic fiction he is likely to find himself plotting different, even mutually incompatible, narrative curves). Most importantly, all three exist in perpetual tension with the texts that have engendered them and which in various more or less aggressive ways they are rewriting: source texts in the case of Chaucer and Milton (and for the latter not just *a* book but *the* Book); the previous books of *The Faerie Queene* itself in the case of Spenser.

Although the greater part of this study will be devoted to investigating the narrative strategies of three poems written before the emergence of the novel as an established form, a final chapter will pick up the gauntlet thrown down by Mieke Bal and preface its more general conclusions with a brief consideration of Eliot's *Waste Land. The Waste Land*'s extreme consciousness of the voices of other texts and its predilection for apparent closure of significance through self-interpretation (here largely displaced into the notorious Notes) invites comparison with the other poems under investigation, and Eliot's fragmented "anti-narrative" seems to have at least one storyline in common with the three earlier works – namely, the covert account of the difficulties of its own production.

It would be possible, no doubt, simply to impose pre-existing critical taxonomies (such as the elaborate systems of Tzvetan Todorov, Roland Barthes, Seymour Chatman or Gérard Genette) upon narratives which happen to be in verse: one might happily diagram the "grammar" of the narrative under consideration; or dissect out "proairetic," "hermeneutic," "semic," "cultural," and "symbolic" codes; or tabulate the relationship between its Author, Implied Author, Narrator, Narratee, Implied Reader, and Reader; or identify and analyze complex "narrative anachronies."[16] All these approaches would, however, defeat my object of interrogating the poetic narrative on its own terms, and not by way of a critical vocabulary evolved for the description and analysis of prose fictions. Although I shall remain receptive to the large corpus of narrative theory already in existence, I shall ultimately be less interested in extended methodological borrowings than in investigating these poems according to my perception of a particular combination of internal and external dynamics influencing their narrative production and articulation. I will use the remainder of this chapter to suggest how various pressures – some consequent upon the very act of framing a story in poetic form, some associated with the characteristically intricate intertextuality of the poetic narrative, and some deriving from the maker's own anxieties concerning poetic authority – might play a significant part in shaping the narrative strategies of the works under consideration. I am aware of the somewhat arbitrary nature of my three initial avenues of approach to the workings of poetic narrative. I am aware, too, of their almost inevitable entanglement in hermeneutic short circuitry. I will therefore emphasize from the start that they do not so much constitute rigid descriptive categories as represent brief meditations upon what might be particularly useful questions and observations to bring to bear on a reading of the poem-as-narrative.

THE QUESTION OF FORM

In his essay "Thematics," the formalist critic Tomashevsky makes the distinction (since redescribed by many narrative theorists) between "story" (*fabula*) and "plot" (*szujet*).[17] The former is that concatenation of events which constitutes the raw material of narrative; the latter involves the manipulation and deployment of that material to create an artistically satisfying whole. Tomashevsky and his colleagues seem to have considered "story" to be a kind of proto-fable existing solely *in potentia*; one might argue, though, that given the many narratives which retell traditional myth or legend, or which rework other *written* fictions, what was once one person's *szujet* may well become another person's *fabula*.

In its attempt to shape the reader's intellectual and emotional responses as he or she experiences the text, the act of turning "story" into "plot" is inevitably an interpretive one. The energy of the narrative tends to be directed towards the totalizing of significance (and pleasure) at its close.[18] This presumably holds true for a sophisticated poetic fiction as well as for a novel: the long narrative poem is no less an exercise in the controlled release of significance. An additional dynamic is at work in the poetic narrative, however: counterpointing and complicating the linear impulse toward the cumulative production of meaning in such fictions are the local pressures of poetic form.

In one sense the prosodic and stanzaic structure of a narrative poem is obviously dependent on its content: the author will select a form suitable to the mood and pace of his matter. One cannot imagine *Paradise Lost*, for example, being narrated in the rhymed tetrameter of *L'Allegro*. Yet a text that is at once narrative and poem may bring into being a two-way dialogue between what it recounts and the manner of its telling that results in a more tangled relationship between content and form. The "bound language"[19] of the formally constructed poem; its adherence to internal schemes of metrical and verbal patterning; its obedience to the configurative needs of the moment: all these do not necessarily subordinate themselves to the onward drive of narrative. I am not convinced that the requirements of form can ever be reduced to the automatism alienated from content that Northrop Frye seems to identify in verse narrative when he argues that, even as a given meter "prescribes the form of rhetorical organization," the poet "develops an unconscious habitual skill in thinking in this meter and is thereby set free to do other things such as tell stories, expound ideas."[20]

Frye contrasts the submerged, repetitious and mechanical form of "verse epos" (his term for poetic narrative) rather unfavorably with the "distinctively lyrical union of sound and sense" which characterizes "what we think of as typically the poetic creation."[21] He does hint, though, that the more removed "verse epos" is from an era of exclusively oral composition and oral performance, and the more distant its metrical form from automatic linear repetition, the closer its internal dynamics will be to a *lyric* ideal of an almost dream-like interplay of form, matter and sound.[22] While I am uneasy with Frye's literary Darwinism, in which the lyric seems to represent a higher level of poetic evolution than the narrative poem, his basic point is worth pursuing. Certainly the refined and leisurely rhyme royal of *Troilus and Criseyde*, or the complexities of the Spenserian stanza, do seem to temper the linear unfolding of the larger narrative with the more synchronic design of lyric.[23] As a unit of fiction-making the highly wrought stanza offers constant opportunities for narrative elaboration, recapitulation, or delay, shifting the reader's attention from what happens *next* to a reflection upon what *is* the event.

The verse form of *The Faerie Queene* was no doubt fashioned by Spenser to provide a fittingly ornate and imposing vehicle for his projected epic fiction. Whether he anticipated the long-term effects of his new narrative unit on the shape of that fiction is debatable. Spenser's lengthy stanzas, often drawing whole sentences out to span their nine lines; his terminal alexandrines, sometimes muting, sometimes climaxing, but always *closing* the preceding block of pentameter (there is almost no enjambment across stanzas in the epic); his employment of only three rhymes per stanza, an economy which encourages the constant repetition and recombination of certain groups of key words: all these phenomena make it quite understandable that *The Faerie Queene* should be wordy, reflexive, episodic, full of verbal artifice and arabesque, and should retard the grand goal-directedness of the narrative scheme announced by its author in his dedicatory letter to Raleigh.[24] The rhyme scheme of ABABBCBCC gives us a displaced "couplet" in lines 4 and 5 which emphasizes the pivotal function of the fifth line in frequently changing, even reversing, the syntax, direction and pace of the stanza as a whole.[25] This means that *The Faerie Queene* is full of syntactic and semantic climax and anticlimax at the stanzaic level, all the more so because of the alexandrines that invite us to enjoy the satisfactions of formal closure every nine lines and may perhaps briefly distract us from the larger sequences of meaning in which the stanza is merely a unit. The laconic connectives or pronouns ("For," "But," "And," "Meanwhile," "Whom") with which many of the stanzas commence are often momentarily jarring: the narrative unit that went before has decorously sealed off its content with a finality that makes it something of a shock to find that content superseded or subordinated by the hooking on of the subsequent stanza.

The perceived tension in a poetic fiction between its local schemes of elaboration and recapitulation and the more linear thrust of its discursive structure makes it the harder to apprehend such a work simultaneously as poem *and* narrative. This is in part due to the limitations of our own descriptive categories: we find it very tempting to deal in tidy binary oppositions (poetry/prose, lyric/narrative), and the narrative poem can not always rest easily within these systems. If, for example, one tries to locate such a work within the dualistic universe of Roman Jakobson's influential stylistic poetics, the insufficiency of that theoretical taxonomy soon becomes apparent. Jakobson argues that poetry, in contrast to prose, privileges the "axis of selection" over the "axis of combination" in the production of discourse so that "[e]quivalence is promoted to the constitutive device of the sentence."[26] He sees "equivalence" at work in the regulation of meter – the ordering and balancing of syllables and accents – and in the equations of rhyme. These operations, based upon relationships of similarity, necessarily take precedence over and modify the syntactical and teleological unfolding of discourse. Interest in what is signified by language tends to be displaced by the poetic function's concentration upon the sign (or system of signs) for its own sake.[27] Jakobson identifies the poetic language generated by this emphasis on the "axis of selection" with the substitutive trope of metaphor; referential (and "combinatory") prose he associates with the more linear trope of metonymy.[28] He maintains, moreover, that lyric favors metaphor and epic metonymy[29] – and this brings us back to our original problem of classification and simultaneous focus.

If we examine, for example, David Lodge's tabulation of a series of polarities analogous to the metaphor/metonymy opposition, we find that most of his dyads – paradigm/syntagm, selection/combination, similarity/contiguity, etc. – seem logical enough.[30] But some of the other oppositions which Lodge derives directly from the arguments of Jakobson sketched above present difficulties:

Metaphor	*Metonymy*
.	.
.	.
Poetry	Prose
Lyric	Epic

Epic (which for our purposes may here be linked with other narrative modes, like romance, in its opposition to lyric) is not necessarily or even usually a prose form, yet because of the monopoly which the lyric holds over the selection/substitution axis in Jakobson's scheme, poetic narrative is relocated on the opposite pole and its "poetic" aspect glossed over. That sequence defers to substitution, and metonymy to metaphor may hold true for the lyric, but this surely leaves us with a tension between (selective/substitutive) delay and (combinatory) forward movement within the narrative poem.

Any assumption that the metaphor/metonymy opposition can adequately define the poetry/prose or the lyric/narrative divide[31] must confront, furthermore, the argument that all literary texts are "metaphoric" in so far as they tend to proffer an implicit totalizing of significance (experienced by the reader as their unity), which, artificial as it is, may be thought of as "a kind of metaphor applied to reality."[32] Peter Brooks, for example, has appropriated metaphor (metaphorically?) to describe the binding together of narrative episodes through imposed patterns of resemblance in such a manner as to reject "the merely contingent (or unassimilable) incident or action" and ensure movement towards a closure that invites retrospective perception of significant design.[33] Nor is this point of view a new one: long before Brooks' suggestion that the metaphorical function may impose a thematic order on large units of discourse as well as a formal one on smaller rhetorical units, Coleridge surely described the same phenomenon when he wrote that "[t]he common end of all *narrative*, nay of *all* Poems, is to convert a *series* into a *Whole*..." (emphases in original).[34] This seems to return us to the starting point of this discussion, for are we not speaking once more of the unity of significance that the *szujet* attempts to extract from – or impose upon – the *fabula*?

A poetic narrative is not simply a battleground between the metaphoric and the metonymic functions of language. It is rather a text in which the energies directed towards structuring content on an extended scale and in a unified and significant manner are entangled with and perhaps even reconfigured by the local pressures exerted by poetic form.[35] Sequentiality is complicated by the pressure of "micro" units (the line, the couplet, the stanza) that have the power to modify, even temporarily foreclose upon, the aesthetic and didactic ends of the narrative by enhancing the satisfactions – and privileging the claims – of the rhetorical moment. Formal pattern becomes not so much a framing device for the unfolding of a distinct, separable "plot" as a kind of emplotment in its own right.

A more radical version of my account of the two-way dialogue between the matter and manner of poetic narrative is proffered by Paul Alpers in *The Poetry of The Faerie Queene*. Alpers argues that Spenser's poem can be experienced *only* as a series of rhetorical moments (as opposed to an unfolding narrative) because the poet perpetually "transforms his narrative materials not into parts of a fiction but into stanzas of poetry, arrangements of words."[36] This not particularly helpful statement overstates, however, the (undeniably considerable) local pressures of poetic form and scheme. The fact remains that there *is* a narrative line to *The Faerie Queene*, we *can* offer a résumé of its action, and the progression of this action *does* involve causality, sequence and consequence. Yet it is no less true (especially in the later books of the epic) that the aforementioned sequence and consequence often appear to be complicated, perhaps even challenged, by both the local and more generalized "counterplots" generated by the work's dilatory, palimpsestic and reflexive stanzas.

Keeping faith with the requirements of poetic form does not so much prevent as modify the production of narrative. Meter and rhyme both serve to stress – through accent or euphony – certain words above others. Such emphases may reinforce the linear syntactical unfolding of discourse, or, by obliging the reader to recognize a tension between formal equivalence and semantic difference, subvert or rearrange it. W. K. Wimsatt points out that rhyme, while overtly bringing aural similarity to our attention, achieves some of its most eloquent effects by quietly exploiting the fact that shared sound does *not* necessitate shared sense (the more obvious the semantic link between words, the triter in many cases the rhyme).[37] Once they are formally bound by rhyme, however, the emphasizing of a purely phonetic connection between words encourages the reader to look for other relationships between them in the narrative, while the narrative exploits, in its turn, the formal equivalence they have been granted. (A case in point is the series of pathetic and ironic changes rung upon such rhyme pairs as *trouthe/routhe*, *herte/smerte*, and *Troye/joye* in Books IV and V of *Troilus and Criseyde*.)

Even when a poetic narrative dispenses with the closely ordered boundaries of the stanza or has no use for rhyme, its unfolding nevertheless tends to be affected by the deployment of the verse line. In *Paradise Lost*, Milton's rejection of rhyme, his use of the verse paragraph in preference to the stanza, and his strong enjambments invite us to see in his periods much of the onward drive of continuous prose. Yet the meter-determined typographical break terminating each line of the text inevitably imposes its own pattern on the narrative: we are repeatedly tempted to suspend the syntax of long narrative units at the margin, thereby modifying, or inviting new meanings into, the narrative line.[38] To invoke a very obvious example, the very first line of *Paradise Lost*:

> Of man's first disobedience, and the fruit

briefly forces us to entertain both the literal (forbidden apple) and figurative (product of disobedience) senses of "fruit" before the eyes move to "Of that forbidden tree..." and the second line qualifies and limits the significance of the noun.[39] The momentary suspension of fixed meaning that constantly opens up the narrative to plural readings (alternative futures, almost) is not just the result of Milton's idiosyncratic syntax (which admittedly has little regard for contiguity, logical combination and other characteristics of Jakobson's metonymical pole of language); it is also dependent on and emphasized by the formal divisions of verse. We should not underestimate the role of the distribution of a poem across a page in directing our experience of it: even prose passages with no claims to the pressures of rhyme or meter in their generation acquire surprisingly different emphases if they are rewritten as lines of free verse.[40] The redeployment and interruption of syntactical units releases the language of the text into a different kind of semantic space, where new relationships of form and signification, no longer solely defined by syntax and punctuation, may be perceived.

I have thus far discussed no formal unit of poetic narrative greater than the stanza and it remains to say a few words about the role of book division (and, in Spenser, canto division) in structuring the works under discussion. Is it, for example, comparable to the division of a novel into chapters?[41] Admittedly, the structural visibility of the chapter varies considerably. At one extreme we have the discreet partitioning of narrative where the new chapter, marked only by a numeral, silently indicates a change of scene or of narrative focus and provides, in effect, a "megaparagraph." At the opposite pole lie far more overt strategies for directing the reader's attention towards the vagaries of the narrative: the lengthy explanatory chapter heading; the proleptic epigraph; the initiation of a new chapter by extended moralizing upon, digression from, or analysis of what has previously been recounted; and, finally, the corresponding tactic of concluding a chapter either by referring explicitly to the withholding or delay of climactic information or by promising to return to characters or events introduced earlier. It is this kind of self-consciousness – almost metafictionality – that generally characterizes the division of sophisticated poetic fictions: a new section of narrative is frequently introduced by the invocation of a Muse, abstraction, patron; or else by a reference to a source or to the act of composition itself; or else (and this is particularly common at the beginning of cantos of *The Faerie Queene*) by a moral pronouncement or gloss. The book or canto may commence by announcing a projected change in narrative tone or direction; it may conclude with the information that the action initiated therein, or events that have been previously set in motion, must be completed elsewhere. The reader's attention is perforce focused upon the narrative unit as a separate narrative event, a discrete entity within a larger structure.

Although the dimensions and scope of such narrative divisions would seem to be determined purely by plot (for there is no formal limit on the number of lines or stanzas per book in any of these works), the shape of the narrative as a whole may be modified by the poet's construction and containment of his episodes. The authorizing rituals of each small new beginning and the narrative suspensions or promises of each temporary closure become integrated with the narrative process: the formal strategies of division that draw attention to certain large details of plot end up as part of that plot. A play of meaning is initiated between the units of narrative; their insistence on their boundaries ironically but predictably encourages the reader to establish patterns of correspondence and cross-reference that transcend those limits. Milton revises the structure of his epic so that it follows the twelve-book model of Virgil, and simultaneously enhances our sense of a whole range of formal symmetries in the thematic structure of *Paradise Lost*. The six completed books of *The Faerie Queene* offer illuminating parallels and contrasts of narrative form and motif whether approached as contiguous pairs (1/2; 3/4; 5/6), symmetrical pairs (1/6; 2/5; 3/4), or paired triads (1/2/3; 4/5/6). In addition, the organization of narrative across the cantos of each book produces its own diagrams of equivalence or opposition: the vision scene on Mount Acidale in Book VI, canto x, for example, has striking parallels with that on the Mount of Contemplation in Book I, canto x.[42] The narrative of *Troilus and Criseyde* displays less complex plotting and is constructed on a smaller scale, but its five books nevertheless offer a careful symmetrical pattern of ascent and descent, Troilus's desire occupying I and II, its consummation III, and Troilus's fall from happiness IV and V. The manner in which these poems are formally constructed and subdivided not only "paragraphs" their episodes and enhances their graceful and orderly unfolding through time, but also makes available a pattern of meanings revealed in the cross-referencing of motifs over the spread of the narrative. The net effect is to give the text an extra dimension, making it a verbal object with a complex interior space. Although this kind of elaborate concretization of design is by no means peculiar to the poetic narrative, it is perhaps encouraged by the particular pressures of "bound language." The imperative which governs the creation of significant correspondences and symmetries on the small scale may well contribute to the plotting of meaning by means of expanded configurations on the large. In the verse narrative, as in the lyric, poetic form does not merely coexist with the ordering of significance, but, in helping to determine it, becomes part of the sense-making process, part of plot itself.

INTERTEXTUALITY

My three representative poetic narratives exhibit a striking degree of intertextuality: their narrative energy is directed less towards the representation of any external material reality (a reality which we now tend to perceive, indeed, as itself the product of many textual forces)[43] than towards the reappropriation and recreation of previous literary texts. This is not simply because all of them reproduce, to some degree, sources or "pre-texts"[44] (an issue I will be addressing later in this section), but also because they all respond to, interrogate, and in the end perhaps elude, received notions about genre (notions derived in their turn from other poetic narratives, other "pre-texts"). With varying degrees of obliquity, they converse with the systems we have devised for the description and differentiation of literary texts: under perpetual, inevitable pressure from readerly expectations about what a perceived generic allegiance *means*, the polymorphous poetic fiction makes its flirtation with a multiplicity of modes part of its distinctive design.

I am not, to be sure, suggesting that poetic fictions are utterly unique in this respect: such prose works as *Don Quixote*, *Moby Dick*, and *Ulysses* (to cite some very obvious examples) demonstrate a comparably intricate intertextuality. Prose fictions considered *en masse*, however, are less likely to display the kind of *sustained*, minutely textured dialogue with previous works and pre-existing genres that seems to characterize many narrative poems. It is noticeable, furthermore, that the prose fictions whose form and content are strikingly allusive and dialogic have tended to be described in terms of the generic categories (such as epic and romance) we more usually associate with poetic narratives. It is as if their very intertextuality and heteromodality "poeticizes" them.

This is not to say that any of the poems under investigation lends itself to easy classification: all of them are generic mavericks. *Troilus and Criseyde* has attracted a wide variety of (often contradictory) labels: Chaucer calls it his "tragedye," its twentieth-century readers have called it epic, mock epic, romance, tragicomedy, comedy, a mixture of "Boethian" comedy and tragedy, and the first English novel.[45] There has not been quite the same rush to explain *The Faerie Queene* in the terms of a single mode or genre, but even if we call it a mixture of epic and romance and allegory[46] we do not exhaust its generic diversity: its nostalgic romance may all of a sudden, as in Book v, turn into a (barely masked) chronicling of "real history"; its epic may gracefully regress, as in Book vi, to pastoral. *Paradise Lost*, too, embraces a multiplicity of literary kinds: the work's epic machinery and scope do not conceal the fact that it intermittently displays certain characteristics of romance, pastoral, classical tragedy, and allegorical narrative.[47]

The resistance of these poetic narratives to tidy disposal within orthodox schemes of literary classification frustrates the reader who wants to begin his or her interpretation of the work by attaching unto it an unambiguous generic label. We like to come to grips with the new and problematic by assimilating it to what is already familiar: our sense of what kind of narrative is before us will direct the retention or suppression of details in our apprehension of the work as a whole and will help to determine the significance it holds for us. We continue to look for our interpretive labels, even as we recognize that all systems of classification from Aristotle onwards have tended to petrify, to become constitutive and closed definitions rather than exploratory critical tools whose fundamental arbitrariness is not forgotten.[48] Texts may be all too easily adapted to the shape of prefabricated pigeonholes rather than located within systems on their own terms; systems themselves may be far from stable or self-consistent – for the descriptive terminology of genre is generated idiosyncratically, and the connotations of any given category are continually in flux.[49]

I have already suggested that the poem-as-narrative cannot be easily embraced by the critical vocabulary of formal stylistics. Its double nature (poem *and* narrative) makes it equally difficult to locate within familiar taxonomies of genre – taxonomies that quite frequently fail to recognize or invoke even the most minimal "polycentrism" in their category generation.[50] It is true, however, that one of the reasons for the persistent indescribability – or over-describability – of highly wrought poetic narratives stems less from inconsistent or inexact categories than from the absence of a preliminary, tentative one. When discussing prose narratives one may employ the grab-bag term "novel" to label all kinds of works – from *Don Quixote* to *The Ambassadors*, from *Tristram Shandy* to *Ulysses* – so long as they are extended fictions in prose. Casually invited to take its place within such a generous and flexible matrix of texts, the individual narrative can be both assessed as a discrete entity and located according to its special affinities for, and correspondences with, more or less rigorously defined classes of fictions. Its particular relationship with, for example, the picaresque, the realistic, the sentimental, or the satiric novel can be determined without necessarily locating the work within a single one of those modes. In discussing the extended poetic fiction we have no simple holding category comparable with "novel" – the phrases I have been employing thus far, "poetic narrative," "poetic fiction," "narrative poem," possess neither its absolute stability as a canonical term of classification nor its supreme tentativeness as a descriptive category.

Jonathan Monroe, discussing the prose poem, has remarked of that at once unprosaic and non-"lyrical" literary kind that it is "a genre that does not want to be itself."[51] One might suggest that the poetic narrative, by contrast, is never *allowed* to be itself: such terms as "poetic narrative" or "narrative poem" are not accepted as meaningful, and the reader's apprehension of the work tends to be precipitately translated into more limited, and yet more approximate, descriptive categories (such as epic, romance, allegory, *de casibus* tragedy, etc.). Premature taxonomy almost inevitably leads to premature closure of significance; a descriptive category is asserted and all the features of the work that contradict it are ignored or suppressed in the reader's account of the text. The alternative to such interpretative foreclosure, of course, can be equally unsatisfactory, producing all-embracing formulae along the line of Polonius' "tragical-comical-historical-pastoral" which do not necessarily leave us much the wiser.

A useful alternative to the critical vision which attempts to fix the significance of polymorphous poetic narratives by interpreting them through the lens of a single, constitutive generic category would focus upon the creative interplay between authorial (and readerly) preconceptions about genre and narrative-as-*process*.[52] One might propose that, as they unfold, complex poetic narratives enter into a kind of dialogue with the (usually implicit, often rather arbitrary) generic claims and self-definitions of other texts. The more sophisticated the poetic fiction, the more aware of other *kinds* of storytelling it will be, and the more complicated its location of itself with respect to them. Indeed, this holds true even when a narrative explicitly declares itself to belong to a certain category of literary works. At the same time that it invokes the principle of similarity, the sophisticated work may be busily establishing its difference, its uniqueness (indeed, its very insistence upon that similarity may underline a departure from the constitutive norm it has supposedly embraced). The opening stanza of *Troilus and Criseyde* promises us *de casibus* tragedy:

> The double sorwe of Troilus to tellen,
> That was the kyng Priamus sone of Troye,
> In lovynge, how his aventures fellen
> Fro wo to wele, and after out of joie,
> My purpos is, er that I parte fro ye.
>
> (I. 1–5)

Chaucer, however, proceeds to confound the fairly predictable expectations he has aroused, as he manipulates the subtle shifts of tone and narrative perspective and the competing generic allegiances of the ensuing five books. Similarly, even as *Paradise Lost* seems to embrace the conventions of classical epic, all of its more orthodox machinery is ultimately subordinated to the articulation of a revisionary definition of "the heroic." The fiction's redefined relationship with *idées reçues* concerning genre becomes part and parcel of its narrative strategy: Milton plots, as well as presumes, the exhaustion of his pagan models.

The fact that the "non-signifying" term *poetic narrative* will always tend to be pre-empted by narrower generic categories during the interpretive act has interesting and readily exploited consequences for such works at the level of process. Paradoxically, the circumstances that would seem to limit narrative meaning actually encourage its strategic manipulation. The double-tongued, highly wrought poetic narrative, always in some sense beyond the pale of conventional systems and taxonomies (although always liable to be prematurely chastened and reduced by such labels as "epic" or "romance"), can embrace and articulate a unique configuration of generic allegiances that range all the way from epic to lyric. Even as the reader strives to classify and tame the text, the polymorphous and transgeneric poetic fiction exploits and interrogates his or her assumptions about literary kinds – sometimes acquiescing in, sometimes reacting against, sometimes undermining readerly expectations. Indeed the narrative richness of all these works derives in part from their willingness to incorporate into their design a play of kinds that becomes in its turn a play of signification (given that every generic category comes with its own semiotic freight) as they inscribe within the plot the moments when generic boundaries are quietly revised. Nor does this dialogue between text and generic expectation remain fixed at the moment of a given narrative's production. We may also perceive a retrospective interaction between a given text and subsequent texts (or subsequent systems of ordering texts) as the later works locate themselves at new points in the spread of narratives, exerting their own pressures, responding to those already present, and generally pulling the pattern of generic relationships into a new shape. This is why it is not really so incongruous to attempt to define a work like *Troilus and Criseyde* in the light of one's awareness of, say, the psychological novel: it is only an error to suppose that any *one* new category can necessarily confine and explain such a fiction any more completely than any single one of the old terms.

The close and often embattled relationship between narrative process and conventional expectations concerning the genre-specific significance of literary texts has obvious ties with a further set of pressures affecting the production of poetic narrative, namely, those exerted by the prior narratives which they are to a greater or lesser degree remaking. In another version of its simultaneous deference to and self-differentiation from the codes of genre, the poetic fiction will tend to oscillate between embracing (or asserting through similarity) the authority of these "pre-texts" and (through re-ordering, re-interpreting and subverting them) establishing its narrative autonomy and otherness.[53] *Troilus and Criseyde* and *Paradise Lost* are written within certain narrative limits determined by the prior texts of *Il Filostrato* and Genesis: their creation is also an act of *re*creation. The situation is not quite the same for Spenser: prodigal in his intermittent borrowing of, or allusion to, the themes and motifs of other fictions, he nevertheless does not draw upon any single antecedent to shape his narrative as a whole. But the publication of the first three books of *The Faerie Queene* in 1590 generates a certain set of expectations about the narrative form and content of the work and establishes a *modus operandi*. The continuation of the poem in the 1596 edition unfolds in many respects according to the blueprint established six years earlier, and is exceedingly conscious of what has gone before and how it has been received – or misunderstood. For all their shifts of tone, mood and focus, and their increasing problems with narrative closure, Books IV–VI exhibit an array of formal parallels with I–III and sufficient reworking of theme and incident to suggest that Spenser is in effect rewriting – both recapitulating and modifying – his earlier stories in the later books of *The Faerie Queene*.

Even as these three works both return to and revise certain cardinal source texts, they open themselves up to the more discrete influence of a profusion of other makings. *Troilus and Criseyde*, for example, entertains the voices of Dante, Machaut, Petrarch, and Boethius. Chaucer's borrowings range from formal appropriations of other people's lines (the "Canticus Troili" of Book I embeds the translation of a sonnet of Petrarch within the larger fiction) to repeated informal invocations – mainly through Pandarus – of the "texts" of proverbial wisdom. *The Faerie Queene* draws upon the Bible, the classical epics,

Ariosto and Tasso, Ovid, Hesiod, Chaucer, and Malory (to name but a few of its sources). The numerous sub-texts of *Paradise Lost* range across an even wider field than those of Spenser, and indeed include among their number *The Faerie Queene*. The unfolding of narrative and the control of its significance in these works may thus be determined from moment to moment by the layers of allusive resonance in a particular theme or motif; alternatively, the reference may be revised and complicated for the author's own ends. In the tenth canto of Book VI of *The Faerie Queene*, Spenser's account of Calidore's vision of the Graces on Mount Acidale offers an internal allusion to (and a recasting of) Redcrosse's mountain-top glimpse of the workings of divine grace in Book I. In giving us another version of a sacred *mons Veneris* it also refers back to the Garden of Adonis (III. vi). It invokes, furthermore, various external allusions: to the *Shepheardes Calender* in its use of the Colin Clout persona of the poet (which thus links the pastoral beginnings of Spenser's career with his epic's current relapse into pastoral); to various mythographies and iconographies of the Graces; perhaps even to the Actaeon myth through the representation of Calidore as an inadequately concealed and somewhat greedy voyeur. Narrative moments, narrative sequences even, become palimpsests where such layers of implicit reference reverberate against the surface narrative. The stories told by these poets are never entirely independent narrative events: the text inevitably assumes a series of complicated stances in relation to a host of other fictions.

One of the most striking by-products of revisionary repetition within poetic narrative is a phenomenon we might call "significant supplementation." Chaucer more or less doubles the length of *Il Filostrato* in creating *Troilus and Criseyde*; Milton's reworking of Genesis i–iii occupies 10,565 lines. Although both poets submit their narratives to certain radical, source-derived limitations – Criseyde must betray her lover; Troilus must perish; Adam and Eve must fall and be expelled from Eden – the enlarged scale of the "secondary" works suggests that narrative expansion has an important role in establishing their autonomy from their source texts. Narrative supplementation is also characteristic of *The Faerie Queene*: Spenser's elaborate accretion, combination and modification of basic motifs (scenes of vision or instruction, descents into various underworlds, digressions from the quest, etc.) and his generation of a larger fiction out of consecutive, increasingly polysemous plottings of a symbolic journey emphasize the importance of additive functions in the construction of his poem.

The supplementation of a source or the constant recapitulation of a fiction's original ground plan are maneuvers which resist narrative closure. Teleology is challenged by the dilation of the text. When a poetic narrative delays a "necessary," source-determined ending, it asserts its power over how the fiction should reach its terminus, and, even more importantly, over the significance to be found in the manner in which it does so. Peter Brooks has discussed the repetition and multiplication of formal and thematic motif and trope whereby the maker of long fictions interrupts the goal-directed impulse towards the totalizing of pleasure and significance in order to exert a finer control over the discharge of meaning at the end of the work.[54] This strategy is all the more congenial to the narrative already under pressure from the apparent "invariables" within a source, for it offers the opportunity to reinterpret the latter through a series of narrative increments which are simultaneously glosses upon the prior text. Frank Kermode has explored the workings of such interpretation-through-narrative-augmentation (as opposed to interpretation by discrete commentary and exegesis) in the Gospels; I see no reason why narrative supplementation cannot equally be analyzed as a reinterpretive strategy in secular makings.[55] Certainly, when the *re*producer of what was at least provisionally a closed and complete system incorporates significant imaginative expansions into his narrative design, those expansions – which may range from the simple replacement of parataxis by subordinating conjunctions to the kind of dense elaboration of character and motive that make Chaucer's heroine so much more complex and disturbing a character than Boccaccio's Criseida – force even those elements of plot structure which seem most immutable to appear in a new perspective. At the same time, the manipulation of this kind of implicit gloss ensures that the "secondary" text achieves autonomy, differentiates itself from its precursor.

The fact that narrative augmentation demonstrates this reinterpretive bias has different implications for different texts. When Chaucer supplements the plotting of *Il Filostrato*, defiantly delaying and complicating the earlier work's movement towards an unhappy conclusion through his circumstantial dilation of the episodes which describe the growth and consummation of the love between hero and heroine, he is exercising the same kind of authorial prerogative over the material of his fiction that Boccaccio himself had exploited in *his* expansive recreation of the Troilus fable out of scattered episodes in the *Roman de Troie* of Benoît de Sainte-Maure. But when Milton supplements the laconic narrative of Genesis i–iii to create *Paradise Lost*, and introduces a vast quantity of additional matter in order to make a sacred text more aesthetically and didactically accessible to fallen humanity, his interpolations are in effect glossing what (in terms of his own Protestantism) should already be comprehensible to any man or woman of faith. Moreover, the generous scale of his recreation and enlargement of a supposedly self-sufficient and closed text is itself troubling. Representation (*re*presentation) inevitably involves a movement away from, or a displacement of, a definitive authorial presence: in *Paradise Lost* the secular and subjective imagination could be viewed as a threat to, and a potential usurper of, the authority of sacred truth.[56] The sheer magnitude of the narrative elaboration and interpolation may result in a sense of fragmentation and diminution, a sliding away from the pregnant intensity represented by the source.[57] As Terence Cave has suggested, the *copia* produced by the celebrative expansion of a sacred text is always perilously close to becoming merely an inadequate copy.[58]

Supplementation as a narrative device produces a related set of pressures and problems in *The Faerie Queene*, a text which unfolds expansively through movements of substitution or repetition. The poem tends to elaborate itself reflexively by means of a continual process of self-interpretation as each narrative incident comments on the one preceding it. At the same time, however, the goal-directed plot of each book's master quest seeks to impose a limit on supplementation: a crisis must be reached, revelation experienced, a victory won.[59] It is noticeable that the further Spenser proceeds with his poem, the shakier becomes its teleology. After the relative self-containment of the narratives of Holiness and Temperance, Books III and IV generate a multiplicity of interlaced plots (which overlap into V as well). All the later books are prone to substitute one protagonist for another as the temporary focal point of the action; all of them are subject to failed or postponed climaxes. By the time we read the Book of Courtesy, the constant supplementation and elaboration of narrative sequence has become disturbingly entropic. The hero of Book VI will disappear from the action for several cantos to be replaced by a somewhat less effective knight bearing a similar name. The heroic quest is diverted back into a pre-heroic pastoral universe, turned away from completion and back to beginnings. Closure of any episode becomes problematic; the very goal of the quest, the Blatant Beast, has "already" escaped into a prior book and assaulted its hero. The augmentation of the fiction seems at once to provoke and be predicated upon the undercutting of its authority: the *telos* that would totalize the significance of the quest, aesthetically and didactically, is increasingly threatened by the sheer productivity of the narrative process.

AUTHORIZED VERSIONS?

A third pressure shaping the production of the poetic narrative is born out of the maker's need to authenticate or authorize the creating self, the creating act, and the text created – to make sure that we acknowledge the fiction to be (in its own way) a true story. This is not to ignore the fact that prose writers have often sought to present *their* fictions as more than "mere stories." The nineteenth-century novelists who offer the reader the illusion of complete immersion in an unmediated and richly textured redescription of the familiar and circumstantial are employing different conventions to the same ends as their predecessors who gave their fictions to the public masked (or half masked) as autobiography (*Robinson Crusoe*), biographical history (*The History of Joseph Andrews*) or as collections of letters merely edited by their author (*Clarissa*). All of these fiction makers wish us to forget we are dealing with imaginative constructions rather than faithful transcriptions of reality, verisimilitude rather than *veritas*. The poetic narrative, however, is less likely (and less able) to deflect our attention from the fact that it is a "making": its reordering of language into a discourse that is emphatically artifical and *other* emphasizes its separateness from the normal continuum of experience. At the same time, its author may evolve his own strategies, not merely to authenticate, but also to privilege the world bound up in his words, the particular vision embraced by his poem.

The very notion of a poetic fiction, to be sure, may translate into either a tautology or a disturbing oxymoron. As I noted at the beginning of this chapter, the bare etymology of fiction seems synonymous with that of poem: something that is *made*. At the same time, however – and despite Touchstone's profound observation that "the truest poetry is the most feigning" – fiction making in the sense of "feigning" has always tended to be sharply differentiated from the ideal of *poesis* as a truer making, a substantial and vital creation. Sidney, for example, asserts, in his *Defence of Poetry*, that "where all other arts retain themselves within their subject and receive, as it were, their being from it, the poet alone bringeth his own stuff, and doth not learn a conceit out of a matter but maketh matter for a conceit,"[60] and feels obliged to insist that the poet never deals merely in fictive versions of reality: his narrative forms "an imaginative ground-plot of a profitable invention," a hypothetical construct whose essence it is to be generative of more profound truths.[61]

The maker of the long narrative poem has traditionally been perceived as a *deus artifex* who authors (and authenticates) his own world, "another nature," as Sidney has it.[62] Tasso in fact suggests that such a poet "is called divine for no other reason than that as he resembles the supreme artificer in his workings he comes to participate in his divinity."[63] But in a Christian universe the poet is also a creature, and a fallen one at that. His artificial creation, his second nature, may be merely an inferior copy or superfluous supplementation of a prior reality, and the fact that this "reality" may be that of another text, itself perhaps a secondary construct, only serves to complicate the matter further.[64] At least one early theorist simply tries to brazen out the ambiguities of the poet's position. In *The Arte of English Poesie*, Puttenham insists that he is both a "maker" and a "counterfaitor," arguing that although poets, in bringing forth their work "of themselves without any subject of verite" are "as creating gods," they can attain that stature either through "divine instinct" for *new* creation or through excellent imitation "of any president or paterne layd before them."[65] Puttenham, of course, manages to embroil himself in contradiction. If poets lack "any subject of verite" are they not therefore feigning?[66] Alternatively, if they are appropriating a "president or paterne," surely their own work may become not so much an original making as merely the discovery of that which already exists: an *objet retrouvé*, perhaps?

The poetic fiction inevitably incorporates into its own narrative discourse its author's anxiety about the possibility of reconciling the ideally authoritative and autonomous act of poetic making with the common understanding of fiction as a feigning that is at once derivative and (in the sense that it lacks real "presence") illusory. The most obvious narrative strategy engendered by this anxiety is the invocation of the Muse. When the maker, in asking for poetic inspiration, begs the Muse to unfold the material of his fiction (*say* what was the cause of Adam and Eve's transgression, says Milton; *show* me the "antique rolles" where my story is inscribed, says Spenser),[67] he suggests to us that his poem already exists, although occupying a space inaccessible to us, and that he is the privileged medium of its transmission. The poem is already a perfect – perhaps too perfect – conceit which he has to translate in order to make it intelligible; he must recast the prior and transcendent construct in the fictive shape which it requires in order to be brought down to earth. And we see another variation on this theme of creation as accommodation when the poetic fiction explicitly articulates the narrative repossession of a past inscribed in texts suspected to be closer and more faithful to an originary union of artifice and truth. The poet accepts the authority of his sources, but *re*presents their significance in the terms of his own art and his own experience: remembering is achieved at the price of a somewhat radical re-membering.[68] This strategy is inevitably accompanied by the risk that the author will not remake his ties with the writings that lie between him and the True Story, but rather make them up – and this brings us to yet another complication of the relationship between external authority and the creative act. As it reinvents its precursor(s), a poetic narrative may well draw attention to the paradoxical individuality and autonomy of the secondary making through the comments of a self-assertive narrator.[69] When we listen to a speaker who purports to lay bare the process, or fix the moment, of *producing* the poem, who discusses his relationship with his sources, his feelings about the fiction that is unfolding, or the significance that he perceives in his narrative, we may come to perceive the work as a microcosmos ruled over by a thoroughly idiosyncratic controlling deity. And since the mask of the narrator does not necessarily reveal the face of the author, by projecting a version of himself into his work while remaining in silent control over the fiction containing this persona, the author may seem to imitate at one remove the relationship between God as true *deus artifex* and the poet as would-be "creating God."

Each of the works I shall be discussing has its own array of (on occasion contradictory) methods for authenticating or privileging its fictions. Chaucer makes use of a narrator whose alleged inexperience in love tends to shield him from accusations that he is merely making up the events of *Troilus and Criseyde*; furthermore, he is able to refer us, when pressed, to the prior authority of his "auctor." But at the same time, this narrator misleads his audience about the source of his narrative: the suppression of Boccaccio's identity in favor of a shadowy *auctoritee* called "Lollius" undercuts the admission of the authority of a previous text: Lollius' book does not exist, so this one toys with the fiction of being created *ex nihilo*. Furthermore, the complex conclusion of the poem, its narrative movement away from a fictive Trojan world and into a Christian universe whose suddenly distanced perspective radically modifies the significance of what has gone before, allows the tale-teller to assert a new control over his work. The world of the poet is no longer the ontologically hazy world of his Trojan hero: the text has expanded to admit a cosmos in which *that* fiction becomes merely a part of a greater making. The narrator wins this (somewhat Pyrrhic) victory by emphasizing the integrity of the larger creation (the story of Troilus and Criseyde plus Christian gloss) at the expense of the smaller one (the story of the various sorrows of the pagan Troilus and Criseyde – or rather, the story of a more partial narrator's hapless entanglement in the sorrows of his Trojan hero and heroine). But this newly omniscient narrator's retrospective reorientation of the poem inevitably clashes with our previous introduction to a narrator who stressed his emotionally and textually second-hand and slippery grasp of his matter; we must perhaps conclude that the poet who created *both* of these narrative voices has constructed his work out of competing reproductions of his source (one based on silently interpolated narrative modifications that delay, and challenge the inevitability of, Troilus' fall; the other deriving from an explicit terminal gloss that denies any tragic significance to that fall) in his attempt to "make it new" and make it *his*.

In Book VI of *The Faerie Queene* the tension between authentic creation and more suspect paradigms for the writing of fictions is particularly acute. The Book of Courtesy concludes with the claim that the poet will henceforward only "seeke to please, that now is counted wisemens threasure" (VI. xii. 41), as if the author is yielding to an external and degraded evaluation of the worth of poetic fictions. Yet in Calidore's vision of Spenser's avatar, Colin Clout, piping to the Graces on Mount Acidale, we have glimpsed what seems to be a moment of plenary creation, as the poet is directly confronted and inspired by a figure who is simultaneously his beloved, a fourth Grace and a nameless Muse. All the Graces vanish, however, when Calidore intrudes upon the dance, and Colin breaks his instrument. We are obliged to ask ourselves what forces are at work in this last complete book of *The Faerie Queene* that so threaten Spenser's sense of the possibility of transmitting, unviolated, a vision of authoritative making.

The very nature of the projected narrative of *Paradise Lost* generates some particularly daunting obstacles to its authorization. In recreating both the Creation and the Fall, Milton must assume a God-like stance to "explain" God, even as he works to convince his reader that a postlapsarian creature can be inspired to supplement the already Authorized Version of the events in Eden. His invocation of the heavenly Muse, his implicit use of the model of linguistic "accommodation" provided by his account of Raphael discoursing of heavenly events in terms accessible to Adam and Eve, and his deployment of various poetic schemata designed to articulate (or to *appear* to articulate) the indescribable are his necessary yet perilous narrative strategies for accomplishing his ends. They are perilous because the reader is so often conscious of the narrow margin between an inspired poetic illumination of the Origin and a presumptuous augmentation of the Logos. At what point does a fiction cease to mediate between the reader and the inexpressible and develop solipsistically? Can the poet repeat the Muse's works and not bend them to his fallen will and desires, not produce a false copy? Where, ultimately, can one locate the "making" that is *Paradise Lost*: is it secondary to Genesis; does it overlap or coexist with it; or does it usurp its place?

The multiple inscription within these narratives of the poets' strategies for asserting, and anxieties concerning, the authority and authenticity of their fictions may actually generate competing voices – competing stories, almost – within the same work. The vocabulary and values of the narrator who "authoritatively" glosses the conclusion of the *Troilus* are not the same as those of the servant of the servants of love who claims to be faithfully translating his *auctor*. The author who will merely "seeke to please" an unworthy audience on its own terms at the end of the Book of Courtesy does not speak the same language as his *alter ego*, Colin Clout, who will break his pipes rather than sing on without authentic inspiration. As *Paradise Lost* unfolds, the poet who strives faithfully to accommodate the divine Word must also make room for an equally faithful realization of the Satanic voice of rebellious secondariness whose supplementations only defile and obscure the Logos. All three poetic narratives are in fact characterized by the "freedom from a unitary and singular language"[70] that M. M. Bakhtin calls *heteroglossia*: everything they try to say "is always entangled in someone else's discourse about it,"[71] whether that someone else is a previous text or poet or tale-teller, the poet's contemporaries and readers outside that text, or the various and partial narrative personae presented within the work. Bakhtin, of course, uses the phenomenon of *heteroglossia* to distinguish prose fiction, the novel, from poetic writing. Nevertheless, his criteria for thus reconstituting the novel as a modal genre are fluid enough for Pushkin's narrative poem *Evgenij Onegin* to become a favorite Bakhtinian example of heteroglot discourse,[72] and his account of the dialogic, relative, competitive (rather than unified and univocal) nature of "artistic prose" representation has interesting implications for the exploration of the sophisticated (and – as both poem *and* narrative – inherently double-voiced) poetic fiction – implications I shall have cause to reinvoke later in this study.

Having briefly outlined some of the more interesting and problematic responses of my three exemplary texts to forces which seem particularly significant in the construction and unfolding of poetic fictions, I now propose to pass on to a more prolonged consideration of narrative process in each one. But I would first like to offer the following observation. In my attempt to ask some interesting questions about a literary kind which has previously been largely uninterrogated, I am very conscious of the selective focus of my project. Although my theoretical influences and borrowings are fairly eclectic, my investigations are predominantly formalist in their methods and emphases. I am quite aware that other questions could be asked of these texts. One could, for example, delve much more deeply into the relationship between the historical moment and conditions of each poem's production and its particular narrative strategies. One might also inquire as to whether there is anything that appears to be gender-specific about the distinctive designs of these male-authored works. This study is not, however, offered as the last word on the workings of poetic narrative, but as an initial foray into unexplored territory. The three large issues I have sketched out in this introduction – the simultaneous dialogues taking place between the poetic narrative and the constraints of form, between the poetic narrative and the textual matrix, and between the poetic narrative and ontology – are certainly not intended to constitute a definitive list of the forces which inscribe themselves within and help to plot such works, nor shall I offer an exhaustive analysis of each phenomenon in each text (some of them, in any case, being more relevant to some works than to others). My approach to the poems will, however, be governed by the general questions I have raised concerning their potentially dialogic and "duplicitous" designs as I offer readings of *Troilus and Criseyde*, *The Faerie Queene* Book VI, and *Paradise Lost*.

CHAPTER 2

Dilation, design and didacticism in Troilus and Criseyde

Intertextuality, as I have already suggested, plays a particularly prominent role in poetic fictions, and one of its consequences is an inscription within the poem-as-narrative of the creator's dialogue with what has gone before. Chaucer's recasting of *Il Filostrato* in *Troilus and Criseyde* narrates a complicated negotiation with a literary predecessor.[1] Relations between the English poet and his Italian pre-text are constantly in flux; in recreating Boccaccio's poem Chaucer incorporates passages of close translation, of more or less accurate paraphrase, of more or less radical supplementation, interpolation, interpretive omission and interpretive commentary. His poem's multiple narrative strategies, which include a skillful exploitation of the formal possibilities of the rhyme royal stanza and a sophisticated manipulation of the competing generic allegiances of his material, suggest that several fictional designs are jostling for supremacy within the text as the earlier work is both repeated and reinvented.

Il Filostrato is itself, of course, an expansion of scattered episodes in the later stages of Benoît de Sainte-Maure's *Roman de Troie*, but the scheme of amplification within Boccaccio's narrative of passion and betrayal is overwhelmingly determined by the narrator's identification with Troiolo. The hero's story is offered to a beloved but distant female reader in the same spirit that would provoke Astrophil to cry to Stella in a later century and a different tongue, "I am not I, pity the tale of me." Boccaccio's preoccupation with Troiolo's condition (and with Troiolo's rhetorical expression of that condition) is underscored by the fact that in a poem of 5704 lines, 1706 of them are spoken by his hero, who thus has more lines of direct discourse than all the other speakers in *Il Filostrato* put together (and over 250 more than Chaucer's Troilus).[2] Narrative expansion in *Troilus and Criseyde*, on the other hand, is less exclusively linked to the role of one particular character across the course of the whole poem. It is especially evident in the rising action of the story: the lovers' happiness is greatly prolonged, and the narration of the fulfillment of their desire, which occupies only 752 lines in Boccaccio's third book, is allotted 1820 lines in Book III of the *Troilus*.[3] Chaucer's substantial dilation of the courtship, suffering, doubts, and eventual bliss of Troilus and Criseyde, his efforts to suspend "in quyete and in reste" the joy they achieve, challenge the grim conclusion of his source narrative, and tempt the reader to envision an alternative fable and an alternative ending to that offered by *Il Filostrato*.[4]

Nevertheless, although Chaucer's narrator will be supplementing his source up to (and beyond) the very moment of betrayal, interrupting his story to quibble with and cast doubt upon the "received account" of Criseyde's treachery, it would be oversimplifying matters to consider *Troilus and Criseyde* solely as an exercise in subversive narrative augmentation. In fact, dilation of *Il Filostrato* is much less apparent in the later part of the English work: Chaucer's Books IV–V are narrated in only 218 more lines than Boccaccio's Books IV–IX. The effect of this upon *Troilus and Criseyde* in its entirety is to endow it with a symmetry that *Il Filostrato* lacks.[5] Paradoxically, Chaucer's rewriting of Boccaccio involves a repatterning that accepts the narrative whole, even as its augmentations appear to challenge teleology. The sprawl of Boccaccio's diversely proportioned nine books is reorganized within the arching symmetry of Chaucer's five, and a whole series of (at times ironic) parallels and echoes, cast into relief by the fable's pathetic conclusion, distribute themselves across the sweep of the poem.[6] Indeed, many of these parallels are actually generated by the episodic expansion of Boccaccio's text.

The intriguing co-existence of additive, goal-resistant narrative dilation and patterned, goal-determined narrative design in Chaucer's translation and transformation of *Il Filostrato* is further complicated by the leisurely Conclusion-cum-Epilogue-cum-Palinode of *Troilus and Criseyde* which creates a revisionary third narrative stance from which the preceding, carefully developed structure of the work is seemingly vitiated. The narrator's final assessment of the significance of Troilus' betrayal and death – this is not what you thought, the fall from happiness is an illusion, the "double sorwe" not worth weeping about – confounds us with its last minute refusal either to vindicate the challenge to teleology offered by the subversive art of excess or to confirm the sterner satisfactions provided by the consummation of the tragic design. In the course of this chapter I shall be investigating Chaucer's manipulation of retrospective reinterpretation, as well as subversive augmentation and conservative architectonics, in his rewriting of Boccaccio, and shall attempt to determine what pressures these three "designs" ultimately exert (separately and in combination) upon the narrative process.[7]

I should perhaps emphasize that what follows is not a source study of *Troilus and Criseyde*, a mere catalogue of similarities and differences between the English and Italian works. My exploration of *Troilus and Criseyde's* polyphonic remaking of *Il Filostrato* assumes that the strategies Chaucer deploys, the forces he sets in motion in the unfolding of his revisionary design(s), represent just one complex and idiosyncratic manifestation of the characteristic dynamics of poetic narrative. Chaucer's triple-voiced reproduction of Boccaccio manipulates relations between the "schemes" of prosody and the shaping of narrative, sets in motion a multiplicity of internal dialogues involving other people's texts and other *kinds* of texts, and records its own quest to supplant *Il Filostrato* as the "authorized version" of the history of the Trojan lovers. While the author orders his poem's heteroglossia and heteromodality to achieve his own, very specific narrative ends, the palimpsestic text he brings into being offers an excellent starting point for a larger consideration of the duplicitous artistry and multifarious ends of other makers of poetic narrative.

REVISIONARY AUGMENTATION

Chaucer's amplifications of *Il Filostrato* are hedged about by equivocation. *Troilus and Criseyde's* voluble narrator[8] loudly proclaims his inexperience and blindness in matters of love – and his consequent inability to augment or alter his source (II. 18–21)[9] – even as he misrepresents both the language of *Il Filostrato* and the identity of its author (II. 14; I. 394). Characteristically, he invokes Clio, the Muse of History, at the beginning of the book in which his most extensive departures from Boccaccio's "history" are about to commence (II. 8). One comes to recognize, indeed, that when our storyteller insists most noisily upon his accurate translation and transcription of his "auctour," he is almost certainly introducing new matter into his work, assiduously postponing the unhappy ending promised by his opening stanza's summary of "The double sorwe of Troilus... In lovynge, how his aventures fellen / Fro wo to wele, and after out of joie" (I. 1–4). For all the narrator's protestations that he is faithfully reproducing his source, Books I–III of *Troilus and Criseyde* constitute an elaborate indirect challenge to Boccaccian authority which climaxes in the suspended moment at the close of Book III when Troilus, "in lust and in quiete / Is with Criseyde, his owen herte swete" (III. 1819–20). The lovers enjoy their bliss for unnumbered joyous nights, and the final stanza of the third book of *Il Filostrato*, which anticipates the turn of the wheel of "fortuna invidiosa" (*Fil.* III. 94), is held off until the Proem of Book IV.

The supplementary strategies of the *Troilus* are legion. I have already suggested that poetic form has its own power to shape plot, and in choosing to substitute rhyme royal for Boccaccio's *ottava rima*, Chaucer ensured that even on the level of the stanza his narrative would be dilatory.[10] Given the tendency of all translations to be wordier than their sources, the employment of a shorter stanza guarantees that, even when the Italian is being followed quite faithfully, the content of a single stanza of *Il Filostrato* will almost invariably overflow into, but not complete, a second stanza in *Troilus and Criseyde*: there will be room for its further elaboration. Moreover, the actual dynamics of the rhyme royal unit provide a sub-structure of dilation. Its rhyme scheme of ABABBCC in effect offers a sestet, ABABCC, expanded by an extra B rhymed line floating in its middle. The "floating" fourth or fifth line frequently consists of a co-ordinated or appositional clause which amplifies (or complicates) and slows the flow of the narrative within the stanza, but which at the same time tends to be an optional extra, potentially subtractable from the whole. Consider, for example, Troilus' response to Pandarus' request that he compose himself and name his beloved:

> But natheless, whan he hadde herd hym crye
> "Awake!" he gan to syken wonder soore,
> And seyde, "Frend, though that I stylle lye,
> I am nat deef. Now pees, and crye namore,
> *For I have herd thi wordes and thi lore*;
> But suffre me my meschief to bywaille,
> For thi proverbes may me naught availle."
>
> (I. 750–56; emphasis mine)

Line 754 is dispensable in the simplest narrative and syntactical terms, but its elaborative presence near the center of the stanza makes the pace and tone of the whole more leisurely and dilatory, just as, on a grander scale, the expansive narrative embellishments of Books II and III of the *Troilus*, while optional to the underlying fable, dilate, elaborate upon and ultimately reshape the structure of the poetic fiction.[11]

Nor is this expansive redoubling in the rhyme royal stanza restricted to the "floating" fourth or fifth line: it may also be found in Chaucer's terminal couplets, which, far more frequently than those closing Boccaccio's units of *ottava rima*, are used to articulate a supplementary illustration, often in the form of a proverb or aphorism. The narrator, for example, exclaims:

> O blynde world, O blynde entencioun!
> How often falleth al the effect contraire
> Of surquidrie and foul presumpcioun;
> For kaught is proud, and kaught is debonaire.
> This Troilus is clomben on the staire,
> And litel weneth that he moot descenden
> *But alday faileth thing that fooles wenden.*
>
> (I. 211–17; emphasis mine)

The *sententia* of the last line is not necessary to complete the bare narrative import of the stanza and is in fact a repetitive variation on lines 212–13; it is generated by the demands of prosodic form, and it is not in Boccaccio.[12]

Repetition within the stanza mirrors in little an additive dynamic within the rising action of the *Troilus*, where there is constant doubling of narrative units and narrative events.[13] On the small scale, we may remark Chaucer's frequent use of two stanzas for one (or less) of Boccaccio's. Pandarus, for example, lectures his niece:

> "Thenk ek how elde wasteth every houre
> In ech of yow a partie of beautee;
> And therfore er that age the devoure,
> Go love; for old, there wol no wight of the.
> Lat this proverbe a loore unto yow be:
> Too late ywar, quod Beaute, whan it paste;
> And Elde daunteth Daunger at the laste.
>
> "The kynges fool is wont to crien loude,
> Whan that hym thinketh a womman berth hire hye,
> 'So long mote ye lyve, and alle proude,
> Til crowes feet be growen under youre yë,
> And sende yow than a myrour in to prye,
> In which that ye may see youre face a morwe!'
> I bidde wisshe yow namore sorwe."
>
> (II. 393–406)

All this derives from Pandoro's curt "'Non perder tempo, pensa che vecchiezza / O morte torrá via la tua bellezza'." (Lose no time, consider that old age or death will take away all your beauty; *Fil.* II. 54), which Chaucer expands through semi-repetition (II. 393), proverb and *sententia* (397–99), and an additional stanza of exemplary anecdote (400–06).

On the larger scale, Chaucer doubles whole scenes, speeches and songs from *Il Filostrato*. Thus, the moment of Troilus' falling in love is described twice, once figuratively (I. 206–31), and then in more concrete terms (I. 271–80).[14] Shortly after this, Troilus sings two consecutive lyrics, the Petrarchan *Canticus Troili* (I. 400–420) and an apostrophe to love (I. 421–34); Troiolo has only the apostrophe (*Fil.* I. 38–9). Troilus takes two formal rides past Criseyde's window (II. 624–48 and 1248–60); Troiolo has only a single passage (*Fil.* II. 82). Book III of the *Troilus* shifts Troiolo's post-consummation paean (*Fil.* III. 74–79) to the Proem (III. 1–38), and then echoes it, after the lovers' night of bliss, in Troilus' Boethian panegyric (III. 1744–71). Troilus and Criseyde both give voice to *aubades* after their first night together (III. 1422–42; 1450–63); only Troiolo berates the dawn in *Il Filostrato* (*Fil.* III. 44–46). Finally, the consummation scene itself (twice as long as in the Italian work) is expanded by the redoubled attempts of the wondering narrator to articulate its bliss, both from the point of view of the lovers and from his own perspective.[15]

Several of the narrative "doublings" recorded above involve the generation and embedding of new lyrics within *Troilus and Criseyde*. The sympathetic narrator's dilation-through-repetition of *Il Filostrato* seems consciously to exploit the poetic fiction's capacity to complicate narrative progression with the more synchronic patternings of lyric. Certainly, whether he is anatomizing the exquisite agonies of frustrated love in Book I, or staving off the moment of recognition of his loss of Criseyde in Book V, Troilus repeatedly orders, confines, perhaps even distances his pain by turning to this particular discourse of desire.[16] But Boccaccio's Troiolo is equally a devotee of lyric complaint; Chaucer's more innovative and significant move is to introduce the lyric mode into the world of the heroine and to authorize a female lyric voice.[17] If he does not actually show Criseyde composing a love lyric of her own in the scenes of his own invention which follow Pandarus' departure from the heroine's house in Book II, our author does allow her to hear in her niece's song a female celebration of love remarkably different in tone and mood from Troilus' Petrarchan complaints in Book I.[18] His narrative amplifications conjure up a series of sensuous and lyrical experiences in the enclosed world of Criseyde's house and garden; he invents a sequence of transformative repetition which offers the heroine a more and more "unnarratable" apprehension of human passion. The measured arguments of Antigone's lyric in praise of love (II. 827–75) melt into the wordless love song of the "nyghtyngale, upon a cedre grene" (II. 918–24), which is in turn subsumed by the disturbing, yet painless, ravishment and exchange of hearts carried out by the eagle in Criseyde's dream (II. 925–31). The text dilates itself by figuring forth an alternative dream-rhetoric of love to balance the poetics of desire and privation already formulated by Petrarchan Troilus in Book I.

Although we hear no more songs from Criseyde's garden, Criseyde gives voice, in Book III, to her own lyric – the *aubade* berating the departing night which Chaucer adds to the dawn song already given to Troiolo in *Il Filostrato.* The third book is interwoven with further lyrical passages: hymns to love frame it at start and close, and the love-making of Troilus and Criseyde is continually interrupted by speeches which are transformed into songs as they strive to define, elaborate and suspend the joyful moment.[19] The sympathetic narrator, too, prolongs their night of bliss with his own rhapsodic attempts to offer an authentic – and largely "lyricised" – account of their joys. In fact, it becomes increasingly difficult to dissect out discrete passages of lyric from the consummation scene: those critics who, in tabulating the embedded lyrics in *Troilus and Criseyde,* end up disagreeing over their number, kind and location[20] are perhaps being teased by a poetic narrative whose diachronic unfolding repeatedly shifts into moments of lyric elaboration in a manner not always or necessarily marked by explicit rubrics like "*Canticus Troili.*"

Lyric delay is a particularly interesting manifestation of the subversive and reinterpretive art of excess in a narrative which persistently favors rhetoric over action – or rather, as Eugene Vance notes, makes speech its favored form of action.[21] Near the close of Book II, the narrator insists that he *wants* to make haste with his story: "But fle we now prolixitee best is" (II. 1564); however, his somewhat tortured syntax teases us with the alternative suggestion that, as far as he is concerned, "prolixitee" indeed "best is." The hero and heroine of the English poem must articulate their hopes and fears about acting, discuss all the possible results of that action, or be lengthily persuaded to act by the go-between, before any step can be taken. Troilus, in Book I, delays revealing his love's identity to Pandarus by reiterating that his case is hopeless: Pandarus has to summon up far more arguments than Boccaccio's Pandaro in order to persuade him to utter Criseyde's name aloud, and the entire episode, from Pandarus's entry to that moment of revelation, requires 162 more lines in the *Troilus* than in *Il Filostrato*.[22] Even when Pandarus is escorting Troilus to Criseyde's bed, the latter is still engaged in rhetorical delaying actions: a request for Venus' aid (III. 712–14) is elaborated into a prayer to half the Pantheon (III. 715–35).[23]

Inextricably intertwined with the constant retardation of narrative progression by such elaborate set pieces – whether they be "pure" lyric or the highly wrought speeches which, in the mouths of Troilus and Criseyde, approach the status of lyric *compleynte* – is Chaucer's concurrent strategy of weaving into his work other, more or less fragmentary, non-Boccaccian textual borrowings. Such appropriations may be introduced with remarkable sleight of hand: when, for example, Troilus is about to burst into his first song, the narrator interrupts him with the following:

> And of his song naught only the sentence,
> As writ myn auctour called Lollius,
> But pleinly, save oure tonges difference,
> I dar wel seyn, in al, that Troilus
> Seyde in his song, loo, every word right thus
> As I shal seyn; and whoso list it here,
> Loo, next this vers he may it fynden here.
>
> (I. 393–99)

This is the first time that the narrator has named his "auctour," and he does so just before he launches into three stanzas which are a fairly close translation, not of any part of *Il Filostrato*, but of Sonnet CXXXII in Petrarch's *Rime sparse*, "S'Amor non è." We have a double bluff: misnamed author of the main source and misattributed borrowed lyric. The prevaricating stanza, tellingly, is a particularly uneasy one: it seems to lack a main finite verb, the "dar wel seyn... I shal seyn" repetition is clumsy, and the final couplet, with its thudding *rime riche*, sounds like padding. Chaucer is perhaps betraying a failure of nerve as he juggles his awareness of his real "auctour" with the elaborate feints of his dilatory narrator.

The most sustained reproductions of other texts in the rising action of the *Troilus* are the Petrarchan *Canticus Troili*, Antigone's song (which has parallels in the *dits amoreux* of Machaut), and the Boethian hymn to love given to Troilus at the end of Book III. In the descending action, Chaucer's single most extended appropriation is Troilus' Boethian soliloquy on free will. The "end-resistant" narrator thus exploits his poetic narrative's pull towards the patterned language of lyric and its willingness to embrace other makings as he augments the rising action, and even in the later stages of the poem makes manifest his characters' predisposition to substitute rhetoric for action through further borrowings. He does not, however, restrict his interpolations to these fairly prolonged appropriations of others' voices: brief allusions to the *Heroïdes* and the *Metamorphoses*, the *Roman de la Rose*, de Vinsauf's *Poetria Nova*, and Dante's *Commedia* also play a part in the amplification of Boccaccio.[24]

Troilus and Criseyde embraces, moreover, supplementary and dilatory "microtexts" constituted by short passages of mythological allusion and proverbial wisdom. Chaucer introduces an Olympian machinery almost entirely absent from Boccaccio into his narrator's prohemia and invocations and into the discourse of his characters. This strategy is quite closely tied to the formal demands of the rhyme royal stanza: a typical stanza filler, in instances when Chaucer simultaneously paraphrases and augments Boccaccio, is a classical reference condensed into a few lines or less. Troilus, lamenting the decision to surrender Criseyde to the Greeks, cries out:

> "What shal I don? I shal, while I may dure
> On lyve in torment and in cruwel peyne
> This infortune or this disaventure,
> Allone as I was borne, iwys, compleyne;
> Ne nevere wol I seen it shyne or reyne,
> But ende I wol, as Edippe, in derknesse
> My sorwful lif, and dyen in distress."
>
> (IV. 295–301)

The stanza begins by loosely paraphrasing *Il Filostrato* (IV. 34) but ends with an interpolated and original allusion to the blinded Oedipus.

Everybody in the poem invokes the gods at one time or another, but proverbs, the "texts" of popular wisdom, are primarily a feature of Pandarus' expansive rhetoric, and his speeches frequently outrun the corresponding ones of Pandaro because of the piling up of proverbial phrases and *exempla*.[25] When Pandarus tries to persuade the unhappy Troilus to trust in his resourcefulness, he departs from the briefer arguments of Pandaro at I. 631 with his *exemplum* of the dull whetstone that can nevertheless sharpen axes. The narrative does not rejoin the source text for another thirty-five lines, by which time Pandarus is discussing the physician who can heal others but not himself: the expansion of Boccaccio arises out of multiple variations upon a single theme.[26] The dilatory narrator is almost as fond of proverbs as Pandarus, and, in that they are frozen "optative"[27] statements which tell us how we would *like* a consistently predictable, humanly comprehensible universe to behave, his employment of them as a means of textual supplementation hints at his desire to control, stabilize and suspend the articulation of meaning in order to defy the vulnerability of his words and of his fiction of earthly happiness.

The increased use of proverbs in the *Troilus* introduces into the poem a vocabulary of the colloquial and the concrete that complements the more elevated diction of aristocratic love. The "in-eching"[28] of naturalistic detail represents, indeed, yet another of Chaucer's augmentative strategies, and one which once more intersects with the dilatoriness plotted by the rhyme royal form. "Realism" is a loaded term to apply to medieval narrative, but insofar as it refers to an interest in establishing physical surroundings and lively idiosyncrasies of speech and gesture which extends beyond what is actually required by the simple concatenation of events in the source fable, it is certainly evident in *Troilus and Criseyde*.[29] The narrator may insist that he is not bound to record *everything* that happened between his lovers (III. 491–504), but he nevertheless offers us far more of the minutiae of their everyday lives than does Boccaccio. Predictably, his interpolations are more evident in the dilated rising action; such realistic episodes in Books IV and V as the descent of the tactless Trojan gossips upon a wretched Criseyde (IV. 680–730), or Troilus' comic mistaking of a "fare carte" for his lady as he awaits her return on the ramparts of Troy (V. 1156–62) are in fact renderings of events already present in *Il Filostrato* (*Fil.* IV. 80–86 and VII. 8).

"In-eching" is especially evident in Chaucer's descriptions of interior and exterior space; he is also much more interested than Boccaccio in furnishings, clothing and bodily gestures.[30] But particularly fully realized settings are only one aspect of the greater verisimilitude of the *Troilus*; a whole range of other details are scattered in passing as part of small-scale dilatory strategies within the narrative. When Troilus is first struck by love, the narrator devotes two stanzas to proclaiming the vulnerability of all men, however proud, to the vicissitudes of fortune:

> O blynde worlde, O blynde entencioun!
> How often falleth al the effect contraire
> Of surquidrie and foul presumpcioun;
> For kaught is proud, and kaught is debonaire.
> This Troilus is clomben on the staire,
> And litel weneth that he moot descenden:
> But alday faileth thing that fooles wenden.
>
> As proude Bayard gynneth for to skippe
> Out of the weye, so pryketh hym his corn,
> Til he a lasshe have of the longe whippe –
> Than thynketh he, "Though I praunce al byforn
> First in the trays, ful fat and newe shorn,
> Yet am I but an hors, and horses lawe
> I moot endure, and with my feres drawe."
>
> (I. 211–24)

The first three lines follow fairly closely the first three lines of *Il Filostrato*, I. 25, but the narrator then expands more and more concretely upon his theme, first stating Troilus' narrative situation (214), then invoking the somewhat predictable image of the stair (215), recapitulating it with a proverb (217) and finally devoting an entire stanza to the elaborative Bayard simile, which, with its down to earth, often monosyllabic nouns and verbs ("skippe," "corn," "lasshe," "fat," "praunce," "whippe," "shorn," "drawe," "trays") creates a little equine cosmos of its own, and is also comically apt as an analogue for the fate of the young chevalier. Once again, moreover, we encounter formal "doubling" as an augmentative measure: two Chaucerian stanzas do the work of one in the source.

On an even more localized scale, a line or phrase within a single stanza frequently proves to be an expansion of Boccaccio in the interest either of greater concreteness or of more realistic "historical" detail. Let us examine a few specific examples of this strategy; the additional material in each instance has been emphasized:

(a) Troilus in love:

> But whan he hadde a space from his care,
> Thus to hymself ful ofte he gan to pleyne;
> He seyde, "O fool, now artow in the snare,
> That whilom japedest at loves peyne.
> *Now artow hent, now gnaw thin owen cheyne!*
> Thow were ay wont ech lovere reprehende
> Of thing fro which thou kanst the nat defende."
>
> (I. 505–11)

(b) Troilus accepts Pandarus' advice to write to Criseyde:

> Quod Troilus, "Depardieux, ich assente!
> Sith that the list, I wil arise and write;
> And blisful God prey ich with good entente,
> The viage, and the lettre I shal endite,
> So spede it; *and thow, Minerva, the white,*
> Yif thow me wit my lettre to devyse."
> And sette hym down, and wrot right in this wyse:
>
> (II. 1058–64)

(c) Calchas says he was content to abandon all he had in Troy,

> "Save of a doughter that I lefte, allas,
> Slepyng at hom, whanne out of Troie I sterte.
> O sterne, O cruel fader that I was!
> How myghte I have in that so hard an herte?
> *Allas, I ne hade ibrought hire in hire sherte!*
> For sorwe of which I wol nought lyve tomorwe,
> But if ye lordes rewe upon my sorwe."
>
> (IV. 92–98)

In all three of these examples, a stanza of *Il Filostrato* is being paraphrased as well as supplemented.[31] Stanza (a) is a very close rendering of *Il Filostrato* I. 50. The latter contains the snare image, but not the more violent and graphic one of the chained animal. Stanza (b) paraphrases *Il Filostrato* II. 95. Lines 1061–62 are not in the source, but it is the invocation of Minerva – part of the classical coloring that is yet another characteristic of Chaucer's "realism" in depicting *his* Troy – that is the single important addition to Boccaccio's text. Stanza (c) is a reasonably accurate version of *Il Filostrato* IV. 8, which already moves the Italian in the direction of greater specificity when it turns Calcas's "'figliuola... ch'io vi lasciai'" into Calchas's "'doughter that I lefte... slepyng at hom.'" It is Calchas's frank wish that he'd brought Criseyde along in her nightshirt, however, that suddenly turns Boccaccio's representation of verbose paternal regret into a more pointed and pithy sentiment. I do not think it mere coincidence, incidentally, that, in the first and third of my examples, the "realistic" verse is one of those dilatory "floating" verses discussed earlier: in both cases its work is felicitously supplementary rather than integral to the syntactic/narrative line; here, again, Chaucer's narrative is cultivating the subversive art of excess.

I have suggested some ways in which Chaucer's prosodic structures, his weaving of passages of lyric elaboration into his narrative, his preference for rhetoric over action, his interpolation of fragments from other texts, and his amplificatory "realism" dilate the material provided by Boccaccio. The augmentative imperative of these strategies, in combination with the many entirely new episodes of Books II and III, subverts teleology; every one of these narrative gestures works to stave off the turning of Fortune's wheel that concludes the third book of Chaucer's source. But every expansion may also come to offer a silent gloss upon its source, and Chaucer's additions to Boccaccio comprise some distinctly and specifically reinterpretive gestures. This is immediately obvious in the interpolation of lyric material taken from Boethius, Petrarch and Machaut. Prior contexts resonate against new narrative frames, adding multiple perspectives to the courtly romance of Books I to III of

Il Filostrato. While the material appropriated from Petrarch and Machaut sketches out, as I have already hinted, competing poetics of earthly desire, Troilus' Boethian hymn (III. 1744–71) – ironic in context, delivered as it is by an emphatically unregenerate and pagan lover[32] – anticipates the assertion of the transcendent nature of heavenly love in *Troilus and Criseyde*'s Epilogue. And the fragmentary and intermittent Petrarchan, Machauvian, and Boethian recastings of Books I through III are further complicated by Chaucer's introducing into his dilatory narrative not only the purloined texts of other authors but also the characteristics of a variety of literary genres.[33]

Boccaccio, of course, carried on his own revisionary dialogue with genre when he fashioned *his* artful and elegant Troy story out of portions of Benoît de Sainte-Maure's *roman antique*,[34] but the relatively coherent universe portrayed in *Il Filostrato*, where sexual passion and sexual betrayal are simply different sides of the same coin, is made vastly more complex by *Troilus and Criseyde*'s generous entertainment and deployment of heterogeneric material which pulls the story of the Trojan lovers into shifting allegiances with other literary kinds. The romance elements of the original are enhanced (Book II's loving and unBoccaccian delineation of the enclosed "other world" of Criseyde's house and garden, full of romance readers, love lyricists, nightingales, and suggestive dreams, offers a striking example of this), but so are its ties to epic: Chaucer provides additional references to Troilus' bravery in battle (II. 190–203; 625–44), devotes more space to the frame story of the Trojan war, "in-eches" a pagan religious context, and introduces repeated allusions to the bloody history of Thebes.[35] At the same time, even as some of the Chaucerian additions to *Il Filostrato* thicken the pagan and "classical" texture of the narrative, other interpolations weave a visible thread of Christian imagery and discourse into the poem, compounding the contradictory interpretive signals offered by its jostling genres. Chaucer's glancing allusions to Dante, his narrator's quasi-Christian "Bidding Prayer" (I. 15–49), and his introduction of Boethius' celebration of Divine Love into Book III move the work in the direction of Christian epic – or divine comedy. At the same time, his fusion of the language of religion with that of earthly passion (seen most strikingly when Eros, Venus, and the Almighty melt into one another in the prayers of hero and narrator at the conclusion of Book III) is equally characteristic of secular and courtly romance.[36]

The shadowy counter-narratives traced out in Chaucer's unannounced supplementations of *Il Filostrato* are somewhat uneasily complemented by the passages of overt commentary or explication which constitute a quite separate strategy of narrative dilation.[37] These direct interventions represent the sympathetic narrator's least satisfactory challenge to the "authorized version" of his story, and they function in particularly awkward contrast to Chaucer's more discreet reinterpretive expansions of Boccaccio. When, for example, Chaucer interrupts Criseyde's first cogitations about her would-be lover with Troilus' victory ride past her window, he gives her thoughts an objective correlative and the burgeoning of her desire an immediate instinctive expression in her exclamation "Who yaf me drynke?" (II. 651), thus adding a new dimension to her otherwise measured assessment of the advantages and disadvantages of taking a lover. His additions radically revise Boccaccio's characterization of a heroine who, at the end of her equivalent meditation, decides to love Troiolo before she has ever seen him (*Fil.* II. 78) – a heroine who will later doff her mask of *daunger* a mere four stanzas after she has insisted that she will love Troiolo as a brother but never speak to him (*Fil.* II. 134–38) (and will be quite likely, the author implies, to forsake her lover as swiftly as she embraced him). Such quiet supplementations of Boccaccio, which reinvent the heroine and call into doubt the "inevitability" of her treachery, pull the invariables of the Italian pre-text into a substantially different configuration. But whenever the narrator intervenes directly to dispose of any doubts the reader *might* be formulating about Criseyde's behavior (devoting, for example, three stanzas to defending her from the hypothetical accusation that hers was a "sodeyn love" [II. 666–86]), he generally succeeds, as Donaldson has so convincingly argued, in making us question her actions for the first time.[38] And indeed, imaginative supplementation and reinterpretation will decline into mere prevarication in Books IV and V, as the tension increases between the sympathetic narrator's "delaying" interventions and the increasingly un-postponable catastrophe. Chaucer may extend the final meeting of the lovers by some 241 lines and increase the narrative space required for Diomede to win Criseyde from Troilus; the narrator may anxiously interrupt the lovers' parting in Book IV with a whole stanza of assertions that Criseyde "was in purpos evere to be trewe" (IV. 1415–21), insist that Criseyde didn't necessarily give her heart to Diomede (V. 1050) and announce that we have no proof that Diomede won her swiftly (V. 1086–92). In the end, however, the revisionary amplifications of the final books seem all too reminiscent of the bluster directed at the sources of *Troilus and Criseyde* in the Proem to Book IV:

> Allas, that they sholde evere cause fynde
> To speke hire harm! And if they on hire lye,
> Iwis, hemself sholde han the vilanye.
>
> (IV. 19–21)

The augmentative impulse must defer, at the last, to the known conclusion. But before moving on to consider the end-determined design which complements – and competes with – the expansive counter-plot of the *Troilus*, I would like to offer a brief discussion of the personage who seems to epitomize the subversive and supplementary aspect of its narrative unfolding. Pandarus is the character whose part is most expanded from *Il Filostrato*: Troilus' lines of direct discourse shrink to 1462·5 from Troiolo's 1706, Criseyde's increase to 1154 from Criseida's 747, but Pandarus' more than double – he has 1804·5 as compared to Pandaro's 789.[39] His amplified actions are, however, almost entirely confined to the rising action: after Book III he speaks only about sixty more lines than Boccaccio's go-between. This dilatory gentleman is thus the prime agent of dilation in the most dilated part of Chaucer's poem – indeed, the completely new events in *Troilus and Criseyde* are mainly *his* inventions.[40]

Pandarus is a maker of plots who takes pleasure both in scheming and in restructuring life as a delightful fiction. His favorite reading is apparently romance (II. 96–97; II. 106–108; III. 980), and it is not surprising that he offers Criseyde the chance to become the heroine of a romance "aventure" (II. 224). He is indubitably an *alter ego* of the expansive narrator, nearly all of whose amplificatory strategies he incorporates within his own actions.[41] Like him, he says he'll abridge, but expands (III. 295ff.; compare II. 1564); like him, he supplements his own speech with other texts and authorities; like him, he will indulge in rhetorical delaying actions; like him, he will combine verbose colloquialism with an equally verbose high style. He delights in narrative excess, and, as the narrator complicates another man's fiction, Pandarus makes fictional additions to Trojan "reality." Talking to Criseyde, he fashions a *story* out of Troilus' love-longing, exaggerating the prince's (admittedly dire) sufferings, and adding to his tale the fiction of his own imminent demise. His impassioned projection of the double murder of Troilus and himself by a "routheles" Criseyde – for he elaborates remorselessly upon his characterization of his niece as a pitiless beauty, a conventional anti-heroine of romance[42] – is an act of moral blackmail: seduction-by-compleynte. Nor does his fabulation stop here. He invents the misdeeds of the wicked Poliphete in order to arrange the first meeting of Troilus and Criseyde, and later caps this tale with the equally outrageous story of Troilus' supposed rival, Horaste, in order to get them into the same bed. Even when *that* has been achieved, and Pandarus has withdrawn, "As for to looke upon an old romance" (III. 980), the "as for" suggests that he is merely feigning interest in someone else's feigning; his immediate response to Troilus' swoon (III. 1094) proves that his attention is still very much upon his own, vital creation.[43] Pandarus only lies down to sleep when Troilus finally makes his first unprompted move in the poem and embraces Criseyde (III. 1187–89) – but he (like the observing narrator) is nevertheless present in the room all the time the lovers are in bed.

Although the go-between is allowed to initiate a romantic design, he can no more control the end of the affair than can the dilatory narrator, and his creation escapes his control. In Book IV, his capacity to fabricate new episodes falters as soon as it is decided to surrender Criseyde to the Greeks. His first proposal to the stricken Troilus – that the latter should repeat his "aventure" with a second lady, substituting another fair Trojan for Criseyde (IV. 400–27) – is suggestive of the most banal and mechanical kind of plot stretching. His second idea is equally repetitive: Troilus must look to his brother's story, abduct Criseyde just as Paris abducted Helen – enact a new *Iliad* in effect (IV. 530–36). In the end (and in a passage added to *Il Filostrato*) it is Criseyde to whom Pandarus offers the mantle of creativity:

> "Syn ye be wise and bothe of oon assent,
> So shapeth how destourbe youre goynge,
> Or come ayeyn soon after ye ben went.
> Women ben wise in short avysement."
>
> (IV. 933–36)

You must improvise a happy ending for your own story. Criseyde later repeats Pandarus' words to Troilus:

> "I am a womman, as ful wel ye woot,
> And as I am avysed sodeynly,
> So wol I telle yow"
>
> (IV. 1261–63)

She now speaks of the "art" which may order matters to their liking (IV. 1266–67): her intention is to become a Pandarus and use tales of riches hidden in Troy to trick Calchas into letting her return there (IV. 1380–1400). Her control of the art of persuasion will "converte" her father from trusting in his own arts to believing her arguments (IV. 1401–14) – just as Pandarus' speeches helped to turn *her* thoughts from chaste widowhood to love. Troilus, unconvinced, proffers an alternative happy ending to their history, imagining a comfortable and honorable exile together, and the later stages of Book IV become a *logomachia* in which they battle for the right to plot the end of their affair. Criseyde, fatally, wins the victory; Troilus' abandonment of imaginative persuasion with "I kan na more" (IV. 1659) seals their destiny.

The only "making" left for Pandarus to articulate in Book V is the fiction that Criseyde will return to Troy – a fantasy which has no connection with actual narrative events. The newly empowered "plotter" of the final book is Diomede, a debased version of Pandarus as well as of Troilus. When he seizes the reins of Criseyde's horse on the ride to the Greek camp (v. 90; not in Boccaccio), he is asserting the same kind of control over her actions that her uncle strove to maintain. His wooing, like Pandarus' on behalf of Troilus, combines emotional blackmail (the imminent Fall of Troy is narrated at much greater length by Chaucer's Diomede than by Boccaccio's) with the figuring forth (through his own self-portraiture) of a nobly suffering hero of courtly romance for her to love (v. 918–45; compare II. 155–207; 316ff). Diomede's artful speeches in Book v emphasize Pandarus' sudden verbal inadequacy. The latter's optimistic reading of Troilus' prophetic dream is the most unconvincing fiction he produces in the *Troilus*, and Pandarus is finally silenced for good by the proof of his niece's faithlessness. An entire stanza is devoted to his dumbstruck state (v. 1723–29), and when he does manage to speak, it is only to confirm his impotence: "I may do the namore. / What sholde I seyen? ... Right fayn I wolde amende it, wiste I how ... I kan namore seye" (v. 1731–43). Cursing Criseyde, he finally parts company from the narrator who dilated her story so delightfully, for, while the latter struggles with the contradictory demands of his fable and his sympathies until, and past, the moment of betrayal, Pandarus renounces his niece for being the "routheles" beauty of his own romance.

RELENTLESS DESIGN

However dilated, however much supplemented, the story of Troilus and Criseyde ends, like that of Troiolo and Criseida, with a betrayal, a death, and an unhappy acceptance of the radical discontinuity between the hero's faith in the perfect "trouthe" of his love and the hard truths of an imperfect and mutable world. The narrator may temporarily suppress the stanza which, at the conclusion of Book III of *Il Filostrato*, announces the turn of Fortune's wheel, but it will reappear, perforce, to commence the Proem of his fourth book. And despite his assertion that all of the descending action will be encompassed by Book IV (IV. 15–17), two books, not one, will be required to dissipate the joys of Book III, just as two were required to climb towards those delights. For all the efforts of the sympathetic narrator to soften the fall from happiness, a new emotional distance is evident in the poem's steady delineation of the transience of earthly bliss: the increasingly visible (and apparently authoritative) designs of a cooler architect inexorably revise the augmentative strategies of the voluble, partial and Pandaric maker.

As *Troilus and Criseyde* unfolds, it gives evidence of an ever more economical deployment (structured in full awareness of a source whose conclusion is accepted and exploited) of both the material taken from Boccaccio and the supplementary makings presided over by the expansive narrator. When Pandarus tells Criseyde that,

> "How so it be that som men hem delite
> With subtyl art hire tales to endite,
> Yet for al that, in hire entencioun
> Hire tale is al for som conclusioun."
>
> (II. 256–59)

he unwittingly sets a limit on his own powers of creation. Pandarus' mistake is to assume that the end to which *his* "subtyl art" is directed is anything more than a provisional, temporary and vulnerable resting place within a larger design. At the start of Book V, we finally learn the length of the affair between Troilus and Criseyde – three springs have passed since he began to love her (V. 8–13). A terminus has been imposed upon the unnumbered nights of shared joy celebrated by the dilatory narrator (III. 1713), and another shaping force emerges to exploit this sense of an inevitable ending and create (through the manipulation of both scheme and matter) a significant pattern of correspondences across the aesthetic object which is the text of the poem.

The duplicitous designs of *Troilus and Criseyde* permit this totalizing strategy to unfold concurrently with the subversive supplementation of *Il Filostrato*. In Books I through III, for example, a familiar rhetorical "delaying action" is provided by the characters' and narrator's repeated invocations of Fortune and their disquisitions upon the control of supernatural forces over men's lives (nearly all of them Chaucerian interpolations).[44] In context, these tend to be overshadowed by the happy results of Pandarus' highly efficient human machinations. As Books IV and V proceed, however, the questionable workings of the powers above inexorably assume a new significance within the overall design of the fiction. Calchas, whose belated retrieval of his daughter from Troy provides the turning point of the narrative, is wholly motivated by what he knows destiny holds in store for his city. The priestly unfolder of Fortune's plot is the fictional equivalent of the maker who acknowledges the force of his fable's destined end – just as Pandarus, who recognizes the existence of supernatural forces which can overturn men's best efforts, but who nevertheless puts his faith in human schemes, is the *alter ego* of that aspect of the poet represented by the dilatory narrator. Early in Book I, *that* narrator had at once acknowledged, and proceeded to ignore, the fate of Troy:

> But how this town com to destruccion
> Ne falleth naught to purpos me to telle,
> For it were a long digression
> Fro my matere
>
> (I. 141–44)

But the city's sack reappears at the beginning of Book IV in a stanza added to Boccaccio's version of Calchas' speech to the Greek leaders:

> "the tyme is faste by
> That fire and flaumbe on al the town shal sprede,
> And thus shal Troie torne to asshen dede."
>
> (IV. 117–19)

Since Calchas' foreknowledge of this provides him with a convincing argument that one Trojan warrior can be spared to exchange for Criseyde, the future Fall of Troy is no longer a "digression" from the "matere" of *Troilus and Criseyde* at all.[45]

The rise and fall of Fortune's wheel influences Chaucer's complication and reshaping of Boccaccio's fiction: form seems remarkably congruent with content in the narrative patterning of the *Troilus* as *de casibus* tragedy on the grand scale.[46] Pandarus' cheerful remark (not to be found in *Il Filostrato*) that Fortune must eventually work in Troilus' favor and give him joy after sorrow (I. 841–54) will be ironically echoed in the prince's plaints against that mutable lady in Book IV, when, joy having followed sorrow, sorrow once again succeeds joy (IV. 260–87; 323–29; somewhat expanded over *Il Filostrato* IV. 30–32). The climbing and descending arch of Chaucer's five books departs radically from the rather untidily divided narrative of *Il Filostrato*, where eight units of disparate length are framed by lyrical dedications to the maker's lady (*Fil.* I. 1–5; IX. 1–8; the ninth book is the end frame).[47] Moreover, the newly symmetrical division of rising and falling action in the *Troilus* is accompanied by a proliferation of structural and thematic parallels distributed across the upward and downward slopes of the work. These present a variation upon the additive repetitions at the level of line, stanza or episode that characterized the augmentative strategies of the expansive narrator; they tend to be more widely spaced "doublings," ironic recastings of events and images in which the energetic expansions of Books I, II and III often constitute, in retrospect, portents of misery to come.

The wooing of Criseyde establishes the initial elements of a series of ironic repetitions or inversions in Books IV and V. We have already seen how Pandarus' arguments on behalf of Troilus are echoed by Diomede's arguments on behalf of himself, and this is only one of many doublings. In the rising action, the lovelorn hero's Petrarchan image of himself as a rudderless boat, tossed by hostile winds, in the first *Canticus Troili* (I. 415–18) is transformed by Pandarus into the conceit that, in loving Criseyde, he has reached a happy port (I. 969) and the Proem of Book II reinforces this by describing Troilus as sailing free of the storm-tossed waves of unsatisfied desire (II. 1–7). In Book V, however, the second *Canticus Troili* recapitulates the original image, and renders it even more gloomy than on its first appearance: the hero declares, "Toward my deth with wynd in steere I saille" (V. 641). Nor is this the only time that the lovers' rhetoric is reinvoked to mark the downward curve of Fortune's wheel. When the hero and heroine are in bed together for the first time, Troilus says Criseyde's eyes are "nettes" that have entrapped him (III. 1355), and the narrator afterwards expands the image to describe how utterly the hero's heart is "yknet" in a "net" of which not one "knotte" may be loosened (III. 1730–36). Diomede, in contrast, will be seen in Book v plotting to bring Criseyde's heart within his "net" (v. 775), and by then the narrator is all too aware that "bothe Troilus and Troie town / Shall *knotteles* thorughout hire herte slide" (v. 768–69; emphasis mine). In a similar manner, the arguments favored by Pandarus when he tells Criseyde she must accede to his wishes to save Troilus (and himself) from death come back to haunt the reader when Criseyde herself appropriates such discourse in a successful bid to make sure that Troilus accepts her doomed scheme of action:

> "trusteth me, and leveth ek youre sorwe,
> Or here my trouthe: I wol naught lyve tyl morwe."
> (IV. 1616–17)

One does not have to look far for other ironic parallels. Pandarus's fictions in Book III require Troilus to forgive Criseyde for an act of faithlessness she has never committed and Criseyde to pardon Troilus for jealousy he has never felt. But when Criseyde's faithlessness is all too evident, and Troilus' jealousy (v. 1212–18) all too justified, Book v will demonstrate that these fictions were grimly prophetic.[48] In Book v, in an ineffectual attempt to rebuff Diomede, Criseyde resorts to the same plea of celibate widowhood (v. 975–80) that she earlier invoked with as little success against Pandarus' insistence upon the love-rites due to May (II. 113–19) – a plea now based on the outright lie that she has no mind to love. Finally, in that second wooing of Criseyde, Chaucer offers a telling echo of his heroine's letter to Troilus in Book II, in which she promises to be a sister to the prince (II. 1224), even though she has already shown herself to be interested in a rather different kind of attachment: Diomede offers himself as a brother to Criseyde (v. 134) when he has far from fraternal service in mind.

Nearly every one of these end-conscious doublings (and triplings) is *created* by Chaucer. Either one or both elements will be absent from Boccaccio's text: the *Troilus* does not merely reproduce a configuration already present there. None of the boat/sea/wind images cited above appear in *Il Filostrato* and the "death threat" passages are less marked in the Italian. Criseida *does* invoke her widowhood as a defense against the arguments of Pandaro (*Fil.* II. 49) and Diomede (*Fil.* VI. 29), but although she promises to be a sister to Troiolo shortly before she arranges their first assignation (*Fil.* II. 134), Diomede never offers to be a brother to her. The original "net" image appears in Troiolo's address to his lady's eyes (*Fil.* III. 36), but there are no Boccaccian equivalents for the subsequent ones we see in the *Troilus*. And Pandarus' invented story of Troilus' jealousy over Criseyde's supposed faithlessness is entirely original to Chaucer.

The consciously goal-determined narrative designs of *Troilus and Criseyde*, like its more subversive augmentative strategies, are also inscribed at the "micro" level of poetic form, most notably in the patterns of rhyme. The narrator's rather odd petition to the Muse of History that she help him to "ryme wel" (II. 8–10) becomes less incongruous when we realize that the repetition of certain rhymes constitutes an integral part of the overall scheme of this particular history. From the first, Chaucer repeats rhyme endings more frequently than Boccaccio, both accepting and exploiting the more limited rhyme range of the English language – and wringing ironic and pathetic significance from the reappearance of familiar and resonant rhymes in modified settings.[49]

The best example of this narrative procedure is provided by the rhyme pair *routhe/trouthe*, which, together with the related pair *rewe/trewe*, crops up a total of twenty-seven times in *Troilus and Criseyde*.[50] *Routhe/trouthe* represents a particularly important and charged coupling: *trouthe*, for example, has a semantic range encompassing the plighted troth of lovers, personal faith and integrity, Divine Truth, and the hard truth of plain facts.[51] (We might note, furthermore, that the various designs of the *Troilus* set the sympathetic narrator's *routhe* for his characters – and particularly Criseyde – in tension with the troth that must be kept with the invariables of the source fable, as well as the higher Truths invoked at the end of the poem.) Characteristically, the rhyme first appears in association with Pandarus, who is responsible for setting so many of the important events of the narrative into play, not least the verbal ones:

> This Pandare, that neigh malt for wo and routhe,
> Ful ofte seyde, "Allas, what may this be?
> Now frend," quod he, "if evere love or trouthe
> Hath ben, or is, bitwixen the and me,
> Ne do thow nevere swich a crueltee
> To hiden fro thi frend so gret a care!"
>
> (I. 582–87)

The go-between later invokes his own *trouthe* to support his fiction of Criseyde as the cruel fair, the "routheles" beauty:

> "If therwithal in yow ther be no routhe,
> Than it is harm ye lyven, by my trouthe!"
>
> (II. 349–50)

and he gradually moves the coupling of *routhe* and *trouthe* into Criseyde's vocabulary (II. 489–90; 1138–39) until she accepts that her integrity is closely linked to her capacity for pity:

> "A womman that were of his deth to wite,
> Withouten his gilt, but for hire lakked routhe,
> Were it wel doon?" Quod she, "Nay, by my trouthe!"
>
> (II. 1279–81)

In Book III, the words break free of Pandarus' rather glib manipulation and begin to resonate at crucial moments in the narrative: his last participation in the rhyme pair occurs when he brings Criseyde to Troilus' sickbed and reasserts that her pity should complement her *trouthe*:

> "I, What?" quod she, "by God and by my trouthe,
> I not nat what ye wilne that I seye."
> "I, What?" quod he, "That ye han on hym routhe
> For Goddes love, and doth hym nought to deye."
>
> (III. 120–23)

Not surprisingly, the rhyme next surfaces, very emphatically, during the lovers' first night together, in a couplet closing a stanza of Criseyde's climactic and passionate assertion of her love and need for Troilus:

> "Beth to me trewe, or ellis were it routhe,
> For I am thyn, by God and by my trouthe!"
>
> (III. 1511–12)

And towards the end of the central book, Troilus, in his hymn to Love, begs that *routhe* and *trouthe* be universalized:

> "hertes colde, hem wolde I that [Love] twiste
> To make hem love, and that hem liste ay rewe
> On hertes sore, and kepe hem that ben trewe!"
>
> (III. 1769–71)

In Book IV the *routhe/trouthe* pair occurs five times within 200 lines during the lovers' final interview. Troilus argues that Criseyde's plots are doomed; her father will oblige her to take a Greek husband:

> "And Troilus, of whom ye nyl han routhe,
> Shal causeles so sterven in his trouthe!"
>
> (IV. 1476–77)

He repeats the rhyme in a variation on this theme only two stanzas later, again using the emphatic couplet at the close of the stanza to make his point. You will find the Greeks so attractive, he suggests,

> "That ye shal dullen of the rudenesse
> Of us sely Troians, but if routhe
> Remorde yow, or vertu of youre trouthe."
>
> (IV. 1489–91)

The hero anticipates the separation of Criseyde's pity from his (and her) fidelity, and knows that he must keep *routhe* and *trouthe* coupled in her mind. But in Criseyde's struggle to have her way, she seizes the key words and throws them back at him (again in a strong final couplet):

> "Mistrust me nought thus causeles, for routhe,
> Syn to be trewe I have yow plight my trouthe."
>
> (IV. 1609–10)

It is you who, for pity's sake, must accept my troth. Book IV's last *routhe/trouthe* pairing occurs as Criseyde describes why she has loved Troilus – not, she avers, because of his rank or wealth,

> "But moral vertu grounded upon trouthe –
> That was the cause I first hadde on yow routhe!"
>
> (IV. 1672–73)

The sentiment is a particularly winning one, but its phrasing means that, as Criseyde reasserts Troilus's integrity and faith, she can match his *trouthe* only with a reiteration of her own capacity for pity.[52]

Book v ominously shows her entertaining the possibility that she might offer that pity to Diomede:

> "If that I sholde of any Grek han routhe,
> It sholde be youreselven, by my trouthe!"
>
> (v. 1000–01)

Conditional *routhe* for Diomede becomes actual, and her compassion for Troilus reverts to mere, helpless regret:

> "But syn I se ther is no bettre way,
> And that to late is now for me to rewe,
> To Diomede algate I wol be trewe."
>
> (v. 1069–71)

The sympathetic narrator still struggles to absolve her:

> For she so sory was for her untrouthe,
> Iwis, I wolde excuse hire yet for routhe.
>
> (v. 1098–99)

– but his *routhe*, significantly, can now only rhyme with her *untrouthe*.

Troilus' *trouthe*, of course remains the invariable in the equation; writing his plaintive letter to Criseyde, he hopes that, even if she will not pity him, her integrity and pledged word will still stand:

> "and though no manere routhe
> Commeve yow, yet thynketh on youre trouthe."
>
> (v. 1385–86)

But Troilus finally learns beyond doubt that she has betrayed him, and the last, poignant *routhe/trouthe* rhyme in the poem sums up his reaction:

> "Allas, youre name of trouthe
> Is now fordon, and that is al my routhe."
>
> (v. 1686–7)

At the moment when Criseyde's *trouthe* is irretrievable, it is Troilus who expresses the *routhe* she no longer offers. (Boccaccio's Troiolo, incidentally, burns frustratedly because he still desires

Criseida [*Fil.* VIII. 13; 15], declares that her actions will make men doubt all women [VIII. 13], and finally asks Jove to dispatch her with a thunderbolt.)

The rise and fall of the *routhe/trouthe* equation, starting with Pandarus' attempt to marry the two concepts in Books I and II, climbing to the perfect harmony of sound and sense in Book III, and slowly collapsing under the pressure of the ironic and disjunctive modifications of its significance in Books IV and V, mirrors and shapes at every step the events of *Troilus and Criseyde*. Nor is the imprinting of resonant rhyme in the overall tragic design limited to this dyad: even a cursory examination of the poem offers evidence of similar patterned manipulation of such exemplary pairings as *herte/smerte* (23 occurrences) and *Troye/joye* (30 occurrences).[53] In the lovers' debates in Book IV, for example, Troilus' own words (and rhymes) are again used as levers against him by Criseyde. As he reluctantly defers to Criseyde's plots, the prince insists,

> "And but ye come at day set into Troye,
> Ne shal I nevere have hele, honour, ne joye."
>
> (IV. 1441–42)

Criseyde, responding to his fears, asserts:

> "And by my thrift, my wendyng out of Troie
> Another day shal torne us all to joie."
>
> (IV. 1630–31)

Troilus begs her not to go to the Greeks:

> "Yet, er that ye me causen so to smerte,
> Dwelle rather here, myn owen swete hert."
>
> (IV. 1448–49)

Criseyde replies with her own brand of emotional blackmail:

> "For if ye wiste how soore it doth me smerte,
> Ye wolde cesse of this; for God thow wost,
> The pure spirit wepeth in myn herte"
>
> (IV. 1618–20)

Most poignantly, perhaps, the verse of *Troilus and Criseyde* enacts its own version of the "end-conscious" inverted parallelism I have already discussed when the rhymes that are so often on Troilus' lips recur in Diomede's courtship speeches, emphasizing the latter's role as a debased version of Troilus, a mere simulacrum of a man of *trouthe*. Diomede informs Criseyde:

> "we Grekis kan have joie
> To honouren yow as wel as folk of Troie."
>
> (IV. 118–19)

and bids her,

> "Commaundeth me, how soore that me smerte,
> To don al that may like unto youre herte."
>
> (V. 132–33)[54]

Diomede finally asserts, amid artful shows of modesty,

> "I am, al be it yow no joie
> As gentil man as any wight in Troie."
>
> (V. 930–31)

Having appropriated the hero's rhymes, he also appropriates his lady; the narrator may hedge the issue, but the relentless reappearance of key rhyme words contradicts him. Criseyde surrenders to Diomede:

> And for to helen hym of his sorwes smerte,
> Men seyn – I not – that she yaf hym hire herte.
>
> (V. 1049–50)

The same words reverberate sadly in Troilus' final letter to the "swete herte" he has already lost, as he pleads that Criseyde heal *his* suffering:

> "In yow my lif, in yow myght for to save
> Me fro disese of alle peynes smerte;
> And far now wel, myn owen swete herte!"
>
> (V. 1419–21)

The lines I have quoted above represent one of Troilus' final hyperbolic assertions that Criseyde holds power of life and death over him; shortly thereafter, conventional hyperbole turns into reality when, persuaded of her infidelity, Troilus becomes not only intent on slaying Diomede (V. 1702–5) but also desirous of his own death (V. 1718). Of course, the wish for or threat of death is everywhere in the narrative line of the *Troilus*, and Chaucer vastly increases the references to death over those in *Il Filostrato*, especially in Books I–III. Their supplementation is particularly remarkable in the "consummatory" Book III, which contains nearly twenty allusions to death where Boccaccio's shorter third book has but one (*Fil.* III. 45).[55] Paradoxically, even as Chaucer's narrative has been expanded over its main source text in such a way as to hold off the moment of closure, the fiction's "death," a significant quantity of its additional material (material which often contributes to what I have called rhetorical delaying actions) is given over to anticipations of death, thereby figuring forth a much greater "sense of an ending" than that source. This "in-eching" of ending is manifested across the poem as a whole by the steady and carefully orchestrated progression from the merely verbal invocation of death to its gradual reification as the end of Troilus and the end of the *Troilus* approach.[56] The expansive narrator's death-defying manipulations of a dilatory prosody, intertextual interpolation, and the lyrical and rhetorical suspension of action are ultimately defeated by the inexorable advent of that other stasis represented by formal closure.

The initially conventional, rather mawkish coupling of *eros* and *thanatos* in the discourse of Troilus, Criseyde and Pandarus becomes increasingly resonant as the narrative progresses.[57] In Book IV of the *Troilus*, real death enters into the world of the lovers with the resurgence of the Trojan war into the narrative, and, in a few lines added to Boccaccio, Chaucer offers us a graphic sketch of the carnage:

> The longe day, with speres sharpe igrounde,
> With arwes, dartes, swerdes, maces felle,
> They fighte and bringen hors and man to grounde,
> And with hire axes out the braynes quelle.
>
> (IV. 43–46)

This violent picture of what will ultimately be the setting for Troilus' death in battle hovers behind all the descending action; every time the hero expresses a fear that he will die if Criseyde leaves Troy, or if she fails to return, his words come closer to a simple statement of fact. His last speech to Criseyde, "'Now holde youre day, and do me nat to deye'" (v. 84) is a sober and brief recognition of what *must* be – not of what might be, or what he wishes might be – if she fails him. Through the Pandaric images of making, the Art of Poetry presided over the rising action of the *Troilus*; the descending action of the work is in a sense devoted to the Art of Dying. Indeed, Troilus spends three (non-Boccaccian) stanzas instructing his friend how to arrange his tomb, funeral rites, and the disposition of his ashes (v. 295–315). Pandarus' dilatory art – and that of the narrator – can now only be employed in the "devysen" of a sepulchre (v. 299).

In *Il Filostrato*, the references to death are more prominently clustered in the later books, where anticipations of death are in general even more violent than in the *Troilus*. Troiolo falls into a deep swoon upon learning that Criseida is to be surrendered to the Greeks (*Fil.* IV. 18) and attempts suicide after he dreams of her infidelity (*Fil.* VII. 33–35). He threatens suicide in his letter to Criseida in language very much like that of Chaucer's Pandarus: if you wrest all hope from me, he writes, I will slay myself, "'ma come che si sia mio il dannagio, / la vergognia fia tua, ch'a sì oscura / morte recato avrai un tuo suggetto, / non avendo el commesso alcun difetto'" (But though the suffering is mine, let the shame be yours, for you will have brought your servant, who has done no wrong, to such an inglorious death) (VII. 73). This is the tone and diction we find in the earlier rather than the later stages of the *Troilus*; the cruder rhetoric of death-threats and shamings belongs to the fictions of Pandarus, while the reality of a state in which life is not worth living is articulated almost without rancor. Thus, when Troilus has discovered that Criseyde has betrayed him,

> after deth, withouten wordes moore
> Ful faste he cride, his reste hym to restore.
>
> (v. 1672–3)

The "quyete and reste" (III. 1680) of gratified desire having been destroyed, death is the only kind of "reste" left for the hero. At the same time, Pandarus, supremely fluent in the rhetoric of death when persuading Criseyde not to be Troilus' "routheles" killer, becomes increasingly inarticulate in the face of death's actuality. Although he now turns his fiction of a "routheles" Criseyde unworthy of life (II. 349–50) into a real wish for his niece's destruction (V. 1742–43), being no Shahrazad, he does not have the capacity endlessly to postpone death with proliferating narratives: he can invent no supplementary fictions to delay the end of his hero and of the history of Troilus' love.

RETROSPECTIVE REWRITING: THE ENDING OF *TROILUS AND CRISEYDE*

On the one occasion in *Troilus and Criseyde* when the sympathetic and expansive narrator concedes that he may indeed have supplemented his "auctour," he immediately invites his readers to feel free in their turn to amplify – or, for that matter, condense – his fiction:

> if that ich, at Loves reverence,
> Have any word in eched for the beste,
> Doth therwithal right as youreselven leste.
>
> For myne wordes, heere and every part,
> I speke hem alle under correccioun
> Of yow that felyng han in loves art,
> And putte it al in youre discrecioun,
> To encresse or maken dymynucioun
> Of my langage
>
> (III. 1328–36)

It is surely no coincidence that these remarks occur in the very midst of his extended account of the lovers' first joyous night together: even as their pleasures are prolonged by the narrator, we are offered the chance to let our "felyng" and imagination reshape his "makyng." The visible limits of the text offering this particular account of their love are to be viewed as arbitrary and provisional, not definitive. In contrast, the speaker who later bids farewell to his "litel ... tragedye" (V. 1786) is much more anxious that his text remain unaltered and uncorrupted, praying to God "that non myswrite the, / Ne the mysmetre for defaute of tonge" (V. 1795–96). However, *his* insistence on the fixed and final nature of the tragic design he has created is undercut by the final stanzas of the poem.

By the end of Book v, we have already had glimpses of possible endings generated by the events of *Troilus and Criseyde*: the (aborted) premature closure of a double suicide of the lovers (iv. 1149–1241) is one; Troilus' hope that he may slay Diomede and/or meet his death in the attempt suggests another. But Diomede and Troilus are not to cause each other's death, for "Fortune it naught ne wolde, / Of oothers hond that eyther deyen sholde" (v. 1763–64). Fortune, whose rising and falling wheel had seemed to be so bound up in the shaping of the "end-determined" narrative, proves to be a bad artist, an unsatisfying maker of plots. Troilus' eventual death at the hands of the "fierse Achille" (v. 1806) has almost the nature of a *non sequitur*: nothing in the previous action of the *Troilus* explains why Achilles should be Troilus' nemesis. However, Achilles is the slayer of Troilus in all the Troy narratives available to Chaucer, right back to Virgil (*Aeneid* i. 474–75), and this "invariable" within the composite pre-text resists the end-conscious designs of the poetic narrative.

In Book v, the narrator constantly hints at an increasing distance between himself and the fiction he is re-creating – even when he intervenes on Criseyde's behalf it is generally by way of references to his mediating sources. He reinvokes vague controlling authorities: "after this the storie telleth us" (v. 1037); "I fynde ek in stories elleswhere" (v. 1044); "But trewely, the storie telleth us..." (v, 1051), and finally becomes so detached from what the "storie" tells him about Troilus' end that he almost forgets to retell it. After we learn that Fortune will not permit Diomede and Troilus to kill each other, five stanzas intervene before the slaying of Troilus is described – stanzas in which the narrator is already bidding his work farewell and starting to gloss it. The Epilogue of the *Troilus* begins, indeed, before the main narrative is over.

We first learn that our storyteller is not going to recount Troilus' heroic deeds in battle, and we are told that we may find these in Dares (v. 1765–71). The narrator then tries to pre-empt the criticisms of any female reader or hearer whom his tale might offend by saying that he would really *prefer* to write about good women (v. 1772–78). His next stanza avoids reiterating

Boccaccio's concluding polemic against fickle beauties by inverting the most obvious "moral" of the tale and warning the ladies against male betrayers (v. 1779–85). After this, he turns to contemplate his "litel bok," his "tragedye," despatching it, even though Troilus' story has yet to be concluded, to salute the footsteps of "Virgile, Ovide, Omer, Lucan, and Stace" (v. 1786–92). Finally, he expresses the hope that his text will not be corrupted and that it will always be perfectly understood (v. 1793–99). These stanzas are all additions to *Il Filostrato*, and it is only now that the Italian text is reinvoked and the stanza translated that kills off the hero (v. 1800–6; *Fil.* VIII. 27).

This postponing and blurring of the final detail in the arched pattern of the "tragedye" is disconcerting: one senses that, just as the strategy of silent subversive augmentation from within reached its limits and could avail no more against the "necessary" ending, so the counter-strategy that accepted that ending, and, from a position of omniscience, ordered the careful design of the poem-as-object, crumbles at the last moment. (We might also note at this point that, however much the economical patterning impulses of Books IV and V exploited the amplifications of Books I, II and III for their own ironic and pathetic ends, they could never entirely *remove* the reader's experience of – and surrender to – those suspended moments of delight in Book III.) The poetic narrative begets a last-minute shift in stance that will permit the reassessment of all that has gone before – and will introduce a new narrative voice.[58] Roland Barthes suggests that, in the making of a fiction,

> disorder is supplementary, it is what is forever added on without solving anything, without finishing anything; order is complementary, it completes, fills up, saturates and dismisses everything that risks adding on: truth is what completes, what closes[59]

But in the Troilus, "truth" and final closure will be provided, it seems, by a fresh narrative gambit which transcends (or at least seeks to transcend) both "supplementary" disorder and "complementary" order.

The final narrative strategy of the *Troilus* is to insist that the poem is not at all what we thought it was. The circular movement from misery to joy to misery becomes, instead, a spiral: Troilus falls victim to Love's darts in Book I, rises to enjoy the bliss of Book III, falls to despair and to Achilles' sword in Book V, then reascends to a higher state of happiness than he ever found in Criseyde's arms. The end of Book V contradicts the work's announced subject; Troilus' "double sorwe" is dissipated in cheerful enlightenment.[60] On leaving his corporeal existence, the hero gains a new perspective on sublunar events that permits him to reject his own "tragedye." Besides the "pleyn felicite / That is in hevene above," the sorrow of those who mourn him seems risible and his love for Criseyde no more than "blynde lust" (V. 1814–27).

Troilus' acquisition of heavenly enlightenment revises *Il Filostrato* by drawing upon Boccaccio's account of Arcita's ascent to a higher plane of existence in his *Teseida.* Although both Troilus and Arcita are pagans, and Troilus is ultimately directed to parts unknown by Mercury (V. 1827), Chaucer's supplementary use of the *Teseida* permits him an easy transition to a Christian gloss of his poetic fiction. The joys and sorrows of the sublunar plane, its "successioun" of vicissitudes, the apparent power of Fortune over human doings: all these are as nothing compared to the life hereafter (V. 1835–41); earthly passion is but a mere shadow of the love that God offers (V. 1842–48), and our experience of over 8000 lines of poetry concerning the miseries and ecstasies of pagan lovers is ultimately reducible, it seems, to this Boethian moral.

The final narrative voice of *Troilus and Criseyde* seems to be that of Chaucer the Christian narrator glossing his own secular text, but the reader has been exposed to such a plethora of (explicit and implicit) narrative personae in the poem – the translator (II. 14), the historian (II. 22–28), the servant of the servants of love (I. 15), the silent subverter and supplementer of Boccaccio, the overt apologist for Criseyde, the cool aesthete ordering an immutable tragic design, and now the orthodox moralist – that she may wonder why she should give greater credence to this voice.[61] The Protean nature of the maker is further refracted in the heteroglot and multiplying authorities within his work: the mythical "Lollius" masks the real

Boccaccio, who is in turn fragmented by the texts of Petrarch, Machaut, Boethius, and Dante, as well as by the other histories of Troilus, by his own *Teseida*, and by the proverbs and sententiae voiced by Chaucer's Pandarus. Given that all these voices have been unleashed within a single narrative, who, ultimately, gets the last word in *Troilus and Criseyde*? After all, the poem offers "an embarassment of finalities."[62] Chaucer lays before us an entire stanza *talking* about endings:

> Swich fyn hath, lo, this Troilus for love!
> Swich fyn hath al his grete worthynesse!
> Swich fyn hath his estat real above!
> Swich fyn his lust, swich fyn hath his noblesse!
> Swich fyn hath false worldes brotelnesse!
> And thus bigan his lovying of Criseyde,
> As I have told, and in this wise he deyde.
>
> (v. 1828–34)

– but even this labored assertion of finality, culminating in death, does not conclude the poem. Nor, significantly, can its author bear to end it with the dismissal of "feynede loves" two stanzas later (v. 1848), any more than he can draw it to a close with the lines "Lo here, the forme of olde clerkis speche / In poetrie, if ye hire bokes seche" (v. 1854–55) which terminate a stanza scorning pagan and worldly pleasures and make the poet's art suffer from guilt by association. However, a dedication of the work to Gower and Strode – which, we remark, reopens the *Troilus* to correction "ther nede is" (v. 1858), in despite of the "tragic" narrator's previous insistence that it should be transmitted unaltered – slides, at last, into the supplication to the Trinity and the Virgin that finally completes the poem (v. 1856–69).

The Epilogue, then, for all its attempts to close the *Troilus* by means of definitive retrospective glosses, is a pretty dilatory affair: at one point it almost seems that its narrator will launch straight out into another fiction:

> And gladlier I wol write, yif yow leste
> Penelopeës trouthe and good Alceste.
>
> (v. 1777–78)

Significantly, it finally comes to rest upon a prayer that offers a new instance of lyric suspension. Book III's privileged moments of lyric synchronicity, which reflected the narrator's hopes that the earthly passion represented by Venus might "heried ben for ay withouten ende!" (III. 1813), have been defeated by the inexorable movement of Fortune's wheel, but the circular sweep of the latter is itself encompassed and transcended by the Divine Circle of the Trinity (borrowed by Chaucer from Dante)[63] addressed in the last stanza of Book V:

> Thow oon, and two, and thre, etern on lyve,
> That regnest ay in thre, and two, and oon,
> Uncircumscript, and al maist circumscrive
> (V. 1863–65)

Here in eternity, outside the domain of time, chance, and mutability, is the ultimate suspended moment.

The reordering of the significance of *Troilus and Criseyde* in its final stanzas makes yet more intricate the pattern of its shifting generic allegiances.[64] The narrative techniques of amplification and supplementation that dominated Books I, II and III are the strategies that we tend to associate with romance,[65] and Pandarus, the dilatory "maker" of those books, is, of course, an admirer of that genre. At the same time, the invocation of Calliope in the Proem to Book III, Chaucer's greater use of classical allusion, his development of the Trojan background, and his increased emphasis on Troilus' heroic deeds in the earlier part of the poem suggest that his narrative intermittently aspires to the condition of epic. But the narrative voice that insists that the poem is a "tragedye" will not allow the "litel bok" to kiss the steps of any writers *en romaunz* (V. 1791) and refuses to enlarge upon the epic deeds of Troilus in between the latter's realization of Criseyde's infidelity and his death in battle (V. 1765–71): *this* speaker has not undertaken to tell of "arms and the man" (V. 1765–67). In their turn, the final stanzas reject *de casibus* "tragedye." Troilus does not fall from bliss into misery but rises from illusory joy and illusory sorrow into cheerful enlightenment. (It is perhaps significant that there are no repetitions of such significant rhyme pairs as *routhe/trouthe*, *herte/smerte*, *Troye/joye* in the epilogue: Chaucer has abandoned the design which they helped to order.) The narrative has suddenly been turned into a Boethian – or Divine – comedy; heavenly Truth appears to have had the last word over the *routhe* exalted and exacted by romance and the partial truths of the tragedy of Fortune.

Nevertheless, one is still tempted to wonder whether each shift to a new genre represents a superseding, an obliteration, of the previous one, or whether the result is rather a superimposition which, like a palimpsest, still permits other, competing kinds of fiction to peep through. Are any of the designing voices of *Troilus and Criseyde* ever silenced, or is the poem inescapably polyphonic to the last?[66] Can the reader's desire for the infinite prolongation of Troilus and Criseyde's love, or even her admiration for the *almost* perfect design of their "tragedye," be completely rebuked and chastened by the orthodoxies of the Epilogue? That the multiple strategies of the poetic narrative are not easy to reconcile is suggested by the sheer length of the concluding movement of *Troilus and Criseyde*, its repeated attempts, in ending after ending, wholly to contain the significance of what has gone before. It is perhaps a recognition of having failed to do so, a suspicion that what he has made is too richly polysemous to be retrospectively glossed in one or two pat stanzas, that provokes Chaucer's final lines of appeal to the Trinity "that regnest... uncircumscript, and al maist circumscrive" (v. 1864–65). Only by surrendering his work to the truly divine perspective, acknowledging the necessarily incomplete omniscience of the mortal creator and *scriptor*, can the poet hope for it to be adequately "ended."[67] Back on the sublunar plane, however, Chaucer seems to recognize that his Christian palinode only partially silences the narrative voices that celebrate earthly passion or insist upon the aesthetic satisfactions to be found in the acceptance of pagan Fortuna's design. His retraction of his work's seductive and un-Christian aspects may represent the end of the poem but not necessarily the end of its resonant counter-narratives, and it is not, therefore, surprising that in a moment of penitence or panic the whole of the *Troilus*, text and gloss together, is labelled as just one more "worldly vanitee" and re-retracted in the *Envoi* to the *Canterbury Tales*.[68]

CHAPTER 3

The end of questing, the quest for an ending: circumscribed vision in The Faerie Queene, *Book VI*

In dissecting out the competing narrative strategies that inform Chaucer's retelling of *Il Filostrato*, I suggested that the rhyme royal stanzas of *Troilus and Criseyde* both engendered and reflected its dilatory recasting of Boccaccio. A comparable small-scale phenomenon is evident in *The Faerie Queene*: once again, poetic scheme offers a blueprint for a larger plot. The Spenserian stanza (ABABBCBCC) shares with rhyme royal (ABABBCC) a central pair of B rhymes; its fifth line does not, however, function as a "floating line" so much as a pivot about which the stanza doubles back upon itself. The repeated rhyme in line five lays the foundation for a second (BCBC) quatrain which complicates, augments or re-examines the narrative content of the first four lines and thus produces a structural matrix exploiting both repetition (the B rhymes of lines five and seven) and difference (the C rhymes of lines six and eight). Narrative syntax moves forward linearly, but within formal parameters that draw in part upon what has gone before. And this "re-pleating effect," this onward thrust that simultaneously folds backwards to cover old ground in new ways, is as evident in the larger narrative structure of *The Faerie Queene* itself as within the walls of the stanza.

It is that larger narrative structure which I wish to investigate in this chapter, focusing in particular upon the generation of successive books of *The Faerie Queene* out of revisionary recapitulation, a narrative strategy which has some remarkably double-edged consequences for Spenser's didactic epic. On the one hand, the poet's successive repetitions of, and variations upon, a narrative template give rise to an ever richer and more subtle web of resonant allusion informing the quests of his heroes. At the same time, the totalizing moral allegory which the discourse of questing is designed to figure forth becomes increasingly unstable. By the time we reach Books IV, V and VI, Spenser's most elaborate encodings of those qualities which were "to fashion a gentleman or noble person in virtuous and gentle discipline"[1] tend to sever themselves entirely from the linear development of the quest narrative, and as Book VI draws to an end, the poet loses faith in his ability to make that narrative serve the ambitious program of moral instruction outlined in the 1590 *Faerie Queene*'s appended letter to Raleigh. The discourse of the quest and the poetry of the vision which one had supposed to direct and shape the quest no longer speak to one another.[2]

My reading of *The Faerie Queene* assumes that we must discuss the poem as both narrative *and* allegory. While its polysemous fictions are intended to signify and communicate moral, philosophical and theological truths, their copious reproduction not only of the familiar matter of epic and romance but also of *themselves* constantly creates material that resists the totalizing designs of allegory; there is simply too much "story" to be contained by any one allegoresis. The poem's excessive narrative productivity is always *in potentia* the fecundity of "Errours endlesse traine": its elaborate "showes" – the trappings of romance which Spenser so belittles in the letter to Raleigh – take on substance and purpose and supplementary levels of referentiality above and beyond the mediation of "good discipline."[3] I do not believe that in discussing *The Faerie Queene* we can ever subsume "narrative" in "allegory" (or discard the former term for the latter): the work fosters a complicated and evolving dialogue between the two modes.[4] Its earlier books perhaps bear witness to a happy duplicity, a "play of double senses" which permits heroic romance and moral allegory to exercise their coterminous but relatively discrete designs upon the reader.[5] But in the later stages of the poetic fiction, for reasons which I shall explore at some length in the course of this chapter, the quest narrative becomes an increasingly inadequate vehicle for the representation of a coherent and untainted moral vision, and other resources of the poem-as-narrative must perforce be invoked to rescue and redescribe an imperilled ideal.

VERSIONS OF THE FABLE: THE ELUSIVENESS OF ENDINGS

The six completed books of *The Faerie Queene* can be envisioned as both a narrative line and a narrative matrix.[6] The diachronic impetus governs the encounters between the returning hero of one book and the novice quester of the next, the overflow of Book III's interlaced narratives into Books IV and V, and also the movement of Arthur from one book to another. These gestures towards linear progression eventually seem less important, however, than the synchronic overlay of each book upon its fellows in the memory of the reader, forming, as it were, a poetic tapestry twelve cantos long by six books wide.[7] Cantos echo cantos, not without distortion; books mirror or refract books, and one ends with the peculiar sense of a narrative in which "everything is happening at once."[8] To augment, to add to this poetic fiction is inevitably to rewrite what one already possesses of it: after Book I, for all the work's local and temporary invocation and incorporation of other narratives, scriptural, classical and vernacular, it is *The Faerie Queene* that becomes the most important source of *The Faerie Queene*: intertextuality collapses into intratextuality.

The whole of this web of fictions is permanently suspended *in medias res*: "The poem as we have it... is all middle: Gloriana's court, beginning and end of all movement, never appears."[9] The epic is not simply unfinished: by the end of the last canto of Book VI Spenser is strongly hinting to his reader that no more of *The Faerie Queene* could ever be written. A mere four stanzas after his Knight of Courtesy has captured and muzzled the Blatant Beast, that ubiquitous slanderer has escaped again (xii. 34–38); as Book VI finishes, the poet is anticipating a Beastly attack on *The Faerie Queene* itself. He ruefully closes the Legend of Courtesy with much lower aspirations for the future:

> Ne may this homely verse, of many meanest,
> Hope to escape his venemous despite,

> More then my former writs, all were they clearest
> From blamefull blot, and free from all that wite,
> With which some wicked tongues did it backebite,
> And bring into a mighty Peres displeasure,
> That neuer so deserued to endite.
> Therfore do you my rimes keep better measure,
> And seeke to please, that now is counted wisemens threasure.
>
> (xii. 41)[10]

Spenser's bold attempt to join the epic company of Homer, Virgil, Ariosto and Tasso is now his "homely verse, of many meanest," and its author is prepared to subordinate his elevated didactic aims to extra-poetic criteria of what is pleasing (that is, to embrace the degraded aesthetic and moral standards of a world in which the slanderous Beast runs free).[11] This decline follows hard upon the cursorily treated and very limited victory of Calidore; the abandonment of the epic project is implicit in the impossibility of bringing the Knight of Courtesy's quest to a satisfactory close. Reinvoking the stanzaic "plot" of *The Faerie Queene*, one might suggest that the delicate tension between continuity-as-dilation and closure, epitomized by the alexandrines that at once extend and terminate each Spenserian stanza, eventually ceases to be perfectly balanced within the poem as a whole.[12] The dilatory narrative structured around revisionary recapitulation comes to incorporate material which disrupts teleology; the (moral) ends of the narrative no longer inform the increasingly ambiguous end of the quest.[13]

The narrative supplementation by layering which maps each quest across the twelve-canto spread of its predecessors, and which finally brings us to Book VI's anticlimactic cessation without fulfillment, is the product of the retelling and revision in each book of *The Faerie Queene* of what I shall call the Fable – the archetypal narrative represented by the adventures of Book I's Christian Everyman, Redcrosse. The latter's trials, learning experiences, and eventual victory over a bestial enemy constitute the poem's large-scale generative pattern. Jonathan Goldberg has suggested that *The Faerie Queene* "generates itself precisely out of its own instability";[14] I would propose, on the contrary, that it *de*generates into an increasingly unstable fiction by way of the elaboration, multiple repetition and distortion of its most stable, and initiatory, narrative which, as it is recreated, falls further and further away from authoritative certainty, simple linearity, and from the capacity to bring itself to a satisfactory close.[15] The imaginative *copia* of the later books of *The Faerie Queene* never entirely or consistently recaptures the totalizing resonance of its generative Fable.[16]

The narrative of Book I is Christian epic in romance clothing, and in as much as the poet's word rehearses the Logos of the Book of Revelation even this "original" book of *The Faerie Queene* is a secondary text, a *re*-creation. The archetypal design of the Fable traces the travels and travails of Redcrosse, the knight all too errant, whose transgressions first imprison him in Orgoglio's dungeon and then enthrall him to Despair. Rescued by the instruments of divine grace, Arthur and Una, the quester is taken for healing and instruction to Cœlia's House of Holinesse. In canto x, instruction merges with revelation as he progresses from Cœlia's mansion to the Mount of Contemplation: Redcrosse enjoys a privileged moment of respite from his journeyings on its summit, where biblical and classical mounts of inspiration and vision are syncretically collapsed into a single *topos* as the Mount of Contemplation is allied by simile with the Mount of Olives, Mount Sinai and Mount Parnassus (I. x. 53–54). From here he looks forward to the New Jerusalem and the promise of eternal rest, but is also required to confront his own beginnings and his identity as Georgos, the ploughman's fosterling (I. x. 65–66). His earthly and earthy name conjures up an Adamic origin, his vision of the City of God announces a desired end. The climactic tenth canto reconnects the perpetual "in the middest" of fallen narrative with a profound source and a transcendent goal.[17]

early experience/tests → fall/ordeal → Arthurian intervention →
(canto vii on) (canto viii)

scene/locus of instruction → achievement of quest → rest/betrothal
vision: origins/ends (x) (canto xi) (canto xii)

Figure I: The Fable

It is this fleeting sight of a true Origin and true End, even more than the hero's education in Cœlia's house, that seems to authorize and enable Book I's narrative and didactic closure: Redcrosse, aided by canto xi's visitations of personal grace, duly kills his dragon, redeems Una's parents, and, in the book's final canto, rests and plights his faith to Una. But although the design of the epic Fable is so clear in Book I (see figure I), it is not untouched by the urge towards repetitive supplementation that characterizes "mere" romance (and which is emphasized on the local level by the recursive dynamics of the Spenserian stanza). Spenser cannot close the Legend of Holiness without reinvoking the disruptive and duplicitous feignings of Duessa and Archimago, would-be pre-emptors of all felicitous endings (I. xii. 25–34), and we learn that the respite Redcrosse earns by his victory is only temporary; as a knight errant he will continue to wander – and err (I. xii. 18). Neither quester nor poem has quite escaped, it seems, the ever reduplicating folds of "Errours endlesse traine."[18] Yet even if the aspiring representative of holiness can only be pledged in betrothal to Truth in the mean time of the secular narrative,[19] the reader (and quester) can accept the deferment of full union; we have, after all, had our fleeting vision of the New Jerusalem where their marriage will be eternal.

In Book II, *The Faerie Queene* begins to distance itself from the design of Christian epic (and from the latter's imaging of a deferred but perfect End). The Fable now recapitulates the *Aeneid*, with its hero who must learn to reject the temptations of passion and premature rest, descend into the underworld, and destroy the old Latium in order to rebuild the new Troy, and the *Odyssey*, with its sea journeys, the obligations of its hero to overcome delaying female enticements, and its climactic violent cleansing of a defiled terrain. Once again the quester passes through preliminary tests before a major and debilitating ordeal: Guyon's experiences in Mammon's cave in the seventh canto combine the underground confinement and starvation Redcrosse suffers in Pride's dungeon with the relentless *verbal* temptation – Mammon never stops renewing his seductive offers – of Despair. As in Book I, the eighth canto brings Arthur to the hero's aid, although the fact that an angel attends to the initial succoring of Guyon hints that Arthur's powers are not so perfect here.

Guyon and Arthur's joint entry into Alma's house of instruction suggests that a process of narrative redoubling (which in later books will contribute towards an increasingly fragmented and attenuated Fable) has been set in motion. Like Redcrosse, both heroes are presented with narratives of genesis, and they peruse, in canto x, chronicles of their respective racial origins. The concise, linear account of the "Antiquitie of Faerie Lond" is juxtaposed with the erratic "Briton Moniments": disturbingly, the dilatory and repetitious narrative of violent usurpations and failures in linear succession of the latter threatens to displace from canto x the exemplary story of dynastic origins represented by Guyon's text. It is noticeably harder to reconnect British Arthur with his origins than it was to reconnect British Redcrosse with his; there is almost too much fallen "between time" for the poetic narrative to encompass.

Canto ix of Book II offers implicit instruction and canto x chronicles of origins, but neither grants transcendent Pisgah visions – reaching out to ends is becoming a more tricky business. And just as Arthur's chronicle took precedence over Guyon's in canto x, Arthur displaces Guyon from the canto in which Redcrosse fought his last battle: Guyon does not meet Acrasia until canto xii. Spenser's doubling of the long concluding battles against the enemies of Temperance suggests yet again that narrative closure is harder to attain in Book II. Even when Guyon purges the Bower of Bliss, he cannot utterly regenerate the landscape of excess: Grill will be Grill, regardless (II. xii. 87). Nor does this quester enjoy the respite that Redcrosse enjoyed at the conclusion of Book I – Guyon's rest is deferred until the first stanza of Book III, canto i.

Book III allies itself with the dynamics of Ariostan epic-romance, a more belated, and inevitably less authoritative model than classical epic, and one which further revises the Fable. Britomart, like Redcrosse and Guyon, suffers, learns, fights and destroys an Archenemy, but her story is pushed to the end of the Legend of Chastity and is displaced in cantos iv through viii by various competing narrative lines. The heroine's early fall is a falling in love, but it is not her passion *per se* that produces the physical agonies of III. ii. 37–39 so much as her inability to recognize her feelings for Arthegall in their providential aspect as part of her (divinely ordained) destiny. She chooses, instead, to refigure her love in the terms of the artificial and constraining discourse of petrified Petrarchanism, enemy of chaste union, generation and regeneration, whose protocols will victimize her *alter egos*, Florimell and Amoret, in Book III's multiplying "tales of error."

Britomart eventually learns that her love is approved by the heavens and that her present experience is inextricably interconnected with the past and future of her nation. Like the heroes of Book II she receives a lesson in dynastic history, and this enables her to set her future union with Arthegall, if not in an apocalyptic, then at least in a historical perspective. Yet her "House of Instruction" – Merlin's cave – is a morally ambiguous locus; in borrowing from Ariosto the subterranean setting of Merlin and Melissa's lecture to Bradamante, Spenser risks reinvoking Book II's Cave of Mammon, laboring spirits and all.[20] Descent into this place of instruction may also be a *descensus ad inferos*.

Britomart sees her future in Merlin's mirror, but her vision is limited to Arthegall; the true revelatory core of Book III, which establishes the transcendent pattern of generation (uniting all sources, all ends) behind the erotic confusion of its fragmentary narrative lines, is located in canto vi's Gardens of Adonis, where the *mons Veneris*, like the Mount of Contemplation, thrusts up out of the fallen time of romance narrative to offer its scene of eternal re-creation (III. vi. 43). Britomart wins a lesser version of this vision in Merlin's prophetic account of her progeny, from which she learns of dynastic, if not universal, continuities, but no quester visits the Garden of Adonis: for the first time an important locus of instruction is reserved for the poet and reader alone. The highest vision will no longer inform the actions of the quester – indeed, Book III's canto x, far from being a climactic scene of education, is an excursus into the comic: as if to stress the potential diminishment and refraction of epic fictions through narrative repetition, the war of Troy is reduced to a burlesque, quasi-pastoral romp in the misadventures of Hellenore, Paridell, Malbecco, Trompart and Braggadocchio.

It is not until canto xi – the canto in which Redcrosse

achieved his quest – that Britomart's search for Arthegall gives way to the culminating quest of Book III, the rescue of Amoret. There is no sense of any sustained sequential progression towards the defeat of Busirane. Like Guyon's personal triumph over Acrasia, Britomart's victory is tempered; she captures, but does not kill the sorcerer. Amoret is saved, but in neither the 1590 nor the 1596 edition of the poem does the Legend of Chastity achieve perfect closure. The 1590 text's (almost) concluding image of the hermaphrodite (III. xii. 45a–46a) – the emblematic union of male and female represented by Scudamour and Amoret's rapturous embrace – can only briefly displace Britomart's yearning for the rediscovery of Arthegall (III. xii. 46a; lines 6–9), and the stories of Florimell, Marinell, Timias and Belphoebe remain unfinished. In 1596, matters are even more open-ended: Scudamour is not to be found, and neither Britomart nor Amoret can rest.

Book IV offers further fragmentations of the Fable. The sophisticated interlace of Ariostan narrative is interrupted by Spenser's completion of that dilatory romance to end all dilatory romances, Chaucer's "Squire's Tale." The promise of strongly sequential narrative, with a beginning, middle and end, held out by the embedded revision of Chaucer, does not, however, inform the remainder of this book, the narrative of which is less a line than a congeries of discrete points at which groups of figures appear out of nowhere, clash or make friends, and disappear again. Important episodes, like those involving the House of Ate, the House of Care, and the Temple of Venus, cannot easily be integrated into a coherent and totalizing allegoresis of Book IV. No quester penetrates all of them – indeed only the reader enters Ate's house; it is the first Hell unvisited by any character. Furthermore, from its very first stanzas, which, in describing Busirane's abduction of Amoret, regress to events before those related by the concluding cantos of III, narrative cause and effect, allegorical text and gloss seem curiously disconnected in Book IV. Amoret's painful experiences in Lust's dark cave (IV. vii) may recall the miseries of Orgoglio's dungeon and Mammon's cave in the corresponding cantos of Books I and II, but she does not pass on to any house of instruction which might set them in perspective. And while Arthur does aid Amoret in canto viii, intervening in his proper place in the Fable, he has no dealings with the nominal heroes of Book IV, Cambel and Triamond, whose role in the narrative of Friendship is rather to provide a local exemplum of *discordia concors* than to undertake an extended quest.

In the manner of Books I and II, Book IV's canto x offers a scene of instruction in a sanctum separated from the wanderings of the quest, but rather than reasserting the ties of narrative middle with supratextual source and end, the Temple of Venus represents a merely reflexive "beginning": we are sent back within *The Faerie Queene* to the events preceding both the abduction (IV. i. 1–4) and the rescue (III. xi–xii) of Amoret as Scudamour recounts his winning of that lady. The role of this canto within the disjointed Fable of Book IV is further complicated by its uneasy recapitulation of earlier scenes of vision. Scudamour is exposed to the lessons of Concord and Love in the temple and its gardens, and touches the fringes of mystery as he gazes upon the veiled, hermaphroditic image of the Goddess. But the veil is not lifted and Venus herself remains an object, a representation, into which Scudamour can read what he wants – namely, approval of his seizure of Amoret (IV. x. 56). He reinterprets the visionary landscape so that it conforms with the narrative trajectory of his solipsistic desires.

Canto x thoroughly undermines the teleology of Book IV, for the beginning of Scudamour and Amoret's story supplants what should have been its end. In the last stanzas of canto ix, Arthur and Amoret had met up with Scudamour, but the reunion and closure we might have expected has been displaced by the backward turn represented by the husband's nostalgic tale; he never quite recognizes his lady.[21] This postponed end is subordinated to another in the final cantos of Book IV, as the history of Marinell and Florimell is resumed, only to be pre-empted in its turn by the elaborate treatment of the Thames/Medway marriage, whose guest-list seems capable of a potentially infinite augmentation which would defer for ever the meeting between captive lady and melancholy knight. That the "victory" canto of Spenser's Fable is here given over to a huge pageant celebrating a concord thrust upon us almost *ex nihilo* after the abortive reunion of Amoret and Scudamour (and delaying the rapprochement of Florimell and Marinell) only confirms how radically the precarious teleology of that Fable has been subverted.

In Book v, narrative interlace is somewhat reduced as Ariostan epic-romance bows to an even more belated pre-text – contemporary history. At the same time, Ariostan providential dynastic history, though briefly reinvoked in the Church of Isis, is gradually displaced by the contingencies and compromises of Renaissance *Realpolitik*. There is an apparent return to the design of Books I and II: the hero falls and suffers imprisonment; a scene of instruction and revelation follows his fall; Arthur enters in canto viii; both questers fight victorious battles in the two final cantos. But the apparent re-membering of the initiatory narrative of Holiness does not preclude a dissipation of the totalizing moral thrust of the Fable. Arthegall's experiences are displaced and oddly marginalized in cantos vi and vii by the reappearance of Britomart – it is she, not the nominal hero of Book v, who has the vision and receives the instruction in Isis Church. While Britomart apprehends the ideal union between Justice and Mercy, the lessons of the Church play no part in Arthegall's violent triumph in canto xii: her vision fails to redeem or reorder the errancies of the quest narrative. Even in Mercilla's castle, a secondary and secular version of Isis Church, no lengthy scene of instruction unfolds for Arthegall. The subtext of history is so close to the surface here that Mercilla/Elizabeth can be mercifully just in name only; she can pity, but not spare, Duessa/Mary. And although Britomart's mediating role in the troubled "mean time" between Britain's bloody past and glorious future is reasserted, Arthegall never has to remember *his* origins or look beyond the immediate moment; his *enfance* has already been described in the first canto and by the eleventh he is abashed to realize that he has lost sight of his journey's end (v. xi. 40).

The climactic battles of Book v occupy three cantos and its final episodes become a long series of bloody single combats interspersed with scenes of mass carnage. Arthegall's battles are less prolonged than Arthur's, but also less conclusive: he is almost too late to help Irena, and is ordered home before he can complete his pacification of her land. On his way back to Gloriana's court, beginnings and ends are thrown into further confusion as the Knight of Justice is attacked by the Blatant Beast. Even as untidy historical circumstance – Lord Grey's recall from Ireland – revises the Fable, Arthegall is already being pushed aside by the intrusive "content" of Book VI.

Book VI's Legend of Courtesy, divided between chivalric and pastoral romance, and abandoning scriptural, epic and contemporary histories for "the Poet, his Story", marks the last recasting and final disintegration of the Fable. As in Book III, the protagonist's adventures are displaced into the beginning and closing cantos; from midway through canto iii until the start of canto ix the deeds of other wanderers wearily and somewhat repetitively dilate Calidore's quest. Arthur meets neither the hero of Book VI nor his surrogate, Calepine; in the "Arthurian" eighth canto he merely rescues his own trouble-prone squire. Calidore's telling absences at crucial points in Book VI result in a peculiar deflection on to other characters of various experiences of physical suffering, degradation and captivity: Serena and Timias receive festering wounds from the Blatant Beast (and Serena is almost sacrificed by the Cannibals), Pastorella nearly perishes in the Brigands' cave, and Calepine is hounded and slandered by Turpine. Calidore, meanwhile, remains unscathed, although he does seem to err, to "fall," when he sits down "in middest of the race," abandoning the quest for the Blatant Beast in canto ix to court Pastorella. Yet his apparent truancy paradoxically permits him to bear witness, on Mount Acidale, to the most sublime manifestation of Courtesy. Willed premature stasis (the rejection of the quest and of the narrative of the quest) is privileged in the pastoral retreat, and the chivalric quest is never really rehabilitated: when Calidore finally returns to his pursuit of the Beast, his mission is brought to the most cursory conclusion, and has the most limited success, of any in *The Faerie Queene*.

Even as the linear unfolding of the Fable is being undermined, Book VI offers a tenth canto which (more than any other scene of vision and instruction) recapitulates that of I. x, although on Acidale it is the dance of the Graces, not the operation of divine grace, that is disclosed. Canto x also represents the poem's supreme moment of self-reflexivity: Calidore and the reader glimpse a secret source of poetic inspiration mediated by an avatar of Spenser himself. Yet the hero's intrusion destroys the timeless, suspended moment of the Graces' dance – in a radical revision of the Fable, Spenser has Calidore falling and suffering privation at the very moment of enhanced vision. The taint of his transgression infects and devalues the rest of the quest: after Acidale, the orderly retracing of the final stages of the Fable becomes irrelevant to the true ends of the poet. At this point, not surprisingly, the supplementation of *The Faerie Queene* ceases to be possible and the Fable is never rehearsed again.

To be sure, the third edition of *The Faerie Queen* offers us an alternative to the enfeebled conclusion of Book VI. The expanded text of 1609 no longer finishes with the diminished aspirations and expectations of an author who can only "seeke to please" a worldly audience; the final stanzas of the appended *Mutabilitie Cantos*, rejecting the "loue of things so vaine" (VII. viii. 1), affirm the mortal maker's yearning for both the *sight* of a promised day of rest and the *site* of transcendent stillness in a universe of flux:[22]

> Then gin I thinke on that which Nature sayd,
> Of that same time when no more Change shall be,
> But stedfast rest of all things firmely stayd
> Vpon the pillours of Eternity,
> That is contrayr to Mutabilitie:
> For, all that moueth, doth in Change delight:
> But thence-forth all shall rest eternally
> With Him that is the god of Sabbaoth hight:
> O that great Sabbaoth god, graunt me that Sabaoth's sight.
>
> (VII. viii. 2)

We are belatedly provided with what looks like a felicitous and apposite terminus to a poem which has repeatedly striven to encompass apocalypse: Spenser seems to be back on Book I's Mount of Contemplation as he pleads for a personal vision of the sublime End to all questing, his own version of the New Jerusalem. And yet, a closer look at the relationship between

Book VI's dubious conclusion and the more promising end of the *Mutabilitie Cantos* suggests that the latter tell a story marked by certain narrative dislocations and evasions which may very well have their source in Book VI's history of the failure of significant sequence. Later in this chapter I shall argue that the *Cantos* do not unambiguously recover or redeem Spenser's secular scripture. Even as they reach out to a higher End, they continue to bear witness to the disintegration of the poetic narrative's quest to mediate an uncompromised vision. But I am running ahead of myself here, and I am well aware that my tracing of the increasingly goal-resistant and dislocated versions of the almost-apocalyptic Fable through successive books of *The Faerie Queene* has necessarily been somewhat sweeping and reductive. Narrowing my focus, once again, to the Fable's recasting as the Legend of Courtesy, I will begin to consider why the figuring forth of this particular poetic narrative is so inimical to the continued articulation of Spenser's allegorical epic-romance.[23]

THE QUEST OF COURTESY: MEANS AND ENDS

As an index to the problems that beset the narration of the Legend of Courtesy, the opening stanza of Book VI is quite suggestive:

> The waies, through which my weary steps I guyde
> In this delightfull land of Faery,
> Are so exceeding spacious and wyde,
> And sprinckled with such sweet variety,
> Of all that pleasant is to eare or eye,
> That I nigh rauisht with rare thoughts delight,
> My tedious trauell doe forget thereby;
> And when I gin to feele decay of might,
> It strength to me supplies, & chears my dulled spright.
>
> (Proem 1)

The poet informs us that the exquisite distractions of his Faery Land more than compensate for the labor of charting a path through it. But as Paul Alpers points out, he tells us this when we have just emerged from Book V, the harshest, least "ravishing" book of *The Faerie Queene*.[24] It appears that the "rare thoughts delight" which rewards Spenser for his travail in describing the travel and travail of the quester will not necessarily be communicated to the reader in the narrative representation of that journey. These are private joys, the "secret comfort" that the Muse offers to the poet alone (Proem 2).

In the 1596 *Faerie Queene*, Spenser is increasingly aware that, even as he attempts to figure forth certain abstract goods by means of the repetition-and-variation of the Fable, his quest narrative may also speak to (and for) the compromised and contingent morality of the world outside the allegorical text.[25] This didactic anxiety is already manifest in the narrative fragmentation of Book v, where the exemplary union of Justice and Mercy, enacted in the allegories of Astraea in the Proem, Isis and Osiris in canto vi, and, to a lesser extent, Mercilla's court in canto ix, seems oddly irrelevant to the actual narrative progress of Arthegall and his automaton-slave Talus from one victory of *force majeure* to another. If the still moment of privileged vision is separated from the goal-directed action of the quest (as Britomart's dream in Isis Church is kept apart from Arthegall's completion of his mission), if the synchronic discourse of vision can no longer converse with the diachronic discourse of that quest, then the retracing of the epic and didactic design may be bereft of its aesthetic and moral energy and will indeed become "tedious trauell."

In the Proem to Book II, Spenser encouraged his royal reader to see in the world he had created in *The Faerie Queene* a reflection of her own realm (II. Proem 4), a Sidneian "second nature" that was nevertheless a recognizable version of the familiar, namely, a triumphant and virtuous nation ruled by a glorious Queen. As the poem unfolds, relations between the text and context of Faery Land become more complex. The Knight of Justice moves through a fallen universe from which Astraea has fled and his adventures mirror in part the turbulent events of the 1580s and 1590s. His cosmos does not lend itself to the ideal designs of the Fable, although it may still embrace numinous spaces, like the Church of Isis, which offer sanctuaries from disorder and error. Entering Book VI, the reader suspects that the most privileged territories of Faery Land have come to represent escapes from, rather than ideal reflections of, the world beyond the text. And as the quest narrative (and the quest to narrate) becomes increasingly detached from the experience offered by these loci of illumination and peace, the temptation for the poet to abandon the "weary steps," futile repetitions, and deferred satisfactions of an increasingly entropic discourse is very great indeed.

In the Proem to Book VI, Elizabeth's looking-glass is doubled, finding its false twin in the distorting "glasse so gay" provided by the worldly representatives of courtesy who deceive and blind their beholders into thinking they offer authentic reflections of that virtue (Proem 5). The single remaining true mirror of antique courtesy is Gloriana/Elizabeth's "pure minde" which "doth inflame / The eyes of all, which thereon fixed beene" (Proem 6). The Book of Courtesy, Spenser claims, derives from the wellspring of her inner virtue alone, and he proffers his queen its redescription of her exemplary courtesy as part of a closed system of emanation and return which parallels her illumination of the inner circle of her most favored courtiers and their creation of a courteous setting for her goodness (Proem 7). The Proem announces that its vision of true courtesy will not be dependent on "fayned" or "outward" showes (Proem 4–5); it is to be apprehended by penetrating to a secret inner space and its dynamics are based on the circle. Fittingly enough, its supreme enactment will be in the round dance of the Graces atop their private *locus amoenus*. All this, however, puts in hazard the linear unfolding of the Fable: if the "triall of true curtesie" (Proem 5) is something other than the goal-directed pursuit of the Blatant Beast (Calidore must stop chasing him in order to have his Acidalian vision), will not the quest narrative merely reproduce the hunt for the "shadowes vain / Of courtly fauour" (x. 2), the false versions and distorted reflections of courtesy lauded by those outside the circle of influence of Elizabeth's "pure minde"?

Spenser acknowledges in Book VI's Proem an extra-poetic world containing true and false mirrors of courtesy, mirrors which have become sadly indistinguishable to many of their beholders. While the poet emphasizes the visual deceptions of the "fayned showes," his account of their misleading "colours faire" slides punningly towards a co-indictment of false rhetoric, especially when he goes on to celebrate the silent, "inward thoughts" that define true courtesy (Proem 4–5). He locates his act of making, then, in a "present age" where all visual and verbal representations are pre-emptively fallen and potentially duplicitous. How is he to authenticate *his* acts of naming amid the perverse usage of a world where "that which all men ... did vertue call / Is now cald vice; and that which vice was hight, / Is now hight vertue and so us'd of all" (v. Proem 4)?[26]

Spenser's anxieties about this very issue have already been incorporated into the poem in his repeated representation of the monstrous enemies of his questers as monstrous abusers of language; even in Book I, Envy, riding in the pageant of the Seven Deadly Sins, is an embryonic Blatant Beast, with his backbiting of "the verse of famous Poets witt" (I. iv. 32; compare VI. xii. 40). As book after book of the poem unfolds, the power of missayers increases. Book IV's Archenemy is Ate, who fashions discord from "the seedes of euill wordes" (IV. I. 25); Arthur, Amoret and Aemylia meet another version of her in Sclaunder, whose "words [are] not, as common words are ment, / T'expresse the meaning of the inward mind" (IV. viii. 26), but are poisoned weapons which, like the teeth of the Blatant Beast, wound inwardly. Revealingly, as soon as he inscribes Sclaunder within his narrative, Spenser worries that some "rash witted wight" will suspect the worst of the ladies for conversing with Arthur unchaperoned (IV. viii. 29): the imagined obstacle of the defamatory reader literally holds up narrative progress. In Book V, an even more disturbing version of the abuse of speech is represented by the double identity of the slanderous poet at Mercilla's court, who, as if to emphasize the potential duplicity of all highly wrought language, is at once Bon Fons and Malfont (V. ix. 26). The evil poet is silenced forcibly (V. ix. 25), but by the end of Book V Arthegall is being assaulted by the hags Envy and Detraction and bitten by the Blatant Beast (V. xii. 33–42). The latter's invasion of Book V. xii from Book VI suggests the anarchic ubiquity of misspeaking: his multiple tongues reproduce envy and detraction a hundredfold.

Arthegall passes stoically on, however, and linguistic abuse remains unchastened and omnipresent as Calidore's quest begins.

Isabel MacCaffrey has argued that the allegorical poet cheerfully exploits the fall of language away from the ideal union of word and thing. As he deliberately dislocates sign from referent, his continual implicit admission of his "fiction's lying fictiveness" paradoxically allows him to get closer to truth than the poet who attempts verisimilitude.[27] While agreeing that the allegorical narrative concedes the absolute divergence of sign and referent in its use of a material fiction to represent an abstract truth, I feel that MacCaffrey's conclusions are a little too tidy, assuming as they do that the narrative representation of the abstraction in question will itself be semantically stable. Her account of Spenser's allegorical method does not admit the possibility that the poet's fictions are already so tangled up in the equivocal discourse of his readers that they can never quite speak with even the contingent authority one might confer upon the knowing alterity of the didactic "making."

Certainly, Spenser himself confronts this issue as his work proceeds. In Book I's Legend of Holiness, for example, the *word* "holiness" is actually employed only twice (and both its occurrences are in Arguments to cantos: it never enters the narrative proper at all). The Book of Temperance has nine direct references to "temperance," seven of which are in the body of the narrative. The words "chastity" and "friendship" each make fourteen appearances in their respective books, but "justice" is used all of thirty-five times in Book V, and "courtesy" on twenty-four occasions in Book VI.[28] The point I wish to establish is that in the earlier stages of *The Faerie Queene* the poet can show rather than tell. He trusts the reader's ability to translate his elaborately allusive and iconic quest narrative into an apprehension of the particular good under discussion – an apprehension that will be reasonably congruent with his own understanding of it. As the poem unfolds, however, Spenser seems to fear that his later allegorical narratives, and especially his retellings of the Fable in relation to social virtues always under negotiation in the public realm of discourse, may be shakily grounded upon arbitrary terms perpetually vulnerable to misprision or deformation. His logocentric allegorical method[29] comes to be less and less centered on the veiled Logos – or, alternatively, finds that Logos to be less and less narratable in the terms of his "darke conceit." Not surprisingly, the narrative progression of Books V and VI is regularly interrupted by direct addresses to the reader which purport to tell just what justice or courtesy *is*: again and again cantos begin with new attempts to characterize the quality under examination.[30] Spenser offers a poetically and thematically complex representation of courtesy in the Proem to Book VI, only to return relentlessly and more and more reductively to its redefinition at the start of cantos i, ii, iii and v. And as the story of Calidore unfolds, we become ever more aware of the discrepancy between the fragile, increasingly ineffable ideal of courtesy and the morally and linguistically ambiguous reality of courtesy-in-action inside and outside the text.

In its most elevated form, courtesy embodies "the secular and natural counterpart of grace,"[31] and certainly its narrative representation invites comparison with Book I's originary Fable in which divine Grace plays such a central role.[32] Calidore's vision of the Graces dancing on Mount Acidale is a secular revision of Redcrosse's glimpse of the workings of divine Grace on the Mount of Contemplation: Redcrosse sees the New Jerusalem, the *Civitas Dei*; Calidore learns that the Graces bring to humanity the manifold gifts which unite in *Civility* (x. 23), a condition which transcends mere "politeness" to encompass all that is best in human civilization and the City of Man. Significantly, a central contention of Book VI seems to be that in a disordered and emphatically fallen world, where one cannot fathom or control the workings of Heavenly Grace, one may mitigate fortune's blows by meeting them with all the (human) grace and graces at one's command. Grace, however, is a word with a disturbingly broad semantic spread: one's "graces" can include the most superficial tricks of *savoir faire*, as Roger Ascham recognized in *The Schoolmaster* (1570), when he censured those courtiers who might say of a pure but unpolished youth that "he is rude and hath no grace, so ungraciously do some graceless men misuse the fair and godly word GRACE."[33] To indicate what are (mistakenly) thought to constitute the courtly graces, Ascham quotes a fragment of current doggerel:

> To laugh, to lie, to flatter, to face,
> Four ways in court to win men's grace.[34]

The virtuous give-and-take of courteous living that is human grace (and our mortal imitation of divine Grace) has become linguistically interchangeable with the debased and marketable accomplishments that gain one worldly grace and favor. Spenser will grant, in an alexandrine afterthought, that "good thewes enforst with paine" are as worthy of praise as the graces that are present "by kind" (ii. 2), but he is afraid that the graces of courtesy, far from being internalized, selfless moral directives, may degenerate into manipulative practical skills – like those of his Blandina, whose pleasing but insincere verbal arts save her unregenerate lord from death at Arthur's hands (vi. 31; 41–43).[35]

In Stefano Guazzo's popular courtesy book, *The Civile Conversation* (first published in English in 1581), the profit motive for courteous behavior emerges in the telling similes of one of his speakers:

> As money well imployd, turneth both to the commoditie of him that receiveth it, and likewise of him that disburtheth it, so woordes well considered bring profit to the hearer and prayse to the speaker.[36]

Similarly, Spenser's own Legend of Courtesy embraces images of the market-place with a frequency which suggests that it is "always already" infected by an extra-textual materialistic ethos and discourse. Its first canto has barely opened when the information that Calidore is naturally graced with courtesy (i. 2) is supplemented by the more troubling information that "his fair usage ... with the greatest *purchast* greatest grace" (i. 3; emphasis mine). And as Book VI unfolds, the wanderings of the quest narrative become further entangled with the world of Mammon. Calidore, offered worldly rewards for his good deeds in canto i, passes on the offered riches to the victims of Discourtesy as their "rightfull meed" – proper compensation for wrongs suffered (i. 47). But once the term "meed" (ideally "due and just reward") has been let loose within the narrative, it is perpetually metamorphosing into, on the one hand, payment for services rendered, regardless of their ethical or unethical nature, and, on the other, personal spoil or booty. Thus we have the scene of young Tristram claiming the arms of the knight he has slain as rightfully won "spoile" (ii. 33), and feeding his "greedie eyes" upon the material rewards of his good deed (ii. 39).[37] More seriously, the services of knights errant become purchasable. Turpine hires Sir Enias with "goodly meed" (vii. 4) to do away with Arthur, and later refers to the Prince as the "bootie" he has "bought" (vii. 16). Arthur, having conquered Enias and slain his fellow assassin restores the proper meaning of the word, informing the former, "Now sure ye well haue earn'd your meed" (vii. 13): you've had your just deserts. Nevertheless, Enias, who perforce switches sides in order to save his life, is soon being called "that courteous Knight" (viii. 4): the epithet has become a remarkably equivocal one in a world where one can be at once courteous and self-seeking.

Even as Spenser seems to be manifestly failing to represent *his* Courtesy in terms that are untainted by the worldly discourse of self-interest, the very figuring-forth of Calidore's enemy subverts the linear integrity of his quest. The Blatant Beast, monstrous abuser of language, cohort of Envy and Detraction, whose "vile tongue and venemous intent...doth wound, and bite, and cruelly torment" (i. 8) is not simply the foe of the virtuous quester but of all virtue: "ne euer Knight, that bore so lofty crest, / Ne euer Lady of so honest name, / But he them spotted with reproch, or secrete shame" (vi. 12). Calidore dismally claims to be following an "*endlesse* trace" (i. 6), and it is true that, unlike the Dragon, Acrasia, Busirane, and Grantorto, the Beast does not await the quester at the end of his book: he rather challenges teleology by his pre-emptive interventions in the narrative,[38] and it is entirely typical that he has assaulted the hero of Book V before Calidore even starts out. Just as slander, scandal, envy and detraction exist wherever good labors to survive in a fallen world, the Beast is a ubiquitous menace in Book VI. Himself a misnamer *par excellence*, he resists the attempts of language to define, confine or chasten him. Even his parentage cannot be fixed: the Legend of Courtesy gives him two contradictory genealogies (i. 8; vi. 10–12).

As a malicious abuser of language, the Beast is predictably the enemy of the proper feignings of didactic poetic narrative (xii. 40). He is a brutish version of the willfully unsympathetic reader whose distortions of meaning menace the narrative integrity of the Book of Courtesy; his omnipresence threatens to implicate Spenser's honorably duplicitous designs in the ambiguities of a debased extra-textual value system. He has been at the poet's heels for a long time. In the verses "To His Booke" printed before *The Shepheardes Calender* in 1579, Spenser anticipates that Envy will "barke" at the work; sixteen years later, in the prefatory letter to *Colin Clouts Come Home Againe*, Spenser thanks Raleigh for his kindness in protecting the poet against "the malice of evill mouthes, which are alwaies wide open to carpe at and misconstrue my simple meaning."[39] The Blatant Beast's avatars in Books IV and V – Ate, Envy, Detraction, Sclaunder – are really versions of that bad reader (whether he is Burleigh or not is ultimately irrelevant) who has completely misunderstood the narrative strategies of Books I, II, and III (IV. Proem 1). Now, in Book VI, Spenser's worst anxieties about his audience – and about the propriety of his own feignings[40] – are embodied by the creature whose sheer uncontainability bespeaks the final unravelling of the Fable.

In a sense, the Blatant Beast is brought into being by the very nature of the Knight of Courtesy. Redcrosse learned on the Mount of Contemplation that all earthly glory is meaningless before the manifestations of God's Grace; Guyon and Britomart enjoyed no public victories when they triumphed over Acrasia and Busirane. Calidore, however, begins his quest by deploring the fact that, since he travels alone, his deeds will "by none be testifyde" (i. 6) – encountering Arthegall, he envies the latter for having achieved a victory "That shall you most renowmed make for euermore" (i. 5).[41] Calidore's interest in worldly fame, and Spenser's preliminary insistence that this hero's skill in battle "him did much renowme, and far his fame display" (i. 2), become disturbing once we recognize that human fame is as subject to abuse as human grace. Thomas Greene, discussing the figure of Virgilian *Fama*, notes that this noisy lady "can be roughly equated with 'rumor' or 'scandal'"; he goes on to suggest that she anticipates Spenser's Blatant Beast.[42] Calidore's "famous quest" (ix. 3) is a double-edged pursuit of both fame and infamy; the gratuitous detraction and ill fame the Beast inflicts on its victims are simply the other face of worldly renown. If the hero of Book VI is not permitted, or cannot be brought to, the humble recognition of the limited value of his earthly actions in the context of a higher end, the very narration of this version of the Fable, this latest revision of the quest that seeks to transcend itself, may engender an adversary to assault its worth, not from the heavenly perspective of the Mount of Contemplation, but from the infernal perspective of the Beastly "Stygian fen" (i. 8).

THE QUEST OF COURTESY: THE FAILURE OF SIGNIFICANT SEQUENCE

Having explored some of the potentially self-subverting aspects of both the quest of courtesy and its narrative/poetic mediation, I now propose to examine more minutely the narrative dislocations that herald the final dissolution of the Fable. The early cantos of Book VI are strikingly prone to reproduce what has gone before in *The Faerie Queene*; at the same time, their rather weary and mechanical iteration of scenes and motifs from earlier books of the poem is nudged along by repeated references to chance and fortune. Calidore's first adventure takes place "when as by chaunce" he finds a Squire lashed to a tree (i. 11), and this sets the pattern for the remainder of Book VI. The words "fortune," "fortuned" ("it fortuned that..."), "chaunce," and "chaunced" appear sixty-two times in Book VI, as compared to their thirty-six occurrences in Book I.[43] And a computation of Spenser's specific use of the terms "fortune(d)" or "chaunce(d)" in generating new narrative incidents or reversals reveals that, while Book I contains fifteen such instances, Book II seven, Book III eleven, and Book V ten, Book VI contains all of thirty-one.[44] I cannot agree with those readers who equate the fortune of Book VI with the providence that guides events in Book I.[45] The providential design of Spenser's originary Fable (where Redcrosse, "chauncing" to fall beneath the restorative branches of the Tree of Life did so because "eternal God that chaunce did guide" [I. xi. 45]) is not evident in the wanderings of the Book of Courtesy. Indeed, in the latter, the supposition that causality is at the mercy of blind chance is wholly congruent with the breakdown of moral cause and effect in a universe where the Beast savages innocent and guilty alike and injury is not necessarily the result of a fall into error.[46]

The anarchic workings of fortune preside over two kinds of subversive narrative iteration afflicting the earlier portions of the quest of courtesy. The first manifests itself in the repetition of *The Faerie Queene*'s past, and it starts out felicitously enough in canto i when Calidore successfully completes his own version of Artegall's first adventure in Book V (i.e. the restoration of an abused lady to a Squire and the punishment of her abductor). Other action-replays, however, are more disturbing. The Cannibals' delight in Serena as their garlanded sacrificial victim (viii. 39) parodies Una's adoration by the satyrs as their garlanded queen (I. vi. 13). Serena wanders into the clutches of the Blatant Beast in canto iii, just as Amoret strayed into Lust's power (IV. vii), but whereas the wounds Amoret sustained in the course of her rescue from Lust responded to Arthur's cordial (IV. viii. 20), Arthur cannot help Serena's hurts. The romance across class-barriers between Priscilla and Aladine echoes that of Amyas and Aemylia in Book IV, but there is no hint here of an eventual union. Book III's rather comic penance of the Squire of Dames (III. vii. 53–60) becomes the miserable and painful quest of Mirabella; the rude, cowardly, yet ultimately harmless false knight, Braggadocchio, becomes Turpine – equally rude and cowardly, but capable of inflicting real hurt. All the fleeing ladies of the poem – Una at the end of I. vi, Florimell throughout Book III, Samient in V. viii – are re-evoked in the form of Serena in flight, but her gallop ends in the Cannibals' territory where she faces a worse fate than any of her precursors. Most disturbingly, perhaps, the narrative returns again and again to the spectacle of a knight open to attack because he has put aside his arms for the purpose of pleasure or ease (Aladine in canto ii, Calepine in canto iii, even Arthur, in canto vii), and thus to

Redcrosse at the nadir of his career, disarmed by Duessa before his trouncing by Orgoglio and the temporary collapse of his quest.

The second kind of repetition enacted by the first seven cantos of Book VI occurs when the quest of Courtesy repeats *itself*.[47] Spenser's anxiously renewed attempts to define courtesy at the beginning of cantos are paralleled by the reworkings of exemplary narrative motifs with less than exemplary results: in both cases his re-versings reverse rather than further his didactic ends. In canto i, for example, Calidore reforms Briana because his courtesies "pearst / Her stubborne hart with inward deepe effect" (i. 45), but in canto ii the Knight of the Barge can only be reformed through a literal piercing by Tristram's spear which "strooke him ... vnderneath the hart" (ii. 12). Enervated repetition is also evident in a series of substitutions of the quest's protagonist. In canto iii, after Calidore has exited in pursuit of the Blatant Beast, Calepine moves to the narrative foreground, but proves to be a weaker and more vulnerable Knight of Courtesy (he is at one point obliged to hide from Turpine's sword behind his stricken lady [iii. 49]). And when Calepine and Serena are separated in canto v, a second substitution of hero is made with the arrival of Arthur, who plays a less impressive part in Book VI than in any other. The prince has to use sleight to enter Turpine's hold, his shield of grace is never used in combat, and, although he has previously acted as a touchstone in matters of true or false seeming, he fails to penetrate the wiles of Blandina. He cannot help his injured squire or Serena, he is never in a position to help Calepine or Calidore because he does not meet them, and he is not allowed to succor Mirabella. The narrative goes out of its way to emphasize the gap between his original role in the Fable and his reduced stature in this, its latest recapitulation – at one point, the shining agent of divine grace who delivered the hero of Book I is discovered unarmed and "Loosely displayd vpon the grassie ground" (vii. 18), just as the armorless and thoroughly fallen Redcrosse was "Pourd out in loosnesse on the grassy grownd" in the corresponding canto of Book I (vii. 7).

Even as the multiplication and substitution of increasingly

ineffective protagonists inhibits the orderly unfolding of the Legend of Courtesy, none of its individual episodes promise much certainty of closure. We do not know what will happen to Tristram, or to the bear baby rescued by Calepine, or whether Aladine and Priscilla will ever marry; the dawn that will make Serena and Calepine known to each other after Serena's rescue from the Cannibals never comes within the text. Cantos iii through vii are dominated, moreover, by Turpine, who represents a kind of evil that simply cannot be ended: Briana's discourtesy was reformed, the Knight of the Barge's was at least terminated, but Turpine bounces back again and again, unrepressed. He torments Calepine and Serena on three separate occasions, Arthur has to punish him twice, and even at the last Discourtesy does not seem to have been destroyed – merely hung up by the heels, left in suspense (vii. 27). Every episode resists the local closure that would allow the larger narrative to move on towards a totalizing *telos*, and this rejection of significant sequence is further emphasized by the proliferation of figures in retreat from the *vita activa* of the quest – the former warrior who has become the Hermit (vi. 4), Aldus, in retirement from worldly battles in his castle (iii. 3), and Aladine and Calepine, who prefer lovemaking in secret bowers to the trials of chivalry.

Book VI's resistance to "significant sequence" may derive in part from the fact that straightforward (and straight, forward) action is no longer of much avail in combatting the forces which complicate the quest of courtesy. There is the question of Priscilla's "good fame," for example. Worried about what her father will say about her overnight absence, she thinks she must "devize / How she the blame might salue with coloured disguize" (iii. 8). Her words recall the Proem's dismissal of worldly displays of courtesy as "fayned showes... / Which carry colours faire, that feeble eies misdeeme" (Proem 4). It appears that in this imperfect world even innocence must exploit the glozes of false virtue, and Calidore readily obliges Priscilla with "a counter-cast of slight / To giue *faire colour* to that Ladies cause in sight" (iii. 16; emphasis mine). By abandoning straightforwardness (indeed, as part of his ploy he retraces his steps to cut off the Knight of the Barge's head) and by telling a partial truth dressed up as a whole one, he preserves her reputation (iii. 17). Calidore was described in canto i as loving "simple truth and stedfast honesty" (i. 3) above all things: it is sadly obvious, however, that "simple truth" will not suffice in the equivocal world of the Blatant Beast.[48]

Even as the narrative of the quest displays an increasing tendency towards iteration-as-subversion, loses its (already shaky) sense of teleology, and becomes enmeshed in unredeemedly duplicitous discourse, a radical solution to the menace of the Blatant Beast is formulated which threatens to disrupt the narrative process as much as the Beast himself. In canto vi, in a scene of instruction at which, in perverse keeping with the fragmented nature of the Legend of Courtesy, neither the nominal quester, his stand-in, Calepine, nor Arthur are present, the Beast-bitten Serena and Timias are lectured by the Hermit. His words are prompted by his discovery that their wounds

> had festered priuily,
> And ranckling inward with vnruly stounds
> The inner parts now gan to putrify.
>
> (vi. 5)

We are reminded of Redcrosse's unregenerate state in Cœlia's house:

> But yet the cause and roote of all his ill,
> Inward corruption, and infected sin,
> Not purg'd nor heald, behind remained still,
> And festring sore did rankle yet within.
>
> (I. x. 25)

Redcrosse's illness is a spiritual condition, the result of his encounters with Pride and Despair. But it is narrated in terms of a physical malady and is cured by correspondingly physical means: special diets, the applications of "corrosiues," the cutting away of "superfluous flesh," whippings, prickings and saltwater baths (I. x. 25–27). The wounds of Serena and Timias, however, which originally seem to be remarkably literal (Serena has been bleeding heavily for three cantos), turn out to be figurative injuries (wounded names, not bodies).[49] They may not, it seems, be cured by any material regimen of Courtesy equivalent to Redcrosse's regimen of Repentance and Holiness: allegory's alterity cannot produce a comparably externalized narrative of recovery.

The Hermit abandons his surgery and in its place urges the repression of the "outward sense" (vi. 7), the avoidance of the "occasion of the ill" (vi. 14), and tells his patients to:

> Abstaine from pleasure, and restraine your will,
> Subdue desire, and bridle loose delight...
> Shun secresie, and talke in open sight.
>
> (vi. 14)

His advice undoes the narrative proceedings of the Book of Courtesy on several levels. It dislocates narrative cause and effect. Detraction can easily criticize a hedonistic existence and slander can pervert all but the plainest and most open speech; only by avoiding the *reason* for the Blatant Beast's attacks will you (paradoxically) cure their consequences. It de-privileges the symbolism of the quest: if, as the Hermit suggests, one can only suppress slander and detraction by shutting down sensory connections with the outside world and retreating from the *vita activa*, then Calidore's "exemplary" journey to destroy the Beast is by definition futile (a supposition which would corroborate, of course, my earlier thesis that the quest to win fame by suppressing infamy is *a priori* "infamous"). Finally, and perhaps most seriously, the advice to "Shun secresie, and talke in open sight" confirms that the very possibility of continuing to write *The Faerie Queene* is imperilled. In its deployment of polysemous discourse, Spenser's poetic narrative, his "continued Allegory or darke conceit," must constantly make use of "secresie," exploiting as it does a kind of enlightened duplicitousness, a "hieratic doubletalk."[50] If we accept the Hermit's teachings, we must recognize that the secretive, ideal courtesy glimpsed in Book VI's Proem can only be articulated unassaulted by the Blatant Beast in a fictional universe *apart* from the world delineated by the early cantos of the quest of courtesy, which has proved all too hospitable to the creature's rampages. Where Book VI has attempted to figure forth the "Allegory of Slander," it has found itself in effect representing and giving body to the "slander of allegory."[51] The duplicitous designs of the Legend of Courtesy will have to undergo significant modification if any part of the Fable's redemptive and totalizing vision is to be saved from its demoralized diachronic unfolding.

THE LEGEND OF COURTESY: THE ENDS OF VISION, THE END OF QUESTING

Half way through canto viii, just after the inconclusive conclusion to the Mirabella episode, the narrative of Book VI does indeed begin to recast itself quite radically. The story of Mirabella's arraignment before the court of Cupid and her subsequent persecution by Scorn and Disdain recalls the mood and techniques of earlier parts of *The Faerie Queene*. Mirabella could easily have wandered in from Book III, tormented as she is by the reification of inner qualities which she has acquired though embracing as courtly – or courteous – an artificial and perverted decorum of sexual conduct. But Spenser seems to recognize that the relative and ambiguous universe of Book VI is no place for her. Arthur's courtesy cannot help to reform her; indeed, we are offered further evidence of his attenuated power in the Legend of Courtesy by the fact that, although Disdain is "sib to great Orgoglio" (vii. 41), Arthur cannot destroy him in canto viii of Book VI as he destroyed his kinsman in canto viii of Book I. At this point the poet abandons his malfunctioning quest narrative, disperses the figures currently occupying its foreground (viii. 30–31), and begins a new exploration of his poetic resources as he labors to refigure, in some unequivocal and unassailable manner, the workings of the virtues with which Book VI is professedly concerned.

Spenser's own flight from the disintegrating Fable is perhaps mirrored in that of the distraught Serena, to whom he now turns his attention. Her headlong gallop "Through hils & dales, through bushes & through breres" (viii. 32) announces a journey into a new kind of fictional space. This initial violent excursus from the line of the quest does not, however, represent a withdrawal into a less vulnerable imaginative landscape so much as a confrontation and reinscription of the very forces that have been menacing allegorical narrative's "significant sequence." Only then can the poet begin to purge them from his work.

Serena lies down to rest in the territory of

> a saluage nation, which did liue
> Of stealth and spoile, and making nightly rode
> Into their neighbours borders...
>
> (viii. 35)

Spenser insinuates that the Cannibals dwell across a *border*, in a territory other than that of the world we have already seen in Book VI. These "salvages," who do not trade, keep animals, or "drive / The painefull plough" (viii. 35) may momentarily recall the Salvage Man of canto iv who "neither plough'd nor sowed" (iv. 14); like him they seem to belong to some prelapsarian age before man needed to gain his food by the sweat of his brow. But whereas the Salvage, "obaying natures first beheast" (iv. 14) neither fed upon flesh nor ate through anybody's efforts save his own, it is the Cannibals' custom "on the labours of poore men to feed" (viii. 35) as well as to "eate the flesh of men" (viii. 36) – the ultimate unnatural act. And, while the Salvage faithfully and civilly protects courteous beauty in the shape of Serena, the Cannibals' relationship with Serena's graceful person is that of mere *consumers*; her "goodly threasures of nature" are valued in that they are edible (viii. 41).[52] Serena's retreat into a superficially more primitive, less fallen world actually reincorporates within the narrative the forces of dissolution and fragmentation already eating up Book VI.

All the familiar disturbing motifs are here. Predictably, the Cannibals are led "by fortune blynde" (viii. 36) to Serena, although they elevate their "good hap" to the status of a providential "heauenly grace" (viii. 37). Their desire to dissect and devour her reflects the extra-textual forces which are unjointing the quest of courtesy: her *sparagmos* would represent the wilful mis-taking or dismemberment for motives of personal profit of the ideals of inner virtue and secular grace, insofar as they are embodied by Serena. The concupiscence of the eye and the obtrusive materialism which have already blemished Book

VI – the Knight of the Barge calling Priscilla his "spoyle" (ii. 17); Tristram looking at the "spoile" of battle with "greedie eyes" (ii. 33; 39); Turpine coveting the "bootie" (Arthur) he has "bought" – return with a vengeance. A spoil of fortune, Serena is stripped before the "sordid eyes" (viii. 41) of her captors, whose gluttonous perspective generates the following *blazon* of her charms as they gaze upon:

> Her yuorie necke, her alablaster brest
> Her paps, which like white silken pillowes were,
> For loue in soft delight thereon to rest;
> Her tender sides, her bellie white and clere,
> Which like an Altar did itself vprere,
> To offer sacrifice diuine thereon;
> Her goodly thighes, whose glorie did appeare
> Like a triumphall Arch, and thereupon
> The spoiles of Princes hang'd, which were in battel won.
>
> (viii. 42)

The description of Serena ignores her face and starts with her neck; she loses her individual identity and becomes a naked animal. Indeed, the parts of her body which are emphasized – neck, breasts, "tender sides," belly, legs – are all cuts of meat. Running in counterpoint to this consumer-determined selectivity, the qualifying adjectives ("yuorie," "alablaster," "white and clere") are the elevated ones of Petrarchan lyric. Donald Cheney has argued that the Cannibals represent a kind of corrupt Petrarchanism;[53] given that their eyes seem to be feeding here upon a disturbing "making" of their own, they may also represent the bad reader who, misprizing true beauty, will subject it to his own prurient gaze, and make it subserve his conspicuous consumption.

In saving Serena from her mis-takers, Calepine in a sense rescues a personal ideal from dismemberment and destruction, but the more universal ideal of a beauty beyond every carnal response, of an aesthetic attraction entirely distinct – and safe – from the urge to consume and possess by detraction, has been forced to the verge of complete dissolution. Serena's escape is a fearfully narrow one. Calepine arrives on the scene "by chaunce, more then by choyce" (viii. 46): his will to rescue her is subordinated to the actions of blind fortune. And the rest is silence: not only do we hear no more of the couple after canto viii, but the naked Serena is speechless with horror and embarrassment as they wait out the dark night together. The mad flight from the narrative equivocations and *faiblesses* of cantos ii through vii has ended in narrative paralysis and aphasia, as if Spenser has been traumatized by the experience of incorporating within his fiction a barely veiled representation of the debased appetites of an uncomprehending outside world. He has admitted just how cruelly a culture of consumers and profiteers might tear asunder the poetic enterprise; has admitted, too, his own anxieties about the very possibility of articulating his vision of courtesy – anxieties which perhaps include a sense of his own complicity in the ethos and discourse of materialism: after all, he is hoping for financial profit (a pension, a position at court) from his "graceful" work. He now has to reinvent, rearticulate, and strive to keep inviolate, the vision of secular grace in action.

When we finally rejoin Calidore in canto ix, one has the impression that the narrative difficulties of cantos ii through vii, and the threats to ideal courtesy (and to the poetic communication of ideal courtesy) confronted in canto viii, have provoked Spenser to start the quest narrative all over again. Calidore's pursuit of the Blatant Beast is not taken up at the point where he abandoned Serena and Calepine, but doubles back upon itself to the court from which knight and reader set out in stanza one of canto one:

> Him first from court he to the citties coursed,
> And from the citties to the townes him prest,
> And from the townes into the countrie forsed,
> And from the countrie back to priuate farmes he scorsed.
>
> From thence into the open fields he fled
>
> (ix. 3 and 4)

Spenser impels his hero on a journey which, like Serena's, moves him out of the narrative space of the preceding cantos of Book VI. Calidore ends up in the pastoral world of shepherds and song (ix. 4). The pursuit of his mission turns into a flight from a misleading "origin," the derivation of courtesy from court ("Of Court it seemes, men Courtesie do call" [i. 1]), to a world which posits an alternative origin of civility in pastoral *otium*. Redcrosse's brief confrontation with his origins in Book I. x, when the quester was reminded that he was also the ploughboy Georgos, a son of the earth and therefore of Adam, is here expanded to form an alternative fictional world to that of the quest. Calidore is not told about his origins, nor does he read of them or dream of them: he actually enters a new landscape (or perhaps an "inscape") where the courtesy he supposedly exemplifies exists untainted by the need to court the world's favor.

This nostalgic retreat to the fields radically revises the generic allegiances of *The Faerie Queene*. In turning to this landscape, Spenser is also returning to the beginning of an artistic journey which commenced with the publication of *The Shepheardes Calender*. The very first stanza of *The Faerie Queene* announced the poet to be abandoning the "Oaten reeds" of pastoral for the "trumpets sterne" of epic (I. Proem 1); is Book VI now rejecting the epic enterprise? Redcrosse's linear progress to victory over the Dragon required a providential pause in canto x in order for the hero to recognize his origins and be graced with a vision of ends which would authorize the achievement of his own limited and human goals "in the middest." Calidore, resting in the primordial world of the shepherds, is tempted to consider his experiences there an end in themselves. The linear drive of Book I's allegorical and eschatological epic (which has already been considerably modified by the interlaced fictions of the intervening books) is supplanted by the relative stasis associated with lyrical pastoral.[54] The generic space which can embrace a "true fiction" of a courtesy as yet uncorrupted by the merely *courtly* graces cannot also, it seems, contain the quest.[55]

To be sure, the Spenserian quest narrative, with its prolific errancy, its revisionary recapitulations and substitutions, its dilatory excess, has always been somewhat at odds with allegory's yearning for totality, for the ultimate subordination of the many to the One.[56] Allegory both requires and exacts a circumscription of significance, a closure that transcends the simple ending of a story. In Book I of *The Faerie Queene* – the Book of Holiness and of Wholeness – the mean time of error, of perpetually wandering narrative middle, is redeemed by that privileged moment of "simultaneity" within the diachronic unfolding of the quest which reconnects the fallen experience of the quester with primal Origin and final End, so that, for one brief instant, he sees things whole. By Book VI, however, the transcendent moment can no longer be recaptured within the quest narrative: too much has supervened; poet, quester and reader alike are locked within the contingencies and substitutions of fallen time and fallen narrative. The logos has moved too far from the Logos, and the altruistic duplicity of allegorical narrative has become indistinguishable from the equivocations of self-seeking dissimulation. In reverting to pastoral lyricism, however, Spenser essays another means of transcending the fragmentation of significance imposed by fallen, diachronic narrative. And it seems to me particularly telling that his chosen strategy exploits the double-voiced nature of the poem-as-narrative.

In Chapter I, I argued that the highly wrought stanzas (or verse paragraphs) of poetic fictions foster a complicated dialogue between the "poetic" and the "narrative" impulse; in the particular case of *The Faerie Queene* one might well contend that the former is privileged in the polysemous and palimpsestic poetry of vision, the latter in the more linear discourse of the quest. In refocusing the central episodes of the Legend of Courtesy about a synchronic, quasi-lyrical meditation within and upon a restricted *topos*, the poet attempts to recapture and contain a unified vision (albeit in the apparently "small-scale" terms of pastoral, rather than the expanded scope of eschatological epic). The unassuming yet intricate designs of pastoral offer a full-fledged counterplot to the narrative and moral ambiguities of the heroic quest; we should be aware, however, that the re-creative lyricism which is so central to these fictions of origin may not quite constitute the last word in the poet's endeavor to find a discourse adequate to the task of at once discovering and preserving his ideal of courtesy.

Calidore's introduction to recreative pastoral takes the form of a recapitulation of canto viii's parody of the rites of the golden age. Instead of the confused huddle of Cannibals about the naked Serena we have "a girland, goodly graced / Of louely lasses" (ix. 8) encircling Pastorella. The rough music of Serena's captors (viii. 46) becomes the melodious pipes and songs of the pastors; the garland which the Cannibal priest wove for Serena now graces Pastorella's head (viii. 39; ix. 7). She is elevated to the status of a goddess (ix. 8–9) – Serena was reduced to the condition of a naked animal. The frozen horror of Calepine's glimpse of the ritual circle with the knife descending on the victim in its midst has been replaced by the sustained delight of Calidore's gaze as he admires the cynosure of the ring of shepherdesses.

In rendering this scene of rural grace, Spenser appears to have revised out of his poem the forces that threatened to dismember it. At the same time, canto ix finally ratifies that urge to lay down one's weapons already manifested in the retreats from the *vita activa* of other characters in Book VI. Calidore is "disarmed" not by a Duessa but by Pastorella, the garlanded queen of pastoral graces, and by Meliboe, spokesman for the ethos of rustic *otium* where virtue can perhaps at last be safe from the assaults of both fortune and the Blatant Beast. And yet Arcadia is not to remain without taint – its corrupter, ironically, being the hero himself. The Knight of Courtesy is too *Court*ly either to read this world aright or to become part of it. Even as he listens to Meliboe's lecture on the simple life, his "hungry eye," Cannibal-like, consumes Pastorella (ix. 26). He is so busy playing the greedy voyeur that he fails to understand Meliboe's words. The latter suggests that in a world of chance and contingency one must internalize one's capacity for happiness; it must not be dependent upon external fortune (hap, or material wealth):

> It is the mynd, that maketh good or ill,
> That maketh wretch or happie, rich or poore
>
> (ix. 30)

Calidore takes this to mean that the will alone can alter the external course of events (ix. 31). Still enmeshed in the manipulative mode of courtly *Realpolitik*, he even assumes that he can purchase a place in the pastoral universe (ix. 32), despite his host's obvious disdain for riches. Rather than accommodating his own manners to the pastoral world, the knight imposes upon Arcadia the values of the imperfect society from which he desires to retreat.

Calidore's stay in Arcadia may educate the reader as to the location of the true origins of civility, but Calidore seems not so much to learn from it as to exploit it through the skills he has brought thither from court. While he manifests a superficial adaptability in his willingness to adopt for a while the garb and pursuits of the other swains, his apparent courtesy and generosity to the discomfited Coridon, his rival for Pastorella's hand, serve only to make the rustic look more oafish (ix. 44).[57] Calidore's condescension to the shepherds is disturbingly reminiscent of a passage in *The Civile Conversation* where Guazzo's Annibal suggests that it is profitable for a gentleman to consort and converse with his social inferiors because, while

> they are induced to love him, to honor him, and to doe him service... the pleasure which the gentleman receiveth is a great deal more, who conversing with other Gentlemen, is faine to frame himself ofttimes to their fancie: knowing that everie one will looke for as much preheminence everie way as himself, but in consorting with his inferiours, he shal be the chief man amongst them, and rule the companie as he list, neither shal he be forced to say or to do any thing contrarie to his mind.[58]

That the primitive virtues of Arcadia may be threatened by Calidore's sojourn in the fields is also suggested by Coridon's feeling that "This newcome shepheard had his market mard" (ix. 40). In the light of this suggestion of Pastorella's "marketability," Calidore's courtesy and graces tend to appear as investments – substitutes for his rejected gold which become his new currency in bargaining for a desired property.[59]

Spenser cannot represent Arcadia as either a safe retreat from, or a complete corrective to, the forces that have debilitated the Quest of Courtesy. Calidore, whom he tellingly compares to "Phrygian Paris" (ix. 36), is only a temporary shepherd; his metamorphosis is partial and self-conscious. His sojourn in the fields simply highlights the discrepancies between the artful, selfish graces of the court and the primitive graces of pastoral, and in canto x the poet renews his attempt to offer Calidore a pristine vision of the sources of true courtesy. The canto starts with a defense of Calidore's truancy: the peaceful stasis of the simple life is again proffered as a superior alternative to the "hunt... after shadowes vain / Of courtly fauour" (x. 2), a hunt for a fame that is only *Fama*, Rumor painted full of tongues, the Blatant Beast. Calidore's first act in Arcady, however, had been to ask the shepherds whether they had seen "a beast... which he had *thether* brought" (ix. 5; emphasis mine): we have already begun to suspect that the duplicities and ambiguities of the quest may have accompanied him into this new universe to assault its serenity. Spenser's own quest to create an imaginative space in which courtesy in action can be rendered without taint thus requires "a digression within a larger digression."[60] Calidore must retreat beyond his current retreat in order to reach Mount Acidale, which is "far from all peoples troad" (x. 5) and defended by an encircling forest and stream.

What Calidore sees on the top of Acidale reworks various scenes of inspiration and generation from previous stages of Spenser's literary career in an effort to concentrate everything the poet wants to communicate about the origins of true courtesy within a densely polysemous scene of vision and instruction.[61] This syncretic and synchronic *tour de force* strives to overleap all the obstacles to the authoritative representation of an ideal social virtue in the equivocal terms of an imperfect society. Retracing in his narrative the scene of vision and instruction in Book I. x, Spenser attempts to tap the plenary authority of the source Fable, even if he cannot put Calidore's quest in the same apocalyptic perspective. Once again we are brought to contemplate truth on a mountain-top, although here the relations of origins and ends are managed somewhat differently. Mount Acidale is, moreover, sacred to Venus (x. 9) and may hold echoes of that other *mons Veneris* and locus of divinely-ordered generation in the Garden of Adonis (III. vi. 43). At the same time, the presence of Colin Clout and his juxtaposition with an exquisite cynosure ringed by the Graces leads us back to Spenser's "Aprill" eclogue and its celebration of Eliza, seated on a hillock and attended by nymphs and Graces.[62] In that she inspires Colin's piping, Colin's lady is as much a tenth Muse as a supernumerary Grace: the scene thus recalls the Proem's location of the seminary of courtesy (and all other virtues) in the "silvre bowres" of the Muses (Proem 3).

The spectacle of the dancing floor of Acidale re-presents for the last time narrative motifs we have already seen in cantos viii and ix. Once more we have the noise of a shepherd's pipe. The circle of maidens about Pastorella has expanded to include the hundred subordinate Graces as well as the inner circle of three. The lady at their center, like Pastorella, is crowned with flowers, and the crown/garland imagery is expanded to embrace the whole company (x. 13–14).[63] Atop the Mount of Contemplation, Redcrosse's sense of his earthly goals was subsumed by the vision of the proper end of all quests and all stories, the End betokening God's endless grace to man, the End that would redeem the long between-time suffered since Adam's fall away from his divinely authored origin. On Mount Acidale, by contrast, Calidore is offered the vision of the *perpetuum mobile* of the endless circle of the Graces, which contains and protects, not only Spenser's primal representatives of secular grace, Thalia, Aglaia, and Euphrosyne, but also their supreme manifestation and summation in the person of the fourth Grace. The Fable of Book I, by invoking both Genesis and Revelation, the beginning and end of the Logos, charged Redcrosse's eventual progression to the earthly conclusion of his quest with divine authority, so that the linear unfolding of his story mimed in little the greater Story. Books II, III, IV, and V recounted ever more fragmentary quests, in which it became increasingly difficult to make these connections with origin and end which would make *significant* the perpetually wandering "middest" of epic-romance. Book VI's substitution of the dynamic circle of the Graces for the linear progress towards grace confirms a major change of narrative strategy. Every point on a circle is both a beginning and end: the diachronic quest movement from initiation at A to achievement at B has been supplanted, and in its place is privileged the synchronic *space* described by the circle.

This new and significant design was anticipated in Book VI's Proem, when the poet celebrated the luminous innate courtesy of Gloriana whose radiance was both delimited and reflected back to the queen by an inner circle of courtiers (Proem 6–7). Yet although the central image of Acidale offers a version of the Proem's concluding stanza, Spenser makes it quite clear that the woman who constitutes the cynosure of this scene is *not* Gloriana and indeed apologizes to Gloriana/Elizabeth for the act of usurpation (x. 28).[64] The poetic space within the circle does not contain the court from which quests emanate, or the public discourse in whose terms (in the universe of most of Book VI) their success is judged. Spenser's insistence on the separate nature of the *locus amoenus* which makes manifest the vision of the Graces concedes the complete dislocation of the Knight of Courtesy's quest from his own attempt to circumscribe and figure forth the unsullied and primitive graces of courtesy.

The circle on Mount Acidale excludes the court; it contains, however, the representatives of secular grace, and a poet, and his Muse. The author's investment in this vision is so great that he has introduced his pastoral avatar, Colin Clout, to make music for the Graces, and Colin is inspired by the fourth Grace, his beloved, to "pipe so merrily, as neuer none" (x. 15). Tonkin has suggested that in showing Colin piping for the dance Spenser is proffering us "the spectacle of the poet creating, the poem coming into being,"[65] but it rather seems that Spenser has enclosed within his digression from the quest of courtesy the representation of a very different kind of poetic making. In the "Aprill" eclogue of *The Shepheardes Calender*, Colin Clout is absent and Hobbinol rehearses Colin's lyric tribute to Eliza. Here, Colin is present, but his actual celebration of the Graces is mediated by Spenser's poetic narration of the scene that inspires Colin and which his song keeps in motion. Although Berger argues that what we have in Book VI is a lyric invasion from the world of *The Shepheardes Calender*,[66] there is no lyric as such embedded within the epic narrative, but rather a narrative description of a nostalgic, synchronic and "lyricized" ideal of courtesy. Spenser may have turned from narrating the diachronic unfolding of the quest to celebrating the space which contains the quest's titular virtue, but the ultimate ordering of that space is carried out by the song we never hear, the song which is "unspeakable" because the identity of its subject – the fourth grace, the Beloved, the figure at the center of the sacred space – is withheld, and is thus for ever protected from the Beastly reader's slander of allegory, from the dismembering misprisions of the cannibal consumers of the graces of poetry and the poetry of grace. The reversion to pastoral does not, in the end, involve a simple substitution of "lyric" for "narrative" as a vehicle for the allegory of courtesy: the significant space of Acidale is constituted by a story about a song about something unspoken: seeing courtesy whole is paradoxically dependent on creating a hole in the picture, in denying the power of *any* fiction to speak the whole truth.

The final divorce of vision from quest, the dislocation of the "poetry of conduct"[67] (and the "conduct of poetry") from the ailing epic enterprise, is emphasized by Calidore's disruption of his own epiphany. David Shore has argued that the discreteness of the Acidalian experience re-emphasizes a general tension within *The Faerie Queene* between the "chivalric quest, devoted to the ongoing struggle, and [the] poetic vision, devoted to the timeless ideal," but his account of canto x, which makes vision and quest separate but equal vehicles for Spenser's allegory, does not recognize Book VI's disturbing resuscitation of the latter at the expense of the former.[68] Looking on from the profane space outside the circles of the Graces, Calidore becomes a greedy voyeur, so ravished by the spectacle that "he him selfe his eyes enuyde" (x. 11)[69] – and utterly intent upon finding out exactly what kind of "enchaunted show" he has happened upon (x. 17). The fact that Calidore can designate his vision a "show" is particularly disturbing if we recall Spenser's repeated condemnation of those mere "shows" all too often associated with "courtly" behavior.[70] Calidore's desire to *know* what he is seeing is so strong that he is prepared to disturb the present vision and sacrifice the instinctive apprehension of secular grace in action in order to win the intellectual comprehension of an absence. He is the well-meaning but limited reader who hungers for clear glosses and neatly-packaged "significance" – and also, perhaps, the slanderer of allegory who abhors secrets because he assumes that mystery is the same as deceit. (Calidore does, after all, suspect that "his eyes mote haue deluded beene" [x. 17].)

When he leaves his covert and intrudes himself upon the sacred space of the Graces, he is briefly at one with all the other rude invaders of privacy in Book VI, including the Blatant Beast itself.

Calidore steps forward, the scene is shattered, the dancers vanish, and Colin breaks his pipes in disgust. Colin's actions mark the moment of Spenser's renunciation of his nostalgic withdrawal from quest narrative into increasingly private, lyric and pastoral space. The fact that the actions of his own hero both precipitate and justify this decision is his announcement that, at this stage in *The Faerie Queene*, even if his mythopoesis can briefly circumscribe a totalizing vision of secular grace in action, its fragile configuration will be destroyed by the first touch of the inadequate interpreter who wants to enjoy it as his own "traine of beauties Queene, / Or Nymphes, or Faeries, or enchaunted show" (x. 17).[71]

Spenser attempts, by way of Colin's mediating gloss upon the dance of the Graces (directed at Calidore-as-quester), to reconnect the narration of the quest of courtesy with the infolded representation of courtesy. Colin, reduced to a version of E.K., essays to redefine courtesy in its most instinctive and natural form. His stress on the nakedness of the virtues which the Graces embody,[72] and on their lack of "false dissemblaunce" (x. 24), emphasizes the discrepancy between courtesy at its purest and the kind of profitable dissimulation in which Calidore has been engaging; his insistence that the Graces are "simple and true" (x. 24) allies them with the "simple truth" that Calidore has found so elusive in his quest. Colin ends his lecture by interpreting their patterned movement:

> them selues so in their daunce they bore,
> That two of them still forward seem'd to bee,
> But one still towards shew'd her self afore;
> That good should from vs goe, then come in greater store.
> (x. 24)

This passage contains a notorious editorial crux. As Roche demonstrates, there is a genuine equivocation as to whether two of the Graces are facing us and one looking away (as in late classical tradition), or whether (via the emendation of "forward" to "froward") the reverse applies, as in the syncretic tradition which conflates the Graces (in Greek, *Charites*) with the triad Faith, Hope and Charity.[73] Roche's proposal that Spenser has incorporated both readings into his ambiguous lines is particularly attractive. Colin, it seems, is exploiting literary "doublespeak" to introject within the profane courtesy of the world the sacred courtesy of the scene of vision. Calidore may understand Colin to be invoking the courtesy-for-gain ethos that has infected his quest: invest a little grace in your dealings with others, you'll profit by the return of a "greater store" of good. But equally implicit in his words is the non-materialistic ideal of courtesy, the dictum that human graces should be selflessly applied to dealings with others without thought of equal or greater return.[74]

Calidore does not take very much away from his scene of instruction. With superb nonchalance, he dismisses his impingement upon the vision of earthly grace in action as a "lucklesse breach" (x. 29). Shrugging off what he has been shown as "that, which I mote not see" (x. 29), he never realizes that it was of supreme importance that he should "see" (apprehend, internalize, reflect upon) the Graces' dance – his error was to demand its translation into his own equivocal discourse. The inadequacy of Calidore's response suggests an admission on Spenser's part that what *he* is trying to communicate may be neither appreciated nor even desired by the imperfect quester or common reader.[75] Calidore would like to linger on Acidale, but only through purely sensuous delight in the landscape, and in Colin's discourse: he "with delight his greedy fancy fed, / Both of his words... / And also of the place, whose pleasures rare / With such regard his sences rauished / That thence he had no will away to fare" (x. 30). The Knight of Courtesy here foreshadows the reader/consumer at the end of Book VI who thinks an artist's only function is to "seeke to please."

By acknowledging Calidore's "greedy fancy," his desire to possess by consuming whatever is lovely that he sees or hears, Spenser hints that, after the brief suspended moment when the beauties of courtesy and the beauties of poetic making were completely interwoven and completely inviolable in their *locus amoenus*, the cannibal morality of canto viii is reasserting itself in the narrative. Redcrosse was turned away from his Pisgah vision to take up his quest and bring it to its proper end. Calidore, on the other hand, departs from Acidale only because of the promptings of his personal desire to possess Pastorella (x. 31–2) – to possess, that is, a version of the cynosure at the center of the dance.

Once Spenser has revealed the incompatibility of the imaginative landscape which contains the vision of courtesy with the fictional space in which the quest of Courtesy unfolds, and has laid bare the limitations of his hero as seer and interpreter, the narrative of Book VI rapidly distances itself from the sacred space of Acidale. The claims of the quest reassert themselves: Calidore returns to Arcadia, but he is swiftly obliged to reassume his knightly identity when he saves Pastorella from the jaws of a tiger (x. 34–36). Although Calidore is still officially "disarmed," by pastoral and Pastorella, the lingering appurtenances of recreative pastoral are fast becoming the weapons of the active quester: Calidore's shepherd's crook can miraculously "hew off" the beast's head. And it is this martial deed that finally wins him Pastorella's love: "From that day forth she gan him to affect, / And daily more her fauour to augment" (x. 37). Spenser hints, however, that Calidore anticipates an official betrothal of courtliness with pastoral grace to possess his lady sexually – a motif all too reminiscent of Redcrosse's erring detour from the route towards chaste betrothal with Truth that brought him "carnal knowledge" of Duessa. We learn that:

> at the last vnto his will he brought her;
> Which he so wisely well did prosecute,
> That of his loue he reapt the timely frute,
> And ioyed long in close felicity
>
> (x. 38)[76]

If the "close felicity" Calidore enjoys is a secret indulgence of his (sexual) "will," his victory would make him more akin to the predatory tiger than one might have anticipated – and if he has indeed consummated his desire and "consumed" Pastorella, it is very fitting that this episode is immediately followed by the rape of Arcadia.[77]

Meliboe's orderly universe, where "bad fortune" could be construed as merely a construct of the malcontent mind (ix. 30), is overturned by an emphatically externalized visitation of mischance: "It fortuned one day" that Brigands raided the shepherds' lands (x. 39). The Brigands "neuer vsde to liue by plough nor spade, / But fed on spoile and booty, which they made / Vpon their neighbours, which did nigh them border" (x. 39). They are not only enemies to the pastoral life but even to simple agriculture, living wholly as a race of consumers who "*fed* on spoile and booty." Like the Cannibals, they dwell in another kind of ontological space, across a "border," and the shepherds are forcibly swept into this new space when they are carried off to the raiders' underground den. In the earlier books of *The Faerie Queene* characters were often "caytiue thralls," symbolically enthralled to one kind of evil or another (as Redcrosse is to Orgoglio at I. vii. 19), but here there is a new literalness to the plight of the rustics. Merchants, who will purchase the Brigands' prisoners, are also to be found across that "border" (x. 43). The mercantilism and profit motives that have tainted so much of the quest of courtesy are now wholly reified. The greedy eyes of the Cannibals and of the imperfect Calidore reappear as the slave traders "greedily... gaze" (xi. 13) upon Pastorella: Calidore's "loues deare spoile" (x. 35) is now mere spoil indeed.

Given the regular guest appearances of Brigands in romance from Heliodorus on, it may seem perverse to identify this particular band and their associates with a thinly veiled narrative response to an extra-textual reality, especially when their cave seems to be just another of the symbolic hells scattered across the landscape of the poem. The Brigands' underground den, in which

> darkenesse dred and night did houer
> Through all the inner parts, wherein they dwelt,
> Ne lightned was with window, nor with louer,
> But with continuall candlelight, which delt
> A doubtfull sense of things, not so well seene, as felt.
>
> (x. 42),

apparently marks a return to the shadows of Mammon's cave, where

> vewe of chearefull day
> Did neuer in that house it self display,
> But a faint shadow of vncertain light;
> Such as a lamp, whose life does fade away:
> Or as the Moone cloathed with clowdy night,
> Does shew to him, that walkes in feare and sad affright.
> (II. vii. 29)

But the Brigands' cave, piled high with stolen and hoarded wealth, is Mammon's cave brought from the "other" world of allegorical narrative into a more material universe. Its odd shadows are caused by real candlelight (whereas lamps as such do not exist in the latter, except when invoked through simile), and its concreteness is further emphasized by Spenser's indication of the palpable nature of those material objects which lie within its shades – in Mammon's poetic space one sees, but may not touch. The thieves' environment seems almost too real: we have little sense of an allegorist's conscious exploitation of otherness, or of the willed distance he establishes between a concept and its representation. And the minimal discrepancy between the world and words of the text and the familiar worldly context in which the poem is written and read suggests that, in this new imaginative space, evil can no longer be ordered, and thus controlled, by a discourse of alterity: its description becomes, perforce, a barely veiled statement of "things as they are." Our sense of this is perhaps strongest in a stanza describing the mêlée in the Brigands' cave:

> Thus as they words amongst them multiply,
> They fall to strokes, the frute of too much talke,
> And the mad steele about doth fiercely fly,
> Not sparing wight, ne leauing any balke,
> But making way for death at large to walke:
> Who in the horror of the griesly night,
> In thousand dreadful shapes doth mongst them stalke,
> And make huge hauocke, whiles the candlelight
> Out quenched, leaues no skill nor difference of wight.
> (xi. 16)

Neither the preliminary account of the fray, nor the metaphor of

Death at large holds as much horror as the final statement that "the candlelight / Out quenched leaues no skill nor difference of wight." Spenser sketches a claustrophobic and chaotic scene, where harm can come to anybody through blind mischance, and human intention is irrelevant. This is the world that is now both inside and outside the narrative of Book VI. The "darke conceit" that at once concealed and revealed truth and whose figuring forth required both "skill" and "difference" has been erased by the shadowy representations of a morality based on contingency and profit motives.

The shattering of Arcadia mirrors the disruption of the Acidalian vision: Spenser traces in reverse the narrative movement that led his unsatisfactory quester to Acidale, in so doing tearing apart each *locus amoenus* he has constructed until we are thrust back into the world of canto viii, with Brigands substituted for Cannibals. Beyond the Brigands lies the resumption of the quest of courtesy, and the fact that the path that leads us there from Acidale traverses the scorched earth of the pastoral universe emphasizes the existence of the moral ambiguities of the one at the expense of the nostalgic graces of the other. Spenser's narration of the captivity and deliverance of Pastorella has been compared to the Proserpina myth,[78] but for all their parallels there is one clear difference between the two stories. When Proserpina comes back from the underworld, new life springs up on the blasted earth, but Pastorella's return leads to no restoration of the green world. Arcadia's only survivors are Coridon, its most boorish representative, and Pastorella herself, who was, like Calidore, a guest and not a native of its fields, and who will now grace it no more.

At the beginning of canto xii, Calidore and Pastorella pass out of the ruins of pastoral and into the world of chivalric romance when they take shelter beneath the roof of Claribell and Bellamoure. Spenser's summary of this couple's history (xii. 3–10) recalls the situation of Aladine and Priscilla, and suggests a return to the narrative continuum of Book VI's early episodes. At this point the quest impulse fully reasserts itself, and with it the claims of those "shadowes vaine / Of courtly fauour" so vehemently rejected at the start of canto x. Calidore now fears that "reprochfull blame" will stain his reputation; intent on winning "so much loos and fame, / As through the world... should glorifie his name" (xii. 12), he departs to capture the Blatant Beast before its slanderous tongues can injure him. The quest of courtesy, it seems, can only conclude by yielding to the dubious standards of its worldly arbiters, although Spenser does delay the final accounting through the interpolation of an episode of pure romance. Pastorella discovers her true identity and her progenitors in an interlude that strives to persuade us that "heauens grace" (xii. 8) still operates in a fallen universe. In the end, however, this episode manifests a retrogressive detachment from the remainder of the Legend of Courtesy: Pastorella stays behind in the world of her parents. The female figure who might be expected to mediate between Acidale and the world of public action,[79] to reconcile the discourse of vision with that of the quest, remains suspended in the generic space of family romance as Calidore's journey continues: pastoral grace is never formally permitted to plight her troth with worldly courtesy.

In the process of catching up with the Beast, Calidore leaves behind him the nostalgic ideals of both chivalric romance and golden age pastoral to enter a cosmos which, with its allusions to sixteenth-century historical realities, is more like that through which Arthegall rode in Book v. As Spenser narrates the pursuit of the Blatant Beast, the monster gets closer and closer to the here and now – Calidore overtakes it in what appears to be the Dissolution of the Monasteries (xii. 23–25). The complete ontological confusion which has now descended upon the poem (leaving indeed "no skill nor difference of wight") makes it unclear whether the Beast is not playing a radically ambiguous role there, for even as he destroys he nevertheless lays bare the abuses of the monks (xii. 24). At any rate, the quest is achieved, the Beast is defeated, muzzled, and leashed. Yet although Calidore, with his "ticker-tape parade through Faerie,"[80] has a more public and extensive triumph than any other quester, his success is the most limited. The sustained chastening of the Blatant Beast which would represent the final closure of the quest and imply at least a partial recovery of the fragmented Fable cannot be achieved in Book vi: the Beast escapes his bonds within a couple of stanzas of Calidore's triumph (xii. 38). Furthermore, when Calidore finally confronts his foe, we learn that among its ever multiplying tongues the most numerous are "the tongues of mortall men, / Which spake reprochfully, not caring where nor when" (xii. 27). The human voices of the monster, the voices of the abusers, misreaders and detractors of truth, the slanderers of allegory, are clamorously censoring and carping even as Spenser pens the last stanzas of canto xii: the Beast is at large both inside and outside the text and is tearing his work apart (xii. 40).

Spenser offers us two strategies for survival in a world where the Beast runs free and they constitute, in effect, alternative endings for both Book VI and *The Faerie Queene*. The first is suggested when he promotes in the Acidalian vision an ideal which is ultimately beyond language – and thus beyond misrepresentation. At the center of the central epiphany of Book VI, at the center of Colin Clout's wordless lyric, is the Beloved, the unnamed fourth Grace. In a consummately centripetal moment which counters the narrative entropy of the quest of courtesy, the *Charites* offer her their gifts of secular grace, and those gifts are implicit within her person. Lila Gella has described the Renaissance tradition (familiar, for example, to E.K., as one of his notes to the "Aprill" eclogue demonstrates) of a fourth Grace, Pasithea, representative of encyclopedic learning and the arts.[81] Spenser's fourth Grace infolds every aspect of these goods as she at once inspires and is celebrated by Colin Clout, the figure of the maker.[82] Within the secret and sacred poetic space of Acidale, a plenitude of generative wisdom and truth resonates about the inchoate form of the Grace/Muse/Beloved and fixes there, beyond the reach of any "beastly" reader's misprision, the circumscribed yet totalizing ideal that lies behind an increasingly dismembered narrative enterprise. But whereas the inscription of revelation within the originary linear narrative of Book I was based upon an imitation of the *Logos*, its preservation here depends upon the *withholding* of the *logos* (the song unheard, the cynosure who is ultimately unidentifiable, who cannot be completely glossed). In Book VI it is the closed circle of secular grace with its unspeakable center and not the broken line and narrative ambiguities of the tired representation of the quest that constitutes the final "version of the Fable."

The second strategy for accommodating oneself to the world of the Beast is the one cynically glanced at in the concluding stanza of canto xii, and it involves an explicit lowering of creative and didactic horizons. The poet must assume that every reader is at best a Calidore and at worst a Blatant Beast and realize that he can only hope to entertain the consumer of the work he produces – just as on Mount Acidale both the vision of the Graces and Colin's teachings could only feed the "greedy fancy" of Calidore. Spenser ruefully hope his "rimes" may "keep better measure / And seeke to please, that now is counted wisemens threasure" (xii. 41): adjusting themselves to the fancy of a less than golden age, they may reap a literal or figurative profit thereby.[83] This pessimistic conclusion announces the end of Spenser's successive revisions of a didactic poetic narrative that had attempted to encompass a moment of revelation transcending all acts of accommodation. And yet, even if it can no longer be named, even if it has to be concealed deeper and deeper within an excursus from the words and the world which misprize the epic enterprise, the totalizing vision of secular grace still survives, kept safe from the untimely end of *The Faerie Queene* within the *perpetuum mobile* of the Graces' dance.[84]

Earlier in this chapter, I alluded to the additional and alternative conclusion to Spenser's poetic narrative offered by the *Mutabilitie Cantos*, whose last lines reach out to the most perfect of all ends, when

all shall rest eternally
With Him that is the god of Sabbaoth hight:
O that great Sabbaoth god, graunt me that Sabaoth sight.
(VII. viii. 2)

But even as the fragmentary seventh book celebrates the possibility of a perfected quest and yearns for the maker's day of rest, its readers cannot fail to recognize a disjunction between the promises and premises of the *Mutabilitie Cantos* and the troubling issues which have been raised in the preceding portions of *The Faerie Queene*. If Nature's invocation of an eternity which will redeem the losses of fallen time (VII. vii. 58–59) recalls the consoling vision of the New Jerusalem proffered to the weary and wandering hero of Book I, the *Cantos* entirely ignore the problems concerning the very possibility of *representing* such visionary moments which have surfaced in the intervening books of Spenser's work, and which have almost overwhelmed the Legend of Courtesy.

Are the *Cantos* really part of the same story; do they really participate in the same narrative continuum as the final stanzas of Book VI? One's first instinct is to say "no." In the Legend of Courtesy, Spenser is less worried by the "natural" inconstancy of the fallen universe than by the obstacles it offers to the communication of any idealizing vision and to the articulation of any moral absolutes. When misprision threatens to translate the enlightened duplicities of the allegorist's "darke conceits" into *mere* duplicity, he exploits his double-voiced poetic narrative to figure forth a circumscribed space of revelation, detached from the imperilled quest narrative. This strategy seems to concede, however, that that narrative is no longer an adequate vehicle for the privileged feignings of Spenserian allegory. Canto x's brief victory over the slander of allegory is achieved at the expense of the larger poetic enterprise: the remainder of Book VI suggests that significant and signifying narrative sequence is no longer a possibility. Yet in the *Mutabilitie Cantos*, the poet's struggle to narrate the quest which will mediate his vision to his reader, and which will redeem the errant "mean time" of human fictions through fleeting glimpses of an enabling Origin and a transcendent End, is no longer very apparent. Although Mutabilitie herself may embody a condition of destructive flux which challenges the providential design of the *deus artifex*, Spenser does not seem to doubt his own ability to articulate the proper response to her menaces. His goddess Nature refigures postlapsarian mutability in a speech of judgment which invokes the power of the redemptive dilation of time to subsume within eternity the inconstancy of fallen creation (VII. vii. 58–59). And in the narrative present, the as-yet-untransfigured Mutabilitie is "put downe and whist" by the poet (VII. vii. 59), reduced to a position comparable to his own chastened situation at the very end of Book VI.

But as soon as Spenser has reported Nature's judgment, he appends to canto vii the free-floating, prayer-like stanzas which, even as they reach out to the highest of all ends, insinuate that the *Mutabilitie Cantos* remain part of the problematic universe of the threatened, silenced poet at the end of the Book of Courtesy. The highly subjective and consciously limited perspective of these stanzas is much closer to the poetic voice we heard in VI. xii. 41 than it is to the magisterial stance of the narrator who mediated Nature's judgment in the previous canto. Nature's triumph over Mutabilitie is transformed into one man's yearning for Last Things – a yearning which must nevertheless acknowledge the material inconstancy of the present moment, the persistent "sway" of that same Mutabilitie. The poet arrests rather than closes the Mutabilitie narrative with his personal desire for a respite from flux.

In hoping to be granted "that Sabaoth's sight," Spenser might seem to have distanced himself completely from his other, question-begging "end" of pleasing a courtly audience. Yet his goal is not as entirely and unequivocally elevated as it might appear. In Book VI, the unheard songs of Colin Clout animated and circumscribed the vision of that unnamed Idea who replaced Gloriana/Elizabeth and her court as the origin and end of secular grace, but this daring act of displacement is not to be repeated. Buried in the *Mutabilitie Cantos*' concluding and lyrical plea for a vision of Alpha and Omega, for the sight of the Maker who presides over the End of all earthly quests, is a triple pun on Sabbaoth/Sabaoth/*Elizabeth*.[85] Grant me, says Spenser, the sight and experience of that day of rest; grant me the vision (or bring me to the site) of the hosts of the blessed; grant me my queen's sight (or even, grant me a return to the site of my queen, to the court). Gloriana/Elizabeth is *not* wholly displaced by the higher vision: the faint trace of the Queen's name brings with it a teasing suggestion that *this* articulation of ending is still informed by a desire for worldly and courtly favor – the very same "seek[ing] to please that now is counted wisemens threasure" ruefully invoked at the terminus of Book VI's deprivileged quest. I am proposing, in short, that the Cantos of Mutabilitie do not simply evade the issue of whether it is possible to continue writing the same poem whose progress had become so imperilled by the time Book VI ground to a halt. They also rearticulate the possibility that the demoralized conclusion of Book VI will inform the future of *The Faerie Queene*. For even when their final stanzas return to the lyricism we have associated with Book VI's redemptive counter-narrative, Spenser's rehearsal of apocalypse cannot quite offer us the absolutely uncompromised, naked epiphany briefly circumscribed by the Acidalian vision.

CHAPTER 4

Inspired duplicity: the multiple designs of Paradise Lost

In dissecting out the competing plots of *Troilus and Criseyde*, in considering the divergent ends of the poetry of quest and the poetry of vision in Book VI of *The Faerie Queene*, I have had occasion to remark upon the inherent duplicity of highly wrought poetic narrative. The narrative poem's tendency to tell more than one story at once may be partly attributed to its formal dynamics, which encourage a dialogue between the representations of linear narrative discourse and the counterplots initiated and infolded by more synchronic and lyrical schemata. But such palimpsestic plotting is probably equally bound up in the multiple generic allegiances that come so easily to poetic fictions, their ability to embrace, simultaneously, several alternative *kinds* of making. There seems, moreover, to be a close relationship between the co-incidence of diverging didactic/aesthetic designs and the poetic narrative's reinterpretive bent: the polyphonic plots of the *Troilus* represent a complicated response to and revision of Chaucer's Boccaccian source text, and it is a frequently revised and reinterpreted originary fable that finally engenders the competing representations of entropic quest romance and recuperative, lyrical pastoral in Book VI of *The Faerie Queene*.

Paradise Lost, of course, is yet another of these "recreative" narratives. It does not, however, remake a secular poetic fiction but rather a canonical, biblical text, and its retellings are correspondingly both more significant and more perilous.[1] When Milton strives to re-present the truth of the origins of the human condition, he presumably hopes to recapture some kind of plenary wholeness. But the poet's "faithful" narrative is inevitably an exegesis, a doubling back upon and multiplication of the Logos: Milton's noblest and most assiduous efforts to speak the unspeakable, to reinscribe the Edenic moment, inexorably give rise to or co-exist with an assortment of richly textured counterplots. I intend, in this chapter, to explore the variously multiple and multiplying plots of Milton's epic; since, however, the work's (often honorable) duplicities are so interconnected with its audacious narrative and poetic assaults upon the limitations of belatedness and the constrictions of postlapsarian time, it is by way of some extended preliminary meditations upon these features of Milton's poetic narrative that I shall circuitously approach the question of the "double vision(s)" of *Paradise Lost.*

BEGINNING LATE

Before unpacking the narrative strategies of *Paradise Lost*, one should perhaps attempt to define the nature of the canonical narrative that Milton was recreating. Erich Auerbach's discussion of the distinguishing characteristics of Old Testament narrative is still a useful guide here: commenting on Genesis 22 (the sacrifice of Isaac), he suggests that the biblical text offers

> the externalization of only so much of the phenomena as is necessary for the purpose of the narrative, all else [is] left in obscurity; the decisive points of the narrative alone are emphasized, what lies between is nonexistent; time and place are undefined and call for interpretation; thoughts and feelings remain unexpressed, are only suggested by the silence and the fragmentary speeches[2]

Milton chose to penetrate the silence, the "nonexistent" (or unspeakable) suspended between the biblical parataxis. In clarifying the obscurity, in filling in the background, every departure he made from scripture was inevitably a gloss on the canonical text as well as part of a new text.[3] C. S. Lewis considered *Paradise Lost* to be a "great ritual mimesis of the Fall,"[4] a marvelous, expansive, ordered working through of what was already familiar and understood, and one to which the reader should surrender willingly in order to appreciate the poem. But Milton's mimesis is not so much a technique of faithful imitation as one of faith-filled redescription,[5] deployed by a creator who devoutly believes that his mythopoesis is a product of the inspired imagination. And the work is really only "ritualistic" if we borrow our definition of ritual from the Kafka parable which tells of leopards invading and desecrating a temple during a certain rite with such regularity that their raids are made part of that rite.

Milton's narrative strategies in *Paradise Lost* invite comparison with *midrash*, the rabbinical exegetical practice which could involve, *inter alia*, "narrative alterations or interpolations, sometimes very free."[6] In a discussion of early Christian interpretive practice, Frank Kermode aligns *midrash* with a tendency almost ubiquitous in the Christian evangelists to enhance the significance of their biographical source material by structuring their narratives around interpolated Old Testament prophecies of the Messiah's coming, thus working from hindsight to redeem the old truth and confirm the new one.[7] Milton's own narrative *midrash*, by contrast, has somehow to speak to all relevant sacred and secular texts produced since the beginning; his retelling must acknowledge, then redeem, absorb, or explode each one. His poem must not only engage with the entirety of Biblical narrative and centuries of Biblical commentary on Genesis and the rest of scripture, but must also invoke and interrogate the pagan epic tradition and a whole alternative canon of myth and fable.[8]

The complicated relationship between redescription and reinterpretation in *Paradise Lost* is closely related, then, to the inherent difficulties of any attempt to produce an authoritative account of Origin, when a consciousness of all the supplementary (sacred and secular) writings that have since come into existence inevitably alters and informs the poet's apprehension of the Beginning. And Milton adds further nuances to his "adventurous song" by incorporating within it the signifying structures of numerous secular genres: in addition to epic, *Paradise Lost* intermittently invokes the characteristic features of romance, tragic drama, pastoral and lyric.[9] Milton's rehearsal of other modes of poetic fiction-making brings with it the danger of inscribing within *Paradise Lost* competing (and sometimes pagan) systems of value, and his incorporation of these makings within his epic dilation of and upon the Logos represents an audacious act of syncretism. The blind poet seemingly exploits his exclusion from the world of visible phenomena to create an independent universe where diverse elements of a vast and heterogenous learning can be juxtaposed within a personal continuum, sometimes jostling each other, sometimes collapsing into one another. Thus, the scales in which Satan's fate is weighed at IV. 997–1004 – which are not, of course, in Genesis – recall the Homeric scales in which Zeus balances the fates of Hector and Achilles, the Virgilian ones in which Jove weighs those of Aeneas and Turnus, but also the divine judgment of Daniel 5:27, in which Belshazzar is "weighed in the balances" and "found wanting."[10] They summon up, furthermore, a more contemporary, secular scripture, Book V of *The Faerie Queene*, in which the Egalitarian Giant finds that "winged words" are too light to be weighed in *his* scales (V. ii. 44). Spenser proposed that epic language soared above mundane reckoning; Milton seems to be revising Spenser from a transcendent perspective to suggest that all the epic boasts of Satan weigh as naught in the divine scheme of judgment.

Supplementing and glossing a laconic canonical narrative with his own comprehensive experience of secular and sacred texts in an attempt to rebuild Truth out of a host of apparently incongruous fragments, Milton seems at times to be as much under the patronage of Hermes, protector of interpreters and thieves, as that of the heavenly Muse. But for all his boldness of aspiration, the most basic aspects of "telling the story" bring with them daunting challenges – for how or where does one begin to tell the story of the Beginning? It is possible, indeed, to suggest that *Paradise Lost* never ceases to begin: in a poem which, as more than one reader has noted, beginnings and ends are remarkably difficult to disentangle from one another, the very last lines of Book XII offer a new start.[11] In contrast to the confined, progressively linear vistas, the relentless "and then," "and next" of fallen time which Michael's narrative of future events has set before Adam, we are once more in a world of choice, of alternative beginnings: "The world was all before them, where to choose / Their place of rest" (XII. 646–47). The fallen couple seem suspended for ever at the threshold of a new history. And while there are narrative "ends" in the poem (most notably the Son's apocalyptic triumph in the war in Heaven, which concludes Book VI, or the vision of the flood and God's covenant thereafter, which closes both the Age of Adam and Book XI), such resolutions only terminate smaller narratives within the larger, more open-ended one.

The characters in *Paradise Lost* are themselves perpetually interrogating or rehearsing the notion of "beginning." Adam and Eve and Sin recount their own origins at great length, Raphael is eager to learn about Adam's creation, a disguised Satan asks Uriel about the creation of the world, and Adam questions Raphael on the same matter. The vocabulary of genesis, of fathering, creating, begetting, establishing, permeates the work: the enormously loaded word "Author" is attached to Satan, God, Adam, the Son, and even the serpent; nearly every figure in the poem is engaged in the process of generation or creation for good or ill.[12] And as they move towards the end of his narrative, Milton's readers, Janus-like, are recalled to the origins of their own immediate condition as representatives of fallen humanity reading about the Fall. The Adam and Eve of the last three and a quarter books of *Paradise Lost* have not only generated but also inhabit the same continuum of postlapsarian time as ourselves: by the end of the narrative they have become our beginning.

Gérard Genette, who has examined the problem of beginning a narrative in authors as far apart in time and intention as Homer and Proust, suggests that "complexly structured openings, mimicking as it were the unavoidable *difficulty of beginning* the better to exorcise it, are seemingly part of the earliest and most lasting narrative tradition."[13] The tortuousness of the twenty-six lines of the first verse paragraph of *Paradise Lost* certainly bears out his thesis. Massive shifts of temporal and narrative focus occur within a relatively short space; light punctuation and heavy enjambments discourage the reader from resting at the close of any of the first fifteen lines and emphasize the building up of an initiatory impulse. We leap from the anticipation of Christ's final victory (I. 4–5) to the "In the beginning" which both announces and mimes the writing of Genesis, the setting-down of the Beginning (I. 9); from the matter of "man's first disobedience" (I. 1) to the manner of the unfolding attempt to achieve in the poetic present "Things unattempted yet in prose or rhyme" (I. 16). We are bombarded with a host of explicit and implicit beginnings and firsts, as if the poet-narrator is indeed trying to desensitize himself to the difficulty of inaugurating his task. Milton creates a kind of montage which collapses together man's first disobedience, the first inspiring of Moses, Moses' first singing of what happened "in the beginning," the Spirit which "from the first" sat brooding on the abyss, and his own ambition to offer the first poetic justification of God's ways to man. Nor is his anxiety assuaged by these preliminary maneuvers. In the address to Light at the opening of Book III, he is again grappling with beginnings – "Before the sun, / Before the heavens thou wert" (III. 8–9); four books later, invoking Urania by name, he is still trying to circumscribe the ineffable moment of creative origin, when,

> *Before* the hills appeared, or fountain flowed,
> Thou with eternal Wisdom didst converse,
> Wisdom thy sister, and with her didst play
> In presence of the almighty Father, pleased
> With thy celestial song.
>
> (VII. 8–12; emphasis mine)[14]

To complicate matters even further, in a kind of equivocal counterpoint to these urgent reinvocations of and appeals to (externally authoritative) priority, Milton secretes his own, distinctly question-begging "moment of origin" within the later stages of Book V of *Paradise Lost*. Near the center of his epic, he uses Raphael as his mouthpiece to describe the action that actually precedes any other in the concatenation of events contained, reordered and redescribed by the poem, the Father's exaltation of the Son (V. 600ff.). Milton's "heroic song" can be viewed, then, as the dilation of and upon an action which, as Mary Nyquist points out, is itself quite uncanonical as the first cause of the war in Heaven.[15]

The rapidity of the shifts between different aspects of beginning in the Invocation to Book I (rendered all the more dizzying by the constant changes in verb tense in these introductory lines) makes the actual *narrative* beginning of *Paradise Lost* come as something of a surprise when the reader comes to rest in the syntactic present of Hell by colliding with the "now" which locates her in the Pit beside Satan (I. 54–56). But for all the elaborate sound and fury surrounding one's apparent initiation into the matter of the poem, Books I and II of the epic of origins constitute a consciously – and riskily – false start. Taking poetic narrative's tendency to engage in a complicated dialogue with pre-existing literary kinds to new lengths, they so successfully entertain the fallen (and now explicitly "Satanic") themes and values of postlapsarian epic and romance, that it becomes a matter for doubt whether pagan and/or secular literary models are ever going to be purged from the work so that Christian epic can finally begin. *Paradise Lost*'s "both necessary and superfluous" precursors engender a remarkably tenacious counter-narrative; Hell's epic resonances can never be completely exorcised.[16]

It is not that Milton's rehearsals of his epic precursors are not thoroughly subversive. To cite just one example, his elaborate "bees in spring time" simile near the close of Book I, which reinvokes the Greeks going to council in the *Iliad* (II. 87–90) and the bustling Carthaginian city-builders (*Aeneid* I. 430–36), diminishes its epic pretexts by entangling them with the literal miniaturization of the fallen angels swarming into Pandaemonium (I. 768–90): the Achaeians and Carthaginians are now mere pygmies and elves. When, furthermore, Satan-as-pseudo-Aeneas sets out on his quest to found a new kingdom, Milton also sends him into a new generic space in which the latter's lingering "epic" attributes will appear disablingly incongruous (for it is a universe which does not yet have to rely on ambiguous and fallen modes of heroism as compensations for the loss of Eden). But Hell itself persistently reverts to (or anticipates) the character of a Homeric or Virgilian underworld. After Satan has departed, his followers explore their domain, and we learn that, although they have yet to become the false gods of Greece and Rome, their home contains the four rivers of Hades (II. 575–86), the Furies (II. 596), and a river which periodically retreats from the lips of the damned "as *once it fled* / The lip of Tantalus" (II. 613–14; emphasis mine). Even though its present description evokes a "now" before the Fall has taken place, Hell seems to be "always already" the habitation of post-lapsarian tormented souls, as well as the fabulous infernal realm of pagan epic. If it contains things "worse / Than fables yet have feigned" (II. 626–27), it also contains *exactly* what those fables have feigned. Indeed, it contains virtually all epic fables – fables which may be "Chimeras dire" (II. 628) from a redeemed perspective, but which are perfectly literal from the infernal one. Hell will still be in existence as *Paradise Lost* progresses, and so will underground epic.

Milton's relations with secular romance are equally perplexed. The mustering of Satan's troops generates comparisons not only with the armies of classical epic but also with those of medieval and Ariostan "fable and romance" (I. 580–87); Pandaemonium is parenthetically the jousting field of chivalric fictions (I. 763–67). At the gates of Hell sits Sin, a figure out of Spenserian romance – a recasting, indeed, of Spenser's Error; unlike Error, however, she does not seek to terminate a quest of holiness but rather helps to initiate the Satanic knight errant's fallen *aventure* when her sire persuades her to aid him in his "wandering quest" to ruin man (II. 830).[17] And fallen romance is never entirely transcended: when the fiend returns to Hell after the Fall, his arrival travesties a romance homecoming: the "great adventurer" (X. 440) is reunited with his infernal family after his "adventure hard" (X. 468). One might even suggest that Adam and Eve's "wandering steps and slow" at the conclusion of Book XII will carry them out of Christian epic and into this most errant of genres.

Milton's long-postponed but explicit announcement in the Invocation to Book IX that he is *not* writing a conventional heroic poem (IX. 14–44) draws careful distinctions between his "higher argument" (IX. 42) and both the concerns of classical epic (IX. 14–19) and the "long and tedious havoc" wrought by the "fabled knights" of romance (IX. 30–31); the gesture encourages the reader to relegate the familiar themes and motifs that permeate the infernal episodes to the realm of the merely Satanic. But this new beginning cannot entirely contain and control the generic polyglossia already unleashed within the poem. Milton's epic of origin seeks to rehearse, revise and ultimately transcend all fallen genres, but it can only articulate its – necessarily belated – alternative song by way of a perpetual incorporation of, and dialogue with, intervening "Satanic" literary kinds – literary kinds in which, for all his protestations to the contrary, the author is obviously "skilled [and] studious" (IX. 42). The proper celebration of "patience and heroic martyrdom" (IX. 32) is consistently defined in relation to the inditing of pseudo-heroic warfare (IX. 27–28). The sublime genres of Eden cannot be comprehended in a vacuum; the praise songs articulated by Adam and Eve in the garden, for example, fall into an inevitable dialogic relation with the fallen seduction lyrics Satan directs at Eve.[18] The advancement of the "higher argument" must always include, in however carefully inflected a manner, the mediating fictions of the between-time: while it is always beginning late, *Paradise Lost* can never offer a completely *fresh* start.

This is further confirmed by Milton's marshalling of a number of alternative narrators within the course of his epic: almost every story of origin is mediated by other voices,[19] and even the most authoritative accounts turn out to have variants, to be already open to interpretation. When Adam relates *his* creation story to Raphael, his account of his first encounter with Eve (VIII. 500–10) revises her relation of the same event (IV. 477–89): where Eve had asserted that she initially turned from him because she found him less attractive than her own reflected image (IV. 479–80), Adam (ventriloquizing an emphatically belated construction of proper female behavior) attributes this action to her modesty and to "the conscience of her worth / That would be wooed, and not unsought be won" (VIII. 501–3). A more dramatic manifestation of the bifurcating story of beginning is evident in the discrepancy between Sin's story of her origins and Raphael's account of the origin of Satan's sin. Two kinds of discourse attempt to accommodate the same event: in the first, Milton defers to the Ovidian family romance narrated by an entity who is herself only a reified abstraction, a "sign" (II. 760); in the second he has Raphael adapt the themes and terms of postlapsarian epic to depict the birth of rebellion and fallen aspiration.

The entanglement of origin in multiplying and variously mediated narratives does not, of course, mean that there is not a hierarchy of authority within the corpus of infolded tales. As the fallen Satan and the postlapsarian Adam and Eve become imprisoned within their own egocentricity they are less and less able to communicate the truth of "what happened."[20] Satan's multiple redescriptions of the war in Heaven are always subordinated to a personal and political agenda, and as soon as *they* have fallen, Adam and Eve recast the events of the last prelapsarian morning to back up the accusations they are making against each other (IX. 1134ff.). Questioned by the Son, they cannot narrate the day's events in the clear and controlled manner in which each previously related their coming into being. Adam tries to delay and confuse his admission with a welter of qualifications and prevarications (X. 125–43); Eve can only make the (canonical) statement about herself which elides narrative cause and effect in a paratactic "and": "The serpent me beguiled and I did eat" (X. 162). As we register the duplicity of these postlapsarian stories, however, we must also confront a question which the very act of composing *Paradise Lost* may seem to beg. Given that the author believes that he is writing the truth, and that his divine history thus makes him one of the fallen sons of Adam (even if he is also the devout poet John Milton),[21] can his attempt to narrate not only the Fall, but also the prelapsarian state have any authority at all? Can a fallen man ever tell a story which will adequately justify the ways of God to men? And when Milton decides to re-word the Logos, to recreate a sacred text in which Truth is already, supposedly, revealed, is he not an undeniably skilled, but inevitably limited, reader-interpreter-rewriter, whose "inspired" supplementation of the Genesis *lacunae* may be merely a false projection, a fanciful amplification of the worm's-eye perspective of postlapsarian humanity?

Milton, in fact, exploits to the full the extra-Edenic hindsight that the reader shares with him, drawing upon it, even as he draws upon his poetic narrative's "supplementary" bent, to generate some particularly poignant dramatic ironies. He makes powerful use of the central, terrible discrepancy in awareness between the unfallen Adam and Eve and the fallen, yet knowledgeable, reader, who, like the spectator of a classical tragedy, knows what will and must come to pass. His most skillful manipulation of this occurs in Book IX, when all the events which took place before our arrival *in medias res* have been unfolded, and the events of Genesis 3: 1–7 have to take their course.[22] An almost unbearable condition of suspense is achieved in this book up to the moment of Eve's fall: the author knows all; we know all; but the story still has to be told.[23] Successive strategies of narrative delay are deployed: we move through Satan's possession of the serpent and subsequent soliloquy, the graceful, extended debate between Adam and Eve, the proleptic comparison of Eve to fallen, pagan goddesses, Milton's lamentations on her behalf, Satan's discovery of Eve and brief moment of half-repentance, a digression on the serpent's beauty, Satan's long, courteous debate with the woman, Eve's own internal debate – in all, 781 lines of verse are produced out of the six verses which take us from the serpent to the Fall in Genesis 3. The laconic scriptural narrative is expanded almost to bursting; it is as if, *pace* Zeno's Achilles and the tortoise paradox, the forward thrust of Milton's narrative takes place in increasingly minute increments – as if the author himself resists articulating the moment when "she plucked, she ate" (IX. 781). Milton seems to forget, in these charged passages, that he has a "higher argument" to unfold; his text partakes of that subversive dilatoriness, that covertly reinterpretive delay of an unwanted but inevitable end which characterizes more profane poetic narratives.

The delaying actions of Book IX follow hard upon the even more prolonged suspensions of narrative movement towards the Fall to be found in Books V to VIII. The conversation of Raphael and Adam dilates the middle of Milton's epic, as if to defer as long as possible the moment when the poet "must change / Those notes to tragic" (IX. 5–6).[24] Adam himself seems conscious of how needful it is to extend this threshold time of dialogue with the divine messenger, remarking to Raphael, "thou seest / How subtly to detain thee I devise" (VIII. 206–07) as he prepares to relate his own beginning. Indeed all of Paradise hangs on Raphael's words as he turns from (or expands) his official mission to narrate the Creation: Adam claims the very sun is "Held by thy voice... / And longer will delay to hear thee tell / His generation" (VII. 100–02). Milton is playing, of course, with more than one audience and more than one speech act here. While the unfolding of supplementary narratives is, from Adam's point of view, an exquisite means of augmenting the pleasure of the present moment of converse with an angel, it is also absolutely essential in terms of epic economy: the reader has to be brought up to date with all that has transpired prior to her entry into the "now" of Book I. 54, which, according to Fowler's dissection of the time-scheme of the work, occurs two-thirds of the way through the period of action actually encompassed by *Paradise Lost*.[25] There is a double thrust *in medias res*: not only does the narrative plunge into the midst of the sequence of events it is to cover, but Milton's action in writing it (and ours in reading it) takes place in the midst of the Fall's consequences. We are ourselves within a narrative, whose projected end – the final triumph of the Son – is in fact revealed to us before the Fall has even taken place in the poem which at once embraces and is embraced by providential history.[26]

Milton made a bold decision when he rejected the more obvious *in medias res* starting position, the moment after the Fall, and chose instead to offer a representation of the prelapsarian condition of Adam and Eve. (In his outlines for the tragedy he originally intended to write on the subject of the Fall, he does not bring the couple on stage until after they have transgressed.)[27] The only scriptural support for an extended treatment of Adam and Eve's quotidian existence in Eden is a single verse indicating their enparadised state: "And they were both naked, the man and his wife, and they were not ashamed" (Genesis 2:25). The rest is silence; Genesis 3 opens immediately thereafter with the serpent and his subtlety; six verses later man has fallen. The Bible thus provides one verse on life in Paradise after the creation of Eve, Genesis 2's account of the topography of Eden, and a resounding ellipsis. Milton, however, keeps the Garden of Eden and unfallen humanity before our eyes for nearly six books of *Paradise Lost*: even when Raphael dilates upon the war in Heaven and the Creation we remain aware of the *moment* of narrating, the conversation in Paradise.

In order to present Paradise and the unfallen – and in order to figure forth Heaven, which we must visit on the way to Eden and revisit in Raphael's narrative of the war in Heaven – the poet must perforce employ a language which is subject to all the corruption of the fallen state. Indeed, where Spenser merely laments that "that which all men then did vertue call, / Is now called vice; and that which vice was hight, / Is now hight vertue, and so us'd of all" (*Faerie Queene* v. Proem 4), Milton actually shows the moment of language's original fall from univocal significance when Satan speaks to Michael of "The strife which thou call'st evil, but we style / The strife of glory" (VI. 289–90), and so privileges an arbitrary act of naming above plenary Truth. The postlapsarian reader is bound to invest the representation of the prelapsarian universe with the ironies which corrupted usage lends to any treatment of the state before corruption; our language is anachronistic as far as Milton's purposes are concerned, but it is all he has.[28]

Obliged, in the Edenic books, to evoke the inexpressible by way of words and images garnered from the resources of a fallen universe, Milton brings several strategies to bear on his task. The most familiar, and one I shall not dwell upon, is his use of a "Latinate" diction which requires the reader to refine the automatism of common usage into an awareness of etymological origins conducive to a rapprochement with the greater Origin under consideration. In addition, the extended replacement of the primary narrative voice by that of Raphael in Books VI, VII, and parts of V and VIII becomes a cardinal tactic for narrating the ineffable. It is almost impossible to distinguish between the voice of Milton the controlling narrator and that of Raphael: Milton may pretend that the angel does not have a completely omniscient viewpoint (Raphael does not know the fine details of Adam's creation, for example, and is eager to hear them), but in the course of narrating the war of Heaven, Adam's visitor describes conversations to which he was not a witness (v. 671ff.; vi. 678ff.) and, seeming to forget that he is a narrating subject, even speaks of himself in the third person (vi. 363). Nonetheless, because Milton at least appears to be using a separate, angelic viewpoint to mediate the particularly challenging narratives of the war in Heaven and the Creation, and because he provides the angel with a convenient accommodation formula – Raphael says he will translate the events he describes into terms comprehensible to the unfallen but fleshly Adam "By likening spiritual to corporal forms, / As may express them best" (v. 573–74) – the poet is able to use Raphael, his superior *and* creature, as a discreet support for his own designs. The very fact that it is so hard to draw a clear line between Milton and Raphael implies an equation of the angel's indirect transmission of heavenly events to an unfallen audience by means of earthly images with Milton's own figuring forth of the framing narrative of prelapsarian Eden to the postlapsarian reader by means of fallen language and images.[29]

For Milton to exploit Raphael as a protective role model he must presume, however, that the angel enjoys perfect authority as a mediator of the ineffable, and I do not believe this to be entirely the case. Raphael (whose important role in the Book of Tobit Milton recalls to his reader at v. 221–23) is an Apocryphal authority; consequently, he may either speak "almost scripture," or something of doubtful authenticity.[30] Furthermore, as he descends to earth in Book v, he is compared to "Maia's son," (v. 285), and, as Davis P. Harding points out, Adam addresses him as "Divine interpreter" (vii. 72).[31] Since Virgil's Mercury is also "Interpres Divum," Raphael can never be completely separated from the fallen reader's knowledge of postlapsarian hermeneutics and profane go-betweens. Nor do our problems with Raphael end here. We may want to ask, for example, whether the Divine Interpreter is not, on occasion, a less than perfect translator. Despite his remarkable "licit transubstantiation"[32] of the creating Word in Book VII, Raphael produces a sense of ontological unease in his earlier mediation of the war in Heaven. He has no sooner announced that he will render the spiritual in the approximate terms of the earthly than he brings the accommodated status of his own narrative into doubt by tossing out the (unanswered) question "though what if earth / Be but the shadow of heaven, and things therein / Each to other like, more than on earth is thought?" (v. 574–76). Striving to render the "invisible exploits" of the warring spirits, he veers from the vague – "deeds of eternal fame / Were done, but infinite" (VI. 240–41) to the clumsily pedantic:

> Their arms away they threw, and to the hills
> (For earth hath this variety from heaven
> Of pleasure situate in hill and dale)
> ... they ran
>
> (VI. 639–42)

He takes five lines to inform us that the combat between Michael and Satan is "Unspeakable" (VI. 297–301) and then proceeds to describe it in great detail (VI. 304–34). Indeed, much of his story tends to be hugely detailed and peculiarly irrelevant: his descriptions of ornate weaponry, flytings, hand-to-hand combats, and courageous endurance present what ultimately seems to be merely a ritualized and superfluous prelude to the victory of the Son. For a fallen reader, the inexpressible has been supplanted by the all too familiar; a gap has been bridged, a substitution made, in such a way that one is paradoxically left with a sense of violent dislocation. Geoffrey Hartman has suggested that accommodation has a double aspect: it may "bring truth down to earth" or "raise an earthly mind to heaven."[33] In Raphael's narrative of accommodation, however, is neither the authoritative condescension that characterizes the former act nor the invitation to aspiration and inspiration of the latter: if Milton, as Marshall Grossman suggests, offers *his* reader a heavenly critique of fallen epic,[34] the angel offers Adam (who only knows the unfallen genre of the hymn of praise) a making that is at once glitteringly splendid and utterly alien. Given that this is the way some of Milton's less devoted readers have no doubt thought of *Paradise Lost* itself, the dangers of angelic accommodation as a model/mask for Miltonic representation of the unfallen are evident. Certainly, in Books V and VI there is always the danger of a shift of perspective whereby Raphael's earnest attempt to convey the heroics of Heaven to the innocent Adam becomes, from the point of view of the overknowledgeable fallen reader, an all too belated mock-heroic narrative – mock-heroic because its tropes are already irrelevant to the redefinition of heroism that Milton is gradually advancing, and which in Books V and VI is represented not by any single martial deed performed by the loyal angels, but simply by their faithfully standing against Satan.

In Book III, by contrast, Milton shows us Heaven unmediated by angelic narrative and relies on the heavenly Muse as Holy Light to illuminate "things invisible to mortal sight" (III. 55). Here, in contrast to the excessively material detail of Books V and VI, which are full of exploding cannon, flying hills and jostling armies, the visual and tangible are almost completely suppressed. Most of the account of the debate in Heaven consists of reported speech of a particularly abstract nature; the Father, in particular, manipulates "a limited number of arbitrary words, meanings and syntactical shapes"[35] in elaborately circular rhetorical patterns. The Heaven of Book III is in the end honestly impenetrable and hermetic rather than improbably reducible to an earthly heroic landscape; at best, the unrepresentable is apprehended or refigured as a resonant oxymoron: holy light at once illumines and obscures, and the environs of the Deity are "dark with excessive bright" (III. 380). If the angelic hymn that follows the celestial council lauds the Son's mediation of the Father's image (III. 384–89), its focus is on the act of *mediating* rather than an ultimate representation of what has been mediated. And Milton, who is by now hymning the Son along with the angels, does not stay in Heaven very long after this brief glimpse of the possibility of perfectly mediated vision. The Son may be the "copious matter of [his] song / Henceforth" (III. 413–14), but the *copia* he chooses to contemplate is the Edenic plenitude, Satan's journey towards which he now rejoins.

Milton lovingly dilates the "white space" between Genesis 2:25 and Genesis 3:1 with this *copia*, filling the silence with words, complicating the design of his mythopoesis not only with events absent both from Genesis and the corpus of commentary upon Genesis,[36] but also with his own interpretations and supplementations of the pre-existing, more or less canonical interpretations of Genesis. The temporal and spatial configuration of the vast *amplificatio* represented by the Edenic books IV–VIII of *Paradise Lost* is intricate and multi-layered. Adam's (non-canonical) conversation with Raphael, for example, occupies the afternoon of a single day in the overall narrative time-scheme. As regards the structural "space" of the poem it takes up roughly a quarter of the lines in the work. Finally, the "written-about time" within that single afternoon – the exaltation of the Son, the war in Heaven, and the Creation, up to the birth of Eve – covers, according to Fowler, another nineteen days of the events encompassed by the epic.[37] There is, moreover, throughout *Paradise Lost*, a perpetual interplay between the eternal present of the act of reading, the architectonically complex and temporally involuted presentation of the events in the poem as a whole, and Milton's own awareness of the vast "mean time" (which holds so many other, belated, fictions and glosses) between the "now" in which he writes and the "then" of which he writes – a mean time both infolded *and* anticipated by his representation of that same "then."[38]

Milton's assaults upon postlapsarian chronology thoroughly exploit the schematic resources of the poem-as-narrative: even at the microcosmic level of the verse line or paragraph, the author refuses to let poetic syntax automatically mime diachronic sequence, and the content of even so small a unit as a sentence is left unfinalized for as long as possible. His constant deferral, through enjambment, of crucial parts of speech allows the typographical end of the verse line to become a pivot of semantic latency until the eyes must shift and the sense begin to complete – and to limit – itself.[39] Furthermore, the postponement of important verbs or qualifications tends to diffuse meaning through quite large blocks of words.[40] Entire verse paragraphs (or significant portions of them) become extraordinarily highly wrought as their content is kept in an elaborately patterned state of suspense: one might deem them, perhaps, the Miltonic equivalent of the Spenserian stanza. Consider, for example, the eight lines which give us our first extended sight of Eve:

> She as a veil down to the slender waist
> Her unadorned golden tresses wore
> Dishevelled, but in wanton ringlets waved
> As the vine curls her tendrils, which implied
> Subjection, but required with gentle sway,
> And by her yielded, by him best received,
> Yielded with coy submission, modest pride,
> And sweet reluctant amorous delay.
>
> (IV. 304–11)

In counterpoint to the actual enjambment of line 305 is the invitation to pause at its close offered by Milton's double syntax, and there is a similar duplicitous invitation at the end of line 306. The narrative content of this "stanza," moreover, could quite happily come to a halt after "received," but the two following lines of qualification circle back upon and amplify the preceding material, rather in the manner in which a Spenserian stanza tends to double back upon itself either after the fourth line or at the alexandrine. Furthermore, the reader's sense that strict logical sequence is being subordinated to dynamic patterning is emphasized by the resurfacing of rhyme into the blank verse. Not only do we have the full rhymes implied/pride and sway/delay, but also the assonance of waist/waved/sway/delay, the alliteration of waist/wore/waved, and the pararhyme of implied/received – all of which draw attention to the line endings and consequently to the interplay of formal design with content. (This is a particularly striking example, with its two full rhyme pairs within the space of six lines, but it is far from the only instance of "the troublesome bondage of rhyming" inveigling its way back into the poem.)[41] Finally, line 311, whose long drawn out syllables mime the delicate prelapsarian dalliance of Adam and Eve, seems both to sum up and to echo Milton's own loving elaboration of this portrait of Eve, if not into a blazon, then at least into something tantalizingly close to a (fallen) love lyric.[42]

That Milton should often choose to articulate the Edenic experience by way of embedded passages of lyric synchrony should not surprise us. Heaven is constantly filled with angelic song and patterned harmony, and Paradise aspires to imitate it; one reader has suggested that "Eden not only contains songs, it is one."[43] When Eve celebrates her love for Adam towards the end of Book IV, she manages to contain the unfallen world within a lyric whose concluding lines circle back upon her opening ones to recapitulate Eden's glories and make them dependent – for her – on Adam's presence within Eden (IV. 641–56). The Morning Hymn of Book V (153–208) also involves a roll call of the delights of the prelapsarian world, this time in order to bid all aspects of created nature praise their Creator. Although continuous with the blank verse narrative of the poem, it has a pronounced tendency to divide into separate stanzas, and furthermore, as John Hollander points out, it generates its own refrain in the process of its impromptu composition.[44] Raphael's Creation narrative – a far more successful "story" than his epic song of Book VI – is really a lyric celebration and dilation of the ineffable moment ("immediate are the acts of God" [VII. 176]) of genesis. Punctuated by songs-within-songs after each day's creation, it finally incorporates a hymn of the attendant angels which in effect repeats it all over again, for, according to Raphael, "Creation and the six days' acts they sung" (VII. 601).

Lyric "translations" are not confined to unfallen Eden: in Book III we find the Son acting as mediator by lyricizing the just but frigid statements of the Father. As God concludes his first, extraordinarily intimidating speech, the Son becomes manifest through the medium of a newly supple poetic discourse:

> Beyond compare the Son of God was seen
> Most glorious, in him all his Father shone
> Substantially expressed, and in his face
> Divine compassion visibly appeared,
> Love without end, and without measure grace[.]
>
> (III. 138–42)

The last line I have quoted does not actually end on a period but with a comma; there is one additional verse to the paragraph: "Which uttering thus he to his Father spake." But the face/grace rhyme invites us to pause and contemplate the equation of the Son's face with grace, and the powerfully balanced quasi-chiasmus of line 142 tempts us to see in its parallelism a small moment of temporary ending that paradoxically permits the *endless* reverberation of the attributes of "love," "grace," and "compassion" about the figure of the Son. As soon as he speaks, moreover, the Son begins to turn the harshly end-stopped rhetorical questions and answers of the Father into the sinuous, melodic, suggesting questions that probe for the promise of mercy for man (III. 144ff.).

In the light of this privileging of lyric synchrony and the equations of rhyme at such significant moments in the prelapsarian narrative, it seems telling that, at the very instant when transgression is made manifest in Eve's gathering of the apple, we read,

> her rash hand in evil hour
> Forth reaching to the fruit, she plucked, she ate:
> Earth felt the wound, and nature from her seat
> Sighing through all her works gave signs of woe,
> That all was lost.
>
> (IX. 780–84)

The particularly jarring half-rhyme ate/seat underscores the fracture of Edenic harmony. By contrast, when the fallen Adam and Eve finally turn from mutual recrimination and despair to true repentance, they learn to sing to Heaven again. At the close of Book X, however, we do not *hear* their prayer: the lyric variation and repetition this time belongs to the summarizing narrating voice, which in the last seven lines of the book repeats in the third person Adam's words of Book X. 1086–92. The lyric confession/prayer is suppressed: it is to be heard by God only, not the fallen reader, although Book X certainly ends on a suspended lyric moment as the couple's pleas wing their way to Heaven (X. 1097–1104).

Book X's climactic *narration of singing* (as opposed to the unmediated quotation of lyric) recalls the occluded lyric of

Colin Clout, and to be sure, the circling harmonious repetitions of Eden's pastoral lyricism (which echoes and recreates the circling dance and song of the denizens of Heaven [v. 595, 618–25; vi. 742–45]) have already recalled Spenser's Acidalian circles. Milton informs us, indeed, that in Paradise, "universal Pan / Knit with the Graces and the Hours in dance / Led on the eternal Spring" (iv. 266–68). The embowered bliss, the unchanging change and dynamic stasis of the Miltonic Eden, recasts the (less unambiguously sacred) landscapes of origin represented by Arcadia and Acidale, and even as the errant Calidore could not stay in either of those versions of Paradise, when Adam and Eve fall they become wanderers who cannot remain in Eden: they are (like Calidore) thrust into the world of diminished earthly goals and diachronic narrative. Of course, if the unfallen world represents the consummate pastoral exploration of the supreme Origin, Hell is a scene of debased pastoral, a forced retreat to a locus where the rebel angels must suffer eternal exclusion from their true place of origin and endure the razing of their original identities. But even in Hell there is music, and indeed there are singers whose "harmony / (What could it less when spirits immortal sing?) / Suspended hell" (ii. 552–54). The songs are fallen and "partial" and unheard by the reader. But they are empowered to grant a moment of lyric delay in the midst of Hell's horrors, to order and to control pain: the Miltonic parenthesis of line 553 literally suspends Hell.[45]

While Hell only offers the briefest suspended instance of ravishment, Milton's representation of Eden defies temporal, spatial and sequential relationships in order to sustain the preternaturally dilated rapture of the unfallen eternal moment. At the same time, Milton inscribes within his narrative the restitutive anachrony of Christian prophecy and typology, tearing events away from merely temporal contingency to set them in a grander design, a transcendent plot.[46] The most obvious example of this is the coupling of the Fall with the promise of redemption from the very start of *Paradise Lost*: in the Invocation to Book i, "man's first disobedience" is followed, four lines later, by the vision of Christ's eventual triumph. The narrative unfolding of Milton's poem involves the reader's seeing the heavenly conference of Book III prior to accompanying Satan to Eden; before witnessing Adam's fall, one has already been assured of humankind's ultimate salvation, and the second and perfect Adam has already pre-empted the role of the original and fallible one. The entropic movement of fallen time has been defeated before it has been begun.

Restitutive anachrony continues to be deployed throughout Milton's representation of unfallen Eden – a representation in which the intertextuality that so often shapes the highly wrought poetic narrative takes on a new significance. Postlapsarian texts, *mythoi* which are as yet not even in being, may be invoked to convey some aspect of The Good: they exist in a seminal continuity with it, and are redeemed by it. Fragments of fallen fictions are anticipated in order to illuminate the Origin: Milton's Heaven partakes of the characteristics of the Elysian fields (III. 358–59) and Eve can be likened to Ceres and Pomona (IX. 394–95). And if Milton's redescription of the prelapsarian world strives to anticipate all the later texts which will aspire to recapture it, his coincident narrative dislocations of time and space encourage *us* to escape diachrony, to enjoy a stance relative to what is circumscribed by the poem which approximates that of its God relative to the infinity and eternity wherein he surveys at once past, present and future (III. 77–78). The reader must constantly accommodate rapid and dramatic shifts of tense and viewpoint as he or she is moved from the contemplation of events that will happen to the witnessing of those that have happened. At the same time, Milton's epic similes range over and conflate vast tracts of history and geography in an effort to elide the gulf between what we know and what we have lost.

The headlong movement of the Miltonic narrative through time and space[47] might seem to comprise an entirely opposite stylistic dynamic to the harmonious local elaborations and circular patternings of lyric I have already identified as crucial to the recreation of origin in *Paradise Lost*. We are not, however, presented with a linear and teleological impulse so much as with the accretion of simultaneous alternatives, suspended and co-ordinated within the perpetual motion of the verse. This phenomenon is evident from the very beginning of the poem:

> Of man's first disobedience, and the fruit
> Of that forbidden tree, whose mortal taste
> Brought death into the world, and all our woe,
> With loss of Eden, till one greater man
> Restore us, and regain the blissful seat,
> Sing heavenly Muse, that on the secret top
> Of Oreb, or of Sinai, didst inspire
> That shepherd, who first taught the chosen seed,
> In the beginning how the heavens and earth
> Rose out of chaos: or if Sion hill
> Delight thee more, and Siloa's brook that flowed
> Fast by the oracle of God; I thence
> Invoke thy aid to my adventurous song,
> That with no middle flight intends to soar
> Above the Aonian mount, while it pursues
> Things unattempted yet in prose or rhyme.
>
> (I. 1–16)

The sixteen lines constitute just one sentence.[48] In the five lines before the imperative "Sing," Paradise is lost, fallen man suffers, and we have had the prospect of Paradise regained: past, present and future are piled together. As soon as we have reached the heavenly Muse, the oracles "Of Oreb or of Sinai...or...Sion's hill...and Siloa's brook" are gathered up and rendered, in effect, co-temporal with Milton's own opening of his poem to the prophetic voice. Furthermore, the original act of composing Genesis has been made, parenthetically, a kind of companion to his initiation of "adventurous song" (I. 8–10). Every time we would pause to evaluate the movement of this process of self-authorization there is some elaboration of the poet's situation, of the complex prophetic moment. One might rest at the end of line 13, but Milton immediately qualifies the phrase "adventurous song" with a relative clause articulating the song's aspiration "to soar / Above the Aonian mount" (I. 14–15) that adds another "top of speculation" to those already mustered; one might also stop after Helicon has been overgone, but the reiterative "while" (I. 15) adds one more assertion of originality to all the other beginnings, and we come to a full stop only at the end of line 16. Indeed, the constant exploitation of the vocabulary of co-ordination – "or," "and," even "while" – is typical of Milton's procedure in such passages: strict subordination defers to suspension-in-simultaneity. As Donald Davie points out, the casual insertion into *Paradise Lost* of all these asides, appositions, and qualifications, each "a sort of footnote," produces a poem where the glosses on a skeletal narrative are wholly integrated into the resultant work: the text's self-interpretation dissolves into the action of telling the story.[49]

In the Invocation to Book I, Milton offers his Muse the choice of where she would prefer to be summoned from (just as he offers Holy Light a choice of descriptive epithets in the invocation to Book III). The Eden she will help him to represent must be a place where choice is absolutely free, where nothing is yet "written," and one way into representing this situation is to oppose or complicate the teleological pull of fallen narrative with the synchronic amassing of ever-burgeoning alternatives.[50] This is particularly evident in the poet's complex similes – which are actually assertions of dissimilarity; after all, the unfallen world cannot in any respect be exactly "like" the universe of his fallen reader. In Book IV, we have the famous "Not that fair field / Of Enna" passage where a series of "nors" compresses within one sentence an epic catalogue of exquisite gardens from fallen myth or history which *cannot* equal Eden (IV. 268–85). Intriguingly, the very inscription of these pseudo-paradises within the Edenic space – and the elaborate care with which Milton assures us of their otherness – helps to defer the loss of Eden; these inadequate substitutions from humanity's fallen future dilate and suspend and strive to illuminate the Edenic moment. As *Paradise Lost* progresses, though, the dilatory multiple choice dynamics of exploded comparison undergoes some modification. Eve leaves Adam's side in Book IX, and:

> like a wood-nymph light
> Oread *or* dryad, *or* of Delia's train,
> Betook her to the groves, but Delia's self
> In gait surpassed and goddess-like deport,
> Though not as she with bow and quiver armed,
> But with such gardening tools as art yet rude,

Guiltless of fire had formed, *or* angels brought.
To Pales *or* Pomona thus adorned,
Likeliest she seemed, Pomona when she fled
Vertumnus, *or* to Ceres in her prime,
Yet virgin of Proserpina from Jove.
(IX. 386–96; emphasis mine)

We have "ors" rather than "nors" now: Eve is "like" or "likeliest" an oread or dryad, or an attendant of Diana, or Pales or Pomona or Ceres. At the same time, nearly every one of these comparisons is carefully qualified: she is like a member of Delia's train, but more "goddess-like" than Delia and without her attributes; she is specifically like Pomona in flight from Vertumnus, or Ceres before she has given birth. The reader, however, is less prone to sort out Eve's precise relationship with such figures than to envision her in Eden as one of a family of nature goddesses, a *genius loci* – even though such false deities will not come into being until after her fall.[51] Indeed the slippage of the rival, postlapsarian fables towards *almost* viable alternatives or substitutions is perhaps all the more evident because in the narrative present of the poem the Fall is now so very close.

I have proposed that when Milton joins the angelic choir in Book III and asserts that the name of the Son shall henceforth be the "copious matter" of his song, the *copia* he actually turns to is the "enormous bliss" of Eden. In the central books of *Paradise Lost*, the encyclopaedic impulse – already evident in the multiply focused similes and polymath digressions of Books I and II – is made manifest both in the Edenic infolding of the war in Heaven and Creation narratives and in the entertainment of all fictions-to-be within the privileged space of the *hortus conclusus*. As Guillory remarks, "Between Christ... and *Paradise Lost* intervenes the whole of Western literature and the heavenly muse is surprisingly not averse to speaking again words whose authority is fundamentally suspect."[52] Guillory goes on to argue that Milton's oblique and negative invocations of post-lapsarian texts prove that he is consciously severing his "omnific word" from the secular literary tradition, but I myself prefer to invoke the suggestion of another reader of *Paradise Lost* that "in poetry all buts are partly ands":[53] to borrow a forensic analogy, Milton as judge may have disallowed the evidence after its introduction into the case, but the reader as jury cannot necessarily hope to forget what he or she has already heard. There is, at any rate, a certain duplicity about *Paradise Lost*'s simultaneous incorporation and repudiation of splendid fragments from alien fictions, and the complicated dynamics of the poet's celebration/purgation of fallen myth and fable permits the occasional glimpse of an authorial thumb in the balance. In the Invocation to Book VII, Milton invokes Ovid's account of the death of Orpheus in Book XI of the *Metamorphoses* when he begs his Muse to "drive far off the barbarous dissonance" (VII. 32) of that poet's inadequate audience (Orpheus's maenads are perhaps Milton's Blatant Beast). Calliope could not protect her son from his foes; Milton, by contrast, may trust in Urania, "For thou art heavenly, she an empty dream" (VII. 39). Yet while Calliope, the (inadequate) pagan Muse is thus banished from the poem, Orpheus, the (fabulous) inspired poet, is not: the comparison between him and Milton stands, and in Book VII the Creation narrative of Milton/Raphael becomes an Orphic scene of making. It is punctuated by the music of angelic harps, nature is moved by heavenly harmony, and on the third day the trees rise "as in dance" (VII. 324) at the Word of God, even as, in the (yet to be written) fables of Ovid, the poet's lyre will summon them to his side.

Milton's evocations of lyric simultaneity and his deployment of redemptive anachronism in recreating an unfallen universe unconstrained by postlapsarian chronology have other equivocal consequences. Because of the reader's fallen hindsight, the comparisons invoked by the Miltonic similes, however oblique, possess, as many commentators have pointed out, an ironically proleptic force.[54] Although we are assured that Paradise is:

> not that fair field
> Of Enna, where Proserpine gathering flowers
> Her self a fairer flower by gloomy Dis
> Was gathered
>
> (IV. 268–71),

Eve, that "fairest unsupported flower" (IX. 432), is to be gathered up by gloomy Satan, and, in sinning, will ally herself with him, even as Proserpine, after her rape and her eating of a fatal fruit, perforce becomes queen of Hell. The scheme of cross-reference repossesses a myth from the postlapsarian world, not only to inform the account of beginning, but also to offer an anticipation of what will happen when man transgresses. Through a circular logic peculiar to *Paradise Lost*, just as Proserpine's rape, and perhaps her eating of the pomegranate, is a warning of Eve's fall, so Eve's fall, once the warning is fulfilled, will be the origin of the Proserpine myth. The tendency of postlapsarian readers to read their own "now versus then" awareness into a Paradise where fatal choices still have to be made and ironic (and invidious) comparisons are still latent is even footnoted within the narrative: later in Book IV, Eve is said to be "more lovely than Pandora," but the denial of similitude is then subverted as Milton adds, "and O too like / In sad event" (IV. 714–16).

Once Eve has plucked her apple, the suspended state of latency that characterizes the hugely dilated and supplemented Edenic moment collapses; all that remains is the linear unfolding of fallen time, the substitution of unredeemed *chronos* for significant *kairos*.[55] The poetic narrative no longer reaches back to beginnings, but races ahead of itself in Books XI and XII to show the waste land of postlapsarian time, the meanness of the meantime between Origin and Apocalypse. The visions and narration proffered to Adam by Michael, and famously dismissed by C. S. Lewis as "an untransmuted lump of futurity," have more recently been subjected to efforts to rehabilitate them: critics have argued that they are carefully structured according to elaborate principles of (generally typological) organization.[56] But such justifications of the ways of Milton to his readers have tended to save these books on intellectual and theological grounds, not aesthetic ones, and Marshall Grossman correctly notes that the anticlimactic poetry of XI and XII "sacrifices the gnosis of the lyric present ... to the proto-prosaic of iterative narrative."[57]

Nevertheless, I consider the somewhat tedious and mechanical poetry which reports the visions of Book XI and mediates the angelic narrative of Book XII to be integral to the larger designs of *Paradise Lost*. Through Michael's rehearsal of human error, Milton redescribes the relentless progress of fallen history, its apparently endless reworkings of Adam's sin, as humanity defaces the Maker's image in every possible way. Although the overall structure of *Paradise Lost* is carefully patterned and full of delicate parallels and symmetries, the division of episodes *within* Books XI and XII, the allotment of narrative space to resonant events in the history of mankind since the Fall, is almost consciously eccentric and asymmetrical. The story of Noah gets 114 lines to itself (XI. 787–901); the same number of lines takes us from Joshua to the Crucifixion (XII. 310–415). David is mentioned only in passing (XII. 326); Isaac and Jacob are almost elided. The narrative is extremely busy, but its encyclopaedic range and method are not really comparable to those of the first nine books: the virtuosity and ease with which places, people and stories were previously drawn together and precipitated out of one another are replaced, in particular in Book XII, by an anxious and clotted diction and by peculiar changes in tempo, as if the narrator is never sure when to dilate upon his subject and when to summarize it: the glorious sense of *perpetuum mobile* is lost. Milton's verse offers us no formal solace as we are thrown into the wanderings and frustrations of postlapsarian time along with the fallen Adam. And until the second Adam comes to defeat entropy, the only hint of a return to the harmony of unfallen time, to the synchronic "now" in which past, present and future simultaneously inform and complete each other, is seen in the vision of God's covenant with Noah that the cycles of seasons will endure, that "day and night, / Seed time and harvest, heat and hoary frost / Shall hold their course" (XI. 899–900).

Given Michael's desire to open Adam's eyes to the full consequences of his transgression, it is not surprising that after his elaborate representation of the mean time between the first Adam's fall and the second Adam's incarnation, his narration of the Passion and final triumph of the Son (XII. 412–65) is relatively muted and cursory. Significantly, the vision of Christ's victory does not arrest the angel's continuing history of humanity's sins: Michael's summary of the ministry of the Apostles swiftly turns into a lengthy indictment of those who have since perverted the Word (XII. 497–530).[58] It is Adam who interrupts – and interprets – Michael's words with a lyrical paean to the good that is to come out of evil: *he* raises the question of whether he should not, in fact, rejoice in his trespass, since its fruits will be so glorious:

> Full of doubt I stand
> Whether I should repent me now of sin
> By me done and occasioned, or rejoice
> Much more, that much more good thereof shall spring,
> To God more glory, more good will to men
> From God, and over wrath grace shall abound.
> (XII. 473–78)

But his question goes unanswered: Michael never quite ratifies Adam's consolatory apprehension of a *felix culpa*,[59] and the prospect of humanity's redemption remains a relatively small part of an exhaustive (and exhausting) narrative of error.

Books XI and XII, then, offer a narrative space in which doctrine triumphs over art, for within them Milton faces, and largely manages to reject, the temptation to make a good story out of fallen history, refusing to confer upon the latter the shape and order of an aesthetically pleasing but *mere* fiction. One of the results of this is to throw into relief the larger beauties of the embracing poetic narrative that strives to contain the history of all the centuries of postlapsarian existence within a providential design. At the same time, implicit in the Christian epic is the suggestion that, once it has gathered into itself human history and our original lapse, and once Adam and Eve have left Eden at the close of Book XII, the poems that now lie in humanity's future, detached once more from the Beginning, can only be escapist compensations for the loss of Eden. The visions and narratives of human history that Michael offers Adam, with their relentless depiction of transgression upon transgression, provide, indeed, a disturbing analogy for a whole range of acts of human fiction making and even for the composition of *Paradise Lost* itself. The supplementation and repetition of original sin that progressively distances humanity from the Logos may be compared to the many supplementary narratives of origin – of which Milton's poem is perforce one – whose copious augmentations of a primordial source involve (as we have already seen in *The Faerie Queene*) its almost inevitable fragmentation and diminution. Milton strives, in the lyrics of Heaven and Eden, to offer a model of unfallen repetition-and-variation, to promote a poetic discourse that may appear to progress forward in time but always circles harmoniously back to its divine source. We see it at its most successful in the exquisite repetitions concluding Eve's song to her "author and disposer," as well as in the refrain of the Morning Hymn which returns its speakers and all of creation to glorifying God, and it is also exemplified by Book III's angelic hymn, which appears to drift away from the Creator only to re-present him in the countenance of the Son and to reinvoke the Father in its final line (III. 415). But *Paradise Lost* also bears witness to the birth of a postlapsarian lyricism in which iteration can no longer recapture plenary presence, but only confirm loss. One of the most poignant instances of such belated repetition occurs when Adam – giving voice, perhaps, to the first pastoral elegy – cries out to his ravaged world:

> O woods, O fountains, hillocks, dales and bowers,
> With other echo late I taught your shades
> To answer, and resound far other song.
>
> (x. 860–62)

He is fully aware that the yearning repetitions of fallen invocation can never restore the harmonious iterations of the Morning Hymn.[60]

PARALLEL DESIGNS: MILTON'S DOUBLE VISION

When Milton depicts Adam's inability to rearticulate the "other song" of unfallen experience, he inevitably reminds the reader of the poet's own alienation from the Edenic moment. Brilliantly exploiting the synchronic and lyric possibilities of highly wrought poetic narrative, idiosyncratically manipulating its intertextual bias, he has attempted to articulate the ineffable. Yet all his gestures towards transcendence (including his lyric invocations of higher inspiration), all his momentary re-evocations of the timeless and the unfallen, are perforce enmeshed in the larger, timebound narration which seeks to "justify the ways of God to men," to bridge a gap between his readers and the both canonical and inscrutable text of Genesis by interposing a fuller accounting.[61] Given that Milton's re-presentations are also explanations, how adequately can he distance and differentiate his recasting of Scripture from solipsistic fabulation; how can he reshape and supplement the Beginning without privileging the (mere) rationalizations of postlapsarian art? Having invoked the heavenly Muse's aid in order to escape the limited perspective of his fallen condition, the author seems to fall quite easily into the role of Poet-Creator, *deus artifex*.[62] Milton's God bids "His Word, the filial Godhead" bring a new world into being (VII. 175); Milton's words create the universe which is *Paradise Lost* – but *his* poetic world is not necessarily the one that God made "in the beginning."

When a bare canonical narrative is paraphrased for avowedly didactic purposes, even replacing the paratactic "ands" of the biblical text with subordinating conjunctions, introducing causality, constitutes an interpretive gloss, and Milton as *deus artifex* expands "ands" not just into "becauses" but into hundreds of lines of additional narrative. Interpretive substitution is already at work in the opening passages of Book I. Milton asks, "what cause / Moved our grand parents... to fall off / From their creator...?" (I. 28–31) and then leaps from "what cause?" to "Who first seduced them...?" (I. 33), answering his own question with the assertion "The infernal serpent; he it was" (I. 34). Narrative focus has been subtly shifted from the motivation of the seduced to the nature of the seducer, and this draws us into the account of Satan's fall and the representation of his desire for revenge. Stanley Fish has insisted that, in *Paradise Lost*, "The unintelligibility [of the movement from sinlessness to sin], and hence the freedom, of the transition is Milton's thesis. Making it intelligible, and hence excusable, either by compromising the sufficiency of the will or by forging a chain of causality, is the reader's temptation."[63] But what do we have here if not the beginning links of a "chain of causality," and one, moreover, that takes us into dangerous territory, for in tracking down causes in the poem one always tends to end up confronting God, the First Cause, who created a Lucifer even though he presumably foresaw from the first that he would fall and then seduce man?[64] Milton supplements the ellipsis between Genesis 2 and the entrance into Scripture of the subtle serpent (whom Genesis, of course, never equates with Satan) with an explanatory narrative; there will be other "rationalizing" stories to come, and the author offers, in addition, authorial comments *within* his poem upon aspects of those same expansions and augmentations: he glosses his own gloss.

We observe a relatively insignificant example of the double gloss phenomenon when Milton pauses in his account of Raphael's mission to Adam and Eve (itself a completely uncanonical addition to Genesis) in order to refute the views of earlier commentators concerning angelic digestion (v. 434–37). There is often a lot more at stake in Milton's double glosses, however, and most notably in those episodes of *Paradise Lost* in which God speaks. Heaven is supposed to be the realm of the literal and absolute; human fictions and tropes have no place there: to paraphrase heavenly words would be to produce emphatically fallen interpretations, equivocations rather than equivalents. But the Heavenly Father who first appears to us in Book III of *Paradise Lost* is *a priori* a covert gloss upon that impenetrable Voice which in Genesis 2 and 3 chooses to lay down an apparently arbitrary prohibition and then punish its infraction severely. Milton has not just paraphrased the scriptural "Word of God"; he has hugely augmented it. He masks his interpretive intervention, however, by conferring upon the Father's omniscient voice the apparent uninflectedness of plain narrative assertion, omniscient authorial commentary. God speaks, as it were, for Milton, not himself; he only exists as the discursive projection of all that the poet feels to be implicit in the Logos but which Genesis does not record. Milton is not so much justifying the ways of God to men as exploiting a poetic (if not very poetical) persona to justify Milton's interpretation of Genesis to men.

We embark on a distinctly circular process, whereby the author presents the disguised gloss, and then reglosses it, overtly and approvingly, in his own voice; *his* comments at x. 5–16, for example, simply recast God's own earlier self-justification (III. 98–134). The Father's repetitive diction reinforces the ritualized and rationalized assertion of what is merely a *donnée* in the biblical text; in *Paradise Lost*, it always seems that the Truth doth protest a little too much. Indeed, Milton himself seems to be half-aware of this, and when the reinforcing, secondary gloss becomes unbearably glib he employs rapid shifts of narrative focus to move the reader's attention elsewhere. In Book v, for example, God instructs Raphael to warn Adam against Satan (v. 224–45) – this incident itself being a non-canonical, silent gloss on Genesis designed to make God appear less arbitrary (and man "inexcusable") – and then the authorial voice approves:

> So spake the eternal Father, and fulfilled
> All justice
>
> (v. 246–47)

Any chance of questioning this assertion is denied us; after only a colon's pause we are in flight with Raphael:

> So spake the eternal Father, and fulfilled
> All justice: nor delayed the winged saint
> After this charge received; but from among
> Thousand celestial ardours, where he stood
> Veiled with his gorgeous wings, up springing light
> Flew through the midst of heaven
>
> (v. 246–51)

– and although we may resist the highhandedness of the transition, we, too, may not "delay" to ponder what we have "received."

To be fair, the *overt* glosses in *Paradise Lost* exhibit a significant variation in the degree of their authorial intrusiveness. At one end of the range we have the dictatorial tone of Milton's cruder comments upon the action, exemplified by the notorious "not deceived, / But fondly overcome by female charm" aside (IX. 998–99) which so inadequately sums up the reasons for Adam's fall (for Adam has decided to sin with Eve after an unvoiced interior monologue [IX. 895–916] that precedes and is completely separate from her blandishments). A similar stridency is evident when the commenting voice abandons all pretence to narrative detachment and discards the inspired poetic overview in order to argue the personal and timebound opinions of John Milton. The abrupt transition in Book IV from a celebration of the "mysterious rites" of Adam and Eve's lovemaking (741–43) to a polemic on the virtues of Protestant marriage (744–70) represents an obvious instance of this, as does the poet's satirical treatment of the inhabitants of the Paradise of Fools (III. 444–97), or the parallel he draws between Satan's wolfish entrance into Eden and his own church's invasion by false pastors (IV. 192–93). At the other end of the spectrum, however, we may remark not only the subtlety of the qualified or subverted similes, whose function as ironic or proleptic glosses I have already touched upon, but also relatively straightforward authorial explication which acquires more delicate resonance as *Paradise Lost* unfolds. Witness, for example, Milton's comments when Satan tricks Uriel into guiding him to Paradise:

> So spake the false dissembler, unperceived;
> For neither man nor angel can discern
> Hypocrisy, the only evil that walks
> Invisible, except to God alone.
>
> (III. 681–84)

At first glance this seems an obvious piece of moralizing, which also provides the necessary rationale for why the good angels are relatively powerless against Satan. On a deeper level, only evident in retrospect, it may be read as an interpretive and anticipatory act in mitigation of Eve's transgression. We are told in advance that in failing to penetrate another disguise of Satan, she will be doing no worse – can do no worse – than the splendid Uriel.[65]

In a poem that so egregiously supplements the Logos it is not, indeed, Milton's most obvious authorial intrusions that cause one to suspect that there may be too much author in this (re)Authorized Version of the Beginning. If we recognize the subtlety of the poet's unfootnoted revisionary interpolations, we must equally recognize their all-embracingness (after all, his silent glosses begin the moment he breaks the silences of Genesis). And Milton deploys more than one strategy of exegesis. *Paradise Lost* is both the rational, didactic justification of God's ways to man[66] – the clarifying of an already revealed truth – and the sensuous, almost intuitive process of "making sense" out of a laconic and troubling myth. There are, in effect, two narratives unfolding in the poem,[67] and both of them are fraught with peril. On the one hand, even as the discursive Milton makes Genesis 1–3 more "reasonable" through his scheme of interpretive and interpolative causality, he raises, and leaves unanswered, an increasing number of new questions: the bottom line of his promised accounting retreats further and further away (or becomes half-buried in its intricately layered unfolding, like the "original" action of the poem, the exaltation of Christ). At the same time, the more the poetic Milton dilates upon the prelapsarian Beginning, passionately rendering it in terms of his inner universe of heterogenous learning and noble music, the more he is in danger of appropriating the Fall as an idiosyncratic and personal fiction.

Paradise Lost is, to be sure, sufficiently explicit on the dangers of ambiguous fiction-making: in giving the Adversary such a prominent place in the narrative of origin, Milton is constantly offering us a dynamic model of the Satanic maker/interpreter. The Archfiend can never relate his own story accurately: he may briefly entertain the truth in his soliloquies (soliloquizing itself being a fallen mode which replaces a unified apprehension of truth with solipsistic dialectic), but will at once reject or revise it.[68] We see Satan paraphrasing within *Paradise Lost* the larger narrative's Authorized Version of events – falsely suggesting, for example, that his army's rout has "emptied heaven" (I. 633), or that God "tempted [his] attempt" (I. 642). Satan turns history into fiction, and Hell itself is the home of the fallen imagination, of "partial" songs (II. 552), of the labyrinthine constructs of unilluminated reason (II. 557–65). It is a universe of persuasive hypothesis ungrounded on fact, a straw-built citadel of non-provable premises whose preferred moods are the conditional and the subjunctive. It is also the seminary of the consoling but deceitful fictions of the postlapsarian word: we have seen how much more comfortably conventional epic fits into Hell than into Heaven. Satan is not only (through Miltonic anachrony) both the original and the perversion of the epic hero: he also becomes the father of fallen lyricism, the corrupter of proper songs of praise. The dream he sends Eve begins with a seduction lyric (and one that happens to be a reinvention-before-the-fact of the canonical Song of Songs):

> Why sleep'st thou Eve? Now is the pleasant time,
> The cool, the silent, save where silence yields
> To the night-warbling bird, that now awake
> Tunes sweetest his love laboured song; now reigns
> Full-orbed the moon, and with more pleasing light
> Shadowy sets off the face of things; in vain,
> If none regard, heaven wakes with all his eyes,
> Whom to behold but thee, nature's desire,
> In whose sight all things joy, with ravishment
> Attracted by thy beauty still to gaze.
>
> (v. 38–47)

When, in Book IX, Satan once more tempts Eve, he is not only the Devil deceiving the mother of mankind but also, proleptically, the urban sophisticate beguiling the country maiden (IX. 445–52) and the Petrarchan lover praising his "sovereign mistress" (IX. 532).[69] Milton's own celebrations of Eve had hovered on the verge of fallen, courtly lyricism; Satan's almost parallel exploitation (or rather invention) of the mode suggests just how fine the line between sacred and profane poetic makings may be.

Even as the poet strives to offer a true fiction of genesis, he shows us Satan propounding egocentric fantasies of origin.[70] As a strategy for containing the demon of fabulation, Milton's incorporation and deflation within his own, higher design of Satan's chimerical creation myths is comparable to his simultaneous invocation/purgation of pagan mythologies in his celebrations of Eden. We have seen how his poetic discourse gathers up all the fragments of fallen knowledge, the better to re-member Truth; Satan, however, refuses to remember his secondariness, the fact that he is a creature and not an authentic creator. Aspiring to be "self-begot, self raised" (v. 860), he falls further and further away from the Origin, the true Word. But does *Paradise Lost* exorcise or merely exploit its Satanic counterplot? For the skeptical reader, the *officially* Satanic narrator may simply be a stalking horse, conjured up to deflect attention from the equally problematic practices of the maker of the (supposedly) more authentic "heroic song." Whenever the latter solicits the Muse's inspiration, and then proceeds to figure forth Hell, Heaven, or Eden, he posits a moment between the act of invocation and the act of speaking the unspeakable that is itself completely ineffable. This is the narrative ellipsis into which a trusting audience reads the granting of the poet's request, the illuminating of his darkness (I. 22–23) the planting of his inner eyes (III. 53). The Miltonic *lacuna* may be judged by others, though, to elide the moment in which the bard is Satanically "self raised" above the Aonian mount rather than authentically inspired – in which case, he, like Satan, may be trying to disguise his far from disinterested exegeses as a true story of origin.

The Satanic counterplot of *Paradise Lost* encourages this anxiety by making the Adversary not only a false poet and false creator but also a false Muse. As Kerrigan points out, the relationship between Eve and her guide in the dream she describes to Adam "elaborately parodies the relationship between the slumbering narrator and his Celestial Patroness."[71] The night-time visit, the singing nightingale (v. 40–1), the promise of an ascent to Heaven (v. 77–81), the soaring aloft to survey the vast prospect of the earth (v. 87–90) are all to be found in the Invocations to Milton's own Urania in Books III and VII.[72] Once again, we are tempted to question the extent to which the poet manages to distinguish the would-be inspired making that is *Paradise Lost* from a product of the fallen imagination.

Milton makes an earnest effort to emphasize the subordination of the subjective "I" of the fallen narrator to divine inspiration. In the Invocation to Book I, the dangerous pronoun is deferred for twelve lines by the baroque syntax of the verse paragraph; the sacred Muse, on the other hand, is bespoken seven lines earlier. In III and VII, "I" resurfaces sooner (III. 3; VII. 3), but in each case it is still preceded by a mediating presence: Holy Light in III and Urania in VII. (In Book IX, Milton's "I" does not appear until line 5; here, however, the mediating "celestial patroness" does not put in her own appearance until line 21 – as if, at the start of the book that brings us to the Fall, fallen subjectivity has reasserted itself.)[73] But the poet must not only hold back the I/eye that hints at the Satanic privileging of solipsistic vision above divine truth; he must also distinguish his address to a Divine Interpreter from profane epic invocations:

> Descend from Heaven Urania, by that name
> If rightly thou art called...
> The meaning, not the name I call
>
> (VII. 1–2; 5)

The circuitous business of adequately naming the Muse suggests that the identity of the Mediator is not easily apprehensible, and indeed, the heavenly Muse is a patroness of infinite variety. In Book I she is more or less conflated with the Spirit of God of Genesis 1:2; in the Invocation to Book III she seems to be interchangeable with Holy Light in her ability to reveal "things invisible to mortal sight" (III. 55); later in the same book it seems to be the Son-as-Muse who will now mediate celestial matters for the poet and furnish the "copious matter" of his song (III. 384–86; 412–14). Urania's plethora of mediating strategies: she will "sing" (I. 6), "illumine" (I. 23); visit (VII. 29), (IX. 22), and be visited (III. 13); "dictate" as the poet sleeps, or "inspire" his "unpremeditated verse" (IX. 23–24), and her varied manifestations partake, perhaps, of the *copia* of Eden itself. But it is a dangerous excess: in attempting not to reduce his heavenly Muse to a merely empty gesture, a fiction of displaced authority, Milton makes her extraordinarily elusive. Indeed he is even prepared to toy with the possibility that his poem is unauthorized by her, remarking, at the start of Book IX, that his work may fail "if all be mine / Not hers who brings it nightly to my ear" (IX. 46–47). The present tense assertion of "brings" clashes oddly with the preceding conditional clause; the suggestion that there may be *no* Muse-determined content in the poem is juxtaposed with the repeated ("nightly") presentness of the Muse's proffered inspiration. The tension between absence and presence is never resolved: we are left in suspense, contemplating the hint of an imperfect synthesis between Urania's permanently present act of bringing inspired verse and the actual production of a poem open to contamination by a fallen authorial (but not authoritative) subjectivity.[74]

The perpetual dialogue between inspiration and limitation left unconcluded in Milton's final conversation with his Muse is paradigmatic of a number of other dialogues (or double plots) which Milton has infolded within *Paradise Lost.* The interplay of his synchronic/lyric strategies for redescribing origin and his discursive narrative justification of God's ways to men, the complicated internal dialectic between redeemed and fallen literary kinds, his work's perilous engagement with – and perhaps incomplete containment of – Satanic counterplots of origin, creativity, and inspiration offer variations upon the same theme. And when one enquires what, exactly, Milton authored in *Paradise Lost*, yet another "doubleness" comes into focus. Isabel MacCaffrey has argued that the poem is "virtual myth": a text whose special "manner of seeing" temporarily recaptures the inexpressible as it reorders a familiar story to make it more meaningful and resonant.[75] But, like C. S. Lewis' assertion that the poem constitutes a ritualistic rehearsal of what is already known, her proposal does not recognize that the mere action of imposing a different narrative structure upon "the familiar" – turning *fabula* into *szujet* – is inevitably an interpretive act, and one, moreover, that tends to issue in novelty, surprise, learning, and discovery – effects MacCaffrey deems of no concern to the producer or reader of "myth."[76] *Paradise Lost* is not exactly scripture (even if its exegeses have retrospectively become canonical texts for some readers),[77] and Miltonic mythopoesis is not quite the same thing as myth, real or virtual. *Paradise Lost* is also a fiction.

In *The Sense of An Ending*, Frank Kermode suggests that

> Myth operates within the diagrams of ritual, which pre-suppose total and adequate explanations of things as they are and were; it is a sequence of radically unchangeable gestures. Fictions are for finding things out, and they change as the needs of sense making change.[78]

The very fact that *Paradise Lost* had to be written, that the pre-existing fable/*fabula* of origin did not suffice, ensures that we cannot read Milton's poetic narrative exclusively as myth. The poet's distinctively audacious program of gathering all truths and all half-truths of fallen experience together to flesh out (or reincarnate) the Word of Genesis guaranteed that his poem would not merely rehearse its pre-text. Moreover, if *Paradise Lost* aspires to the oxymoronic condition of being a true fiction,[79] it is a true fiction that is perpetually reinvented by its readers (including the ones who "find out" that it is a myth). And it is always belated, always *other* than scripture. Milton makes Raphael tell Adam and Eve, "To thee I have revealed / What might have else to human race been hid" (VI. 895–96); in fact, were it not for the supplementary fiction of origin, which created and contains both Raphael and his revelation of the celestial struggles and their aftermath, the scriptural narrative, with all its *lacunae*, would still be hiding the war in Heaven (not to mention Milton's expanded narrative of the Creation). Readers who possess both Genesis and *Paradise Lost* will inevitably read their awareness of the latter into their knowledge of the original narrative: Milton's attempt to encompass the old Beginning results in his generation of a new one.[80]

If Milton's story of beginnings is inextricably duplicitous, his representation of endings is no less double; this ultimate duplicity, however, is a particularly happy one, and it is with an acknowledgement of its characteristically Miltonic saving grace that I wish to conclude this chapter. I have already remarked upon Adam's joyous articulation of the *felix culpa* doctrine in response to Michael's prophetic narrative of the incarnation, death and triumph of the Son (XII. 437–48). Just before Adam and Eve depart from Eden, Eve echoes Adam's optimistic lyricism in a speech which reports the (non-narrative, subrational) consolation sent to her by God in a dream:

> Whence thou return'st, and whither went'st, I know;
> For God is also in sleep, and dreams advise,
> Which he hath sent propitious, some great good
> Presaging, since with sorrow and heart's distress
> Wearied I fell asleep: but now lead on;
> In me is no delay; with thee to go,
> Is to stay here; without thee here to stay
> Is to go hence unwilling; thou to me
> Art all things under heaven, all places thou,
> Who for my wilful crime art banished hence.
> This further consolation yet secure
> I carry hence; though all by me is lost,
> Such favour I unworthy am vouchsafed,
> By me the promised seed shall all restore.
>
> (XII. 610–23)

In the present moment, Eve encloses redemption in her words, as well as, prospectively, in her womb, and the fourteen lines of her affirmation of comfort and hope constitute (as other readers have noted) an embedded, blank verse sonnet.[81] But it is the *narrative* entanglement of redemption and sin, joy and misery, already seen in Michael's discourse to Adam, rather than Adam and Eve's "poetic" insistence that good will be born (quite literally, in Eve's case) out of evil, that informs the counterpoise of affirmation and affliction in the final lines of *Paradise Lost*:

> They hand in hand, with wandering steps and slow,
> Through Eden took their solitary way.
>
> (XII.648–49)

If Adam and Eve, comforted by the prospect of a "happy ending," depart Eden "hand in hand" and capable of offering each other support and solace, the poem still concludes with their "solitary" initiation of a new narrative – that of postlapsarian history. Nevertheless, although his final lines leave the reader at the beginning of *that* unhappy story, Milton has already subordinated Michael's linear history of fallen "mean time" to the larger, foreseen-but-not-yet-completed narrative that is at once embraced by *Paradise Lost* and embraces the poem and its fallen readers.

Michael's history, to be sure, does contain a narrative of salvation, and Stanley Fish has proposed, in a discussion of Book XII. 405–15, that every idea and image articulated within "the entire poem returns to its source and end in the figure on the cross."[82] I would argue, however, that the diachronic unfolding of the epic has been "synchronized" by an earlier and more carefully circumscribed apocalypse. Michael's restrained and discursive relation only offers an indirect and muted rendering of the Passion and a quite summary account of the final triumph of the Son. A far more striking vision is embedded two books earlier, at Book X. 182, and proffered to the reader in a resonantly prophetic moment just after the Son has pronounced judgment upon the serpent:

> So spake this oracle, then verified
> When Jesus son of Mary second Eve,
> Saw Satan fall like lightning down from heaven,
> Prince of the air; then rising from his grave
> Spoiled principalities and powers, triumphed
> In open show, and with ascension bright
> Captivity led captive through the air,
> The realm it self of Satan long usurped,
> Whom he shall tread at last under our feet;
> Even he who now foretold his fatal bruise
>
> (X. 182–88)

In these lines, the fallen Mother of Mankind and her redemptive daughter, the incarnation, death and resurrection of Christ, the narrative "now" of prophetic judgment and Satan's ultimate defeat at the hands of the Son are hurled together in the poem's supremely synchronic moment, and the Messiah, for the first and only time in *Paradise Lost*, is given the human name (the Word made word) of his mortal passage. In this stanza-like instance of narrative compression and totalization,[83] the "poetic" Milton anticipates all the discursive and rational work of the remainder of his poem. Doubling his vision, he has, after his own fashion, already encompassed his – and our – end.

Milton pre-empts Michael's linear discourse of inexorable cause and effect – a discourse in which redemption is almost occluded for the fallen reader by the ever-dilating "between time" of fallen narrative – with his circumscriptive lyricism.

This is one more version of his willingness throughout *Paradise Lost* to play off synchronic/lyric strategies for articulating the ineffable against a more linear narrative justification of God's ways to men. The poet is not quite prepared to proclaim the consolatory doctrine of the *felix culpa* in his own voice, displacing it instead into the interpretive conclusions of the fallen Adam. But he is nonetheless quite willing to exploit his narrative's felicitous duplicity to anticipate not only Michael's prophecies but also an entire mean-time of postlapsarian error as he supplements the Logos – the Son's canonical speech of judgment – with his own representation of the transcendent ending which redeems his readers' fallen beginnings.

CHAPTER 5

The ends of poetic narrative

THE WASTE LAND AS ANTI-NARRATIVE

For all the heteromodality of each of the poems I have so far discussed, few critics would deny that *Troilus and Criseyde*, *The Faerie Queene* and *Paradise Lost* may be classified as poetic *narratives*. The same cannot be said for a twentieth-century work whose internalized dialogue between poetic scheme and narrative discourse, whose self-conscious intertextuality, and whose self-interpretive bent nevertheless suggest a kinship with their practices. While many readers have attempted and will attempt again to map out *The Waste Land*'s "plot," others consider this a futile response to a work that is "[n]ot a seamless narrative but a set of lyric moments,"[1] or, alternatively, "an extended lyric structure in sequence form."[2] Certainly the poem's assembly of frustrated and frustrating epiphanies, its moments of poetic concentration which offer glimpses of a significant design but still fail to propel the reader towards any sustained moment of resolution or revelation, make this point of view understandable, even appealing. At the same time, however, *The Waste Land* seduces its reader into a search for the linear progression of conventional plot, for a structure more logical and unified than simply the "felt relationship" between focal points of emotional intensity.[3] Even if Eliot's citation of Jessie Weston's *From Ritual to Romance* had not suggested that the Grail Quest was to form the *fabula* or groundplot of this poetic fiction, the echoes of the Prologue to the *Canterbury Tales* in the opening lines of "The Burial of the Dead" would immediately invite us to locate the work in the context of goal-directed journeying and storytelling.

Reviewing Joyce's *Ulysses*, Eliot was to suggest that the "mythical method," as distinct from more conventional narrative strategies, offered a useful means of "giving a shape and significance" to the complexities and contradictions of twentieth-century existence.[4] (In welcoming it, he did not mention that this practice was hardly new: we have already seen Spenser attempting to reorder the contingencies of contemporary history and social practice within his apocalyptic quest fable.) In *Ulysses*, however, the Homeric pre-text is an autonomous and already canonical narrative. Readers can trust in their prior knowledge of the plot of the *Odyssey*, even if Joyce's tendency not merely to parallel but also to parody and subvert its episodes in *Ulysses* may complicate the significance of specific allusions. The "myth" that constitutes the *fabula* of *The Waste Land* is considerably less stable; one might suggest, indeed, that Jessie Weston's primary achievement was not so much to uncover the objective existence of a single, originary fertility myth or ritual as to subsume the ambiguous evidence of romance narrative, legend and folk custom within a fiction of her own making.[5] And when we consider that Eliot's own acknowledgement of Weston was made as part of a supplementation-after-the-fact of his text, in endnotes apparently generated by the publisher's desire to bring the format of the poem up to a convenient sixty-four pages, we are faced with what may be a double displacement of authority. The notes that announce the connection between *The Waste Land* and the archetypal quest to renew the fertility of a waste land may be viewed as one questionable fiction, the scholarly redactions and interpretations that have created that archetype as another.

Nor is this the only instance of the equivocal nature of material that might be expected to authorize our pursuit of a linear narrative in *The Waste Land*. We are offered, for example, a thread of allusion linking Phlebas the Phoenician to other avatars of the quester-protagonist (including the Fisher King) by way of Act I, scene ii of *The Tempest*.[6] Madame Sosostris announces, "Here... / Is your card, the drowned Phoenician Sailor, / (Those are pearls that were his eyes. Look!)," and Belladonna's lover, a refiguration of the "you" Sosostris addresses, recalls the same line from Ariel's song (I. ii. 399) in

"A Game of Chess."[7] An echo of the speech that directly precedes "Full Fathom Five" in *The Tempest* is heard in the ruminations of the (fishing) quester in "The Fire Sermon" (191–2), and the next line from Ferdinand's speech, "This music crept by me upon the waters" (I. ii. 392) is interposed between the music of the Typist's gramophone and the music of the Thames-side pubs (257). Phlebas the Phoenician appears at last in "Death By Water," and his sea-change is elegized there. Finally, in the last paragraph of "What the Thunder Said," the Fisher King/Quester's "I sat upon the shore / Fishing, with the arid plain behind me" (423–24) recalls not only lines 189–91 of "The Fire Sermon," but also Ferdinand's "Sitting on a bank, / Weeping again the King my father's wrack" (I. ii. 390–91). Given that the web of allusion extends through all five sections of the poem, it is particularly tempting to identify a narrative progression. The quester is warned that releasing the healing waters (the springs of feeling) may also involve his own dissolution, that if he does not "Fear death by water" he will indeed become the drowned sailor whom the Tarot announces to be his *alter ego*. In the middle of the arid, nervous exchanges in Belladonna's chamber, he recalls the threat of corporeal transformation – a perilous sea-change that perhaps corresponds to the workings of the forces of fragmentation and petrification in his waste land. As the quester's voice becomes that of the Fisher King in "The Fire Sermon," he is now pondering the "wreck" and dissolution of all humanity (synecdochically represented by the father and brother of the allusive lines 191–92); the music he will hear from the Typist's gramophone will again announce humanity's fear of death by water – and its associated fear of the energies of fertility. This fear is foregrounded, shortly afterwards, by the emergence of "Death By Water" as a discrete section of the poem chronicling the disintegration of the Phlebas aspect of the quester in the oceanic whirlpool. Yet the separate lyric that elegizes Phlebas represents *one* end, not *the* end, of the quest. The Fisher King/Quester is reconstituted in the last lines of "What the Thunder Said" so that he can at least think about setting his lands in order; he has moved back to the shore and now contemplates the dangerous water that might refresh the desert wastes (423–25). The apparent progression from the Tarot's warning to the sea-death was perhaps only an inner journey conjured up by his own terror of action – a necessary "trial by water," however, and one that must be suffered before quester and reader may reach even the tentative resolutions of "What the Thunder Said."

Gathering up the references to just one of the fragmented pre-texts of *The Waste Land*, one can thus construct a narrative line. But if we recall in more precise detail the original context of the Shakespearian borrowings, we must recognize that the "death by water" of which Ariel sang was only a fiction. Ferdinand was deceived when he thought his father drowned – Ariel's lyric of re-creative metamorphosis was an exquisite lie. The allusions suggest a proxy authority that might guide us in piecing together a plot, but on closer examination they prove to center upon a fabrication within the displaced source. (The situation is further complicated by Eliot's idiosyncratic endnotes, which only mention the Ferdinand allusions in "The Fire Sermon," ignoring the Ariel quotation completely; the reader has to construct his or her own "unauthorized" cross references.) And even if one argues that, notwithstanding the illusory nature of the "death" commemorated by Ariel, the redemptive sea-change promised by his song *is* fulfilled by the events of *The Tempest* and may consequently constitute a plot matrix for Eliot's poem, one must also recognize that Eliot offers a less redemptive vision of altered states. Phlebas the Phoenician, unlike Alonso, does not metamorphose into anything "rich and strange": the lyric that memorializes him centers, as Calvin Bedient argues, upon a fantasy of dissolution.[8] The final lines of "Death By Water" refigure Phlebas only as a *memento mori* (319–21), a reminder of ending guaranteeing neither rebirth nor continuity. The temptation to view the Phlebas lyric as the poetic ordering and containment of a necessary encounter with entropy which actually initiates and enables the (admittedly ambiguous) epiphanies of the final section of the work should probably be resisted.

Readers of *The Waste Land* are in this fashion both encouraged and rebuffed as they try to construct its plot (or plots). The poem seems to be a "writerly" text, so limitlessly polysemous that one can and must create it for oneself.[9] Its epigraph from Petronius makes the Cumaean Sibyl a presiding deity of the work,[10] and its fragments have certainly seemed as difficult to order and unify as the wind-scattered leaves which held the Sibyl's prophecies. But the poem is also sibylline inasmuch as it speaks with an intermittently and ambiguously vatic voice, which, while never providing a terribly trustworthy focal authority, tends to discourage readers from feeling wholly free to plot the poem as they please. One of the concluding lines of the work reads, "These fragments I have shored against my ruins" (430), but in an earlier draft of *The Waste Land* the line read "These fragments I have *spelt* into my ruins" (emphasis mine).[11] The etymology of "spell" comprises "speech, signifying story, narrative" as well as "incantation"; the final version's suggestion that dispersed intimations and echoes of horror and beauty and banality must suffice to shore up the ruins of post World War I European civilization is superimposed, it seems, upon a suppressed hint of a secret, more unified narrative. The "spelling" of a visionary quest to order chaos is – perhaps – concealed within the very act of rendering chaos.

Yet even as *The Waste Land* offers the reader fragmentary, half-buried glimpses of a goal-directed plot, it unfolds in a manner that partakes less of linearity than of restatement and complication.[12] One does not so much pass on from a given action or situation as repeat it; as in *The Faerie Queene*, there is a sense of endless recapitulation, of travelling over the same territory but examining it from different perspectives. The multiplication of impotent questers, of sterile relationships, of incomplete epiphanies, creates an unhappy *copia*, an excess of examples of dearth. Ezra Pound's description of *The Waste Land* as "the longest poem in the English langwidge"[13] is not mere hyperbole; the work's very compression, its condensed shorthand of historical and literary allusion, gives the poem some of the epic range of, for example, *Paradise Lost*.

However, there is more than one kind of "compression" at work in this text. There is the obvious compression of reference, which, in juxtaposing images and allusions drawn from past and present with prophecies of the future, creates out of poetic concentration and distillation a sense of copious simultaneity which defies teleology.[14] But the poem also entertains strategies of more formal compression, invoking the containing gestures of "bound language" in an apparent attempt to arrest the continual accumulation of supplementary (and fragmentary) content. Eliot is always experimenting with different meters, different kinds of verse paragraph, even different stanzaic forms, as if in search of a framework that would permit him, however temporarily, to impose *some* order upon *The Waste Land's* testament to confusion.[15]

Yet no intimation of a lyric design is ever sustained for long. The first two speeches of the three violated Thames daughters at the end of "The Fire Sermon" (292–99), for example, are ABAB quatrains, rather irregular in rhythm and with some heavy enjambments, yet still recognizable as patterned language. But the third speech breaks the sequence of formal stanzas: it offers six metrically irregular lines, lines 300/303 and 301/304 rhyming, lines 302/305 constituting a *rime riche*:

"On Margate Sands.
I can connect
Nothing with nothing.
The broken fingernails of dirty hands.
My people humble people who expect
Nothing."

(300–5)

The passage might easily have been set out as follows:

"On Margate Sands.
I can connect nothing with nothing.
The broken fingernails of dirty hands.
My people humble people who expect nothing."

– a "stanza" which offers a closer approximation to the previous ABAB quatrains. It is as if a repeated design is purposely suppressed.[16] The frustration of the patterning impulse is emphasized by the line break after "connect": the non-stanza dramatizes *The Waste Land*'s difficulties with maintaining narrative connections, re-enacting the stylistic, syntactical and semantic dislocations of the work as a whole.

Even the most obviously self-contained section of the poem,

"Death By Water," which is basically two ABCB quatrains, unfolds in such a way as to half-question the designs of meter and rhyme:

Phlebas the Phoenician, a fortnight dead,
Forgot the cry of gulls, and the deep sea swell
And the profit and loss.

A current under sea
Picked his bones in whispers. As he rose and fell
He passed the stages of his age and youth
Entering the whirlpool.

Gentile or Jew
O you who turn the wheel and look to windward,
Consider Phlebas, who was once handsome and tall as you.
(312–21)

The passage is arranged typographically in terms of grammatical rather than poetic syntax (the separate sentences take priority over the lines of verse), an enjambment after "fell" undercuts the swell/fell rhyme, and a flurry of extra syllables in the final clause suggests a chafing at the (already somewhat irregular) constraints of meter.

We find yet another example of prosodic "unbinding" in the Typist episode (215–56). In the original draft of *The Waste Land* this was written entirely in rhymed quatrains, but in its final version the stanzas are intermittently broken apart. Lines 218–21 ("I Tiresias, though blind... the sailor home from the sea") offer us what looks like an ABAB quatrain, although it is not a syntactically closed verse unit. Another ABAB quatrain appears at 224–27; this one does end with a period, but the next three lines once more fracture the pattern. A *sequence* of quatrains is only achieved with the arrival of the Typist's callow lover (231), whose appearance initiates a closed ABCB "stanza"; immediately afterwards there are three more closed quatrains rhyming ABAB. W. M. Gibson has suggested that those quatrains actually constitute the first twelve lines of a sonnet which finishes at line 248, when the departing clerk

Bestows one final patronizing kiss,
And gropes his way, finding the stairs unlit
(247–48)[17]

These last lines, however, deviate strikingly from the formal regularity of the previous quatrains: the unrhymed and open-ended "couplet" is as anti-climactic as the sexual encounter Eliot/Tiresias has just described. Gibson maintains that the seduction "sonnet" is immediately followed by another one (249–62), and lines 249–56 do seem to offer us a closed octave. But once again, a pattern surfaces only to be dissolved. Although the next six lines end with an apparent gesture towards finality in the concluding rhyme mandoline/within, we have little sense of a circumscribed lyric whole:[18] the content of this "sestet" (which in any case moves us from the Typist's bed-sit to the Thames docks) overflows into line 263 and the verse paragraph does not come to an end until line 265.

Denis Donoghue is, I think, correct to maintain that *The Waste Land* does not exhibit formlessness so much as "a passion for form, largely unfulfilled."[19] The poem is constantly entertaining different methods of ordering and containing its fragmentary voices and visions, adopting prosodic blueprints as diverse as the blank verse of Renaissance drama, the rhythms of popular song, and the stylized periods of the King James Version. But as soon as any given form is adopted, it is quite likely either to be exploded at the moment when it should attain some kind of closure, or to be suddenly abandoned in favor of less schematic, more disjointed discourse. In the last section of *The Waste Land*, the single sentence beginning "A woman drew her long black hair out tight" and conjuring up a series of nightmarish and surrealistic visions (377–84) constitutes a quite elaborately structured verse paragraph, rhyming ABABCDDE and incorporating an additional cross-rhyme (bells/wells) in its last two lines. The syntactic and prosodic configuration of the verse paragraph which immediately succeeds it, however, is much looser (385–94). And yet there is little evidence that such transitions into free (or freer) verse, where form is not exerting its own pressures, imposing a particular order upon content, foster a more linear and goal-directed narrative impulse. That second and looser paragraph brings the reader and the protagonist to the "Grail Chapel," but only to present them with emptiness, a *lacuna* where there should be illumination or revelation. Similarly, when the form of the Thames nymphs' songs begins to disintegrate at the end of "The Fire Sermon," we are left with mere scraps of language culminating in the final, isolated word "burning" – a laconic index to a suspended and inconclusive purgation (306–11).

The Waste Land's gestures towards formally containing and controlling its sub-narratives of loss and lack are repeatedly frustrated, then, by the generation of alternative designs and supplementary content which do not so much facilitate narrative progression as recapitulate the same old story of dearth, unhappy stasis, aphasia. This phenomenon is most strikingly evident on a larger scale when the lyrical description of Phlebas's death and dissolution, in the section of the poem that is certainly closest to an autonomous lyric, is paratactically juxtaposed, in the opening lines of "What the Thunder Said," with the living dead who await their *quietus* (329–30) and with the endless trek through the arid mountains (331–58). To be sure, all of the poem before the walk among the dry rocks of the reified waste land anticipates or pre-describes that journey. The materialization of the parched and decaying terrain at this point in the poem is not the *result* of the actions of the Typist, the Clerk, Belladonna and her lover, the people who fear April and fertility, or the unseeing London crowds: they are already walking through it. In this context, the watery death and *sparagmos* of Phlebas in the very midst of a superfluity of the forces of life is merely a resonant inversion of the slow death and dissolution of those who cannot invoke or control such forces to bring refreshment, not destruction, to their waste land.

Dearth and excess go hand in hand in *The Waste Land*; the text is at once riddled with *lacunae* and ellipses – missing words, missing links, missing climaxes – and characterized by copious augmentation and restatements. Madame Sosostris mentions Tarot cards she does not find (54–55), but is not allowed to describe one that is present (52–54). The poem is supplemented by notes which were only added to make the text a more convenient length for the publishers, and yet, as Eliot himself admitted, have now integrated themselves so thoroughly with the poem that it would be impossible to remove them from it.[20]

Characteristically, while appearing to provide additional information, these idiosyncratically selective annotations contain as many *lacunae* as the poem itself.[21] Moreover, their interpretive, supplementary information may in the long run actually emphasize narrative absences. Let us glance at a passage from "A Game of Chess":

> "Do
> You know nothing? Do you see nothing? Do you remember
> Nothing?"
>
> I remember
> Those are pearls that were his eyes.
> "Are you alive, or not? Is there nothing in your head?"
>
> (121–26)

The note to line 126 refers us back to line 37 in "The Burial of the Dead," which reads "– Yet when we came back, late, from the hyacinth garden." The specific connection is not apparent until one invokes that speaker's later remarks in lines 39–40: "I was neither / Living nor dead, and I knew nothing." But this is not just an instance of sloppy line counting: in an earlier draft of lines 121–26, line 124 ("I remember") reads "I remember the hyacinth garden" (*Facsimile*, p. 19), making it clear that the hyacinth girl and her lover are avatars of Belladonna and *her* lover. The note is here compensating for a suppressed connection; it retrospectively encourages us to resurrect part of a submerged plot. At the same time, in the context of the final version of *The Waste Land*, its supplementariness can only lead the reader to confront an absence, a gap.

The belatedly imposed scheme within which we are asked to re-read *The Waste Land*'s depictions of loss and failure may posit an alternative narrative – one which the textual machinery quite actively tempts us to uncover – of a quest that reaches some kind of *telos*, that leads to some kind of revelation. At the same time, the design that insists on the absence of design, on the impossibility of ever unfolding the quest plot, seems to be equally powerful within the work: *The Waste Land* is, to an extent, "about" the difficulty of its interpretation. And the reader's problems in apprehending any satisfactory totalizing design are exacerbated by the fact that, although the poem's many points of view, literary allusions and echoes suggest that it is the twentieth-century equivalent of the Renaissance encyclopaedic epic, it lacks any consistent focal point of narrative authority. We are offered neither the poet as controlling *deus artifex*, nor any interpolated "figure of the poet" (like Colin Clout, or Raphael, or even Pandarus). Instead, numerous proxy voices (both invented and borrowed) tell fragmentary tales. Certainly some of these utterances sound more authoritative than others. There are intermittent glimpses of oracular and didactic strains in the poem, passages that seem almost scriptural – such as the address to the Son of Man (19–30) and the sermon-like glosses of the thunder's commands.[22] But even if an unambiguously prophetic voice can be isolated, the poem offers no clear indication that we should privilege it above all the other jostling utterances in *The Waste Land*.

The two explicitly prophetic presences in *The Waste Land* are the Cumaean Sibyl and Tiresias; the Sibyl's leaves provide us with one model for the poem's structure (or lack of it), and, according to Eliot's note to line 218 of the Typist episode, the poem as a whole is the product of Tiresias' preternaturally heightened vision. It is tempting to invest double-gendered Tiresias, who both foretells and pre-emptively suffers the future (228–29; 243), with narrative authority – there would certainly be something very Miltonic about such an empowerment of the blind seer. Yet Tiresias, who is impotent in his way as the superannuated Sibyl, locked in her jar wishing only for death, hardly offers a transcendent prophetic voice; he is less a seer, perhaps, than a helpless voyeur, trapped in a cycle of innumerable and unproductive metamorphoses and enduring the same waste land subsistence as those whose lives, and subjectivity, he temporarily shares. The passages in "The Fire Sermon" in which he parenthetically but explicitly identifies himself as the speaker (218–19; 228–30; 243–46) emphasize his powerlessness: they have little in common with the diction of the episode in "The Burial of the Dead" where the anonymous, magisterial voice addresses and exhorts the Son of Man.

In fact, for all its flirtation with oracles and prophecy, *The Waste Land* is more concerned with moments of aborted or suppressed vision – the thwarted apocalypses that prevent any of its stories from reaching an authoritative resolution. In Eliot's original draft of Section I, the closing lines of the fortune-teller's speech read as follows:

> I see crowds of people, walking round in a ring.
> (I John saw these things and heard them).
> Thank you. If you see dear Mrs. Equitone,
> Tell her I bring the horoscope myself,
> One must be so careful these days.
>
> (*Facsimile*, p. 9)

The parenthetical line which had previously separated Madame Sosostris' final reading of the Tarot from her concluding trivialities was eventually cancelled. It derives from Revelation 22:8, where it appears shortly after the author has described his vision of the New Jerusalem. The suppression of this borrowed apocalyptic voice and consequently of a reference to a supremely resonant eschatological vision (the End explicitly invoked in – and very important to – both *The Faerie Queene* and *Paradise Lost*) is wholly characteristic of *The Waste Land*'s obsession with failed vision, narrowly missed revelation. Nor is the erasure of the line from the apocalyptic text the only instance of Eliot's circumvention of revelation. It has been argued that the hyacinth girl episode in Section I is the poet's rewriting of Book IX of *Paradise Lost*: a wrong choice or betrayal takes place in a garden and leads to a terrible privation.[23] But *The Waste Land*'s reader never even penetrates that *locus amoenus*; she merely learns what happens between the lovers "when we came *back*... from the hyacinth garden" (37; emphasis mine). The dislocation of language and vision (38–40) which the paralysed speaker suffers when he fails to act upon his experiences in the garden functions, from the reader's point of view, as a double suppression of the *numen* which emanates from the unseen "paradise." In contrast to the poetic narratives which we have seen striving to circumscribe some representation – however questionable, however attenuated – of a privileged experience or vision, Eliot's text elides it completely. I have already mentioned his cancelled second reference to the hyacinth garden at line 124 – the one which confirms that Belladonna and her lover are versions of the hyacinth girl and *her* lover. In the description of Belladonna's chamber in "A Game of Chess," that unseen and undescribable hyacinth garden has been translated into a kind of Bower of Bliss where the natural is submerged in artifice: here "fruited vines" (79) are in reality metallic lamp standards and the phrase "sylvan scene" (98) (lifted, according to Eliot's note, from Milton's description of Eden [*Paradise Lost* IV. 140]) refers merely to a *trompe l'oeil* painting. The occulted *locus amoenus* of heightened experience and vision is finally made visible only to be petrified.

In the fifth section of *The Waste Land*, revelation and Revelation do seem to be invoked in a nightmarish apocalyptic vision which incorporates the collapse of a representative city that may be Jerusalem or Athens, Alexandria, Vienna or London (366–76).[24] The subsequent surreal depictions of the madwoman and the bats among its wreckage conclude, however, with a reference to "empty cisterns and exhausted wells" (384), and this reinvocation of drought implies – once more – that the city's plight is not so much the result of a Last Judgement upon the sins of the waste land, as simply a restatement of the waste land's existence and universality, another version of the excessively familiar story. This reminiscence of the putative grail quest/fertility rite subtext is followed by a passage that sketches an arrival at a desired goal, hints at an opportunity to complete the ritual and release the life-giving waters upon the parched mountains traversed by the protagonist. Yet the skeletal grail chapel (387–89) does not hold the revelation that announces and enables renewal and rebirth, but rather emptiness and absence. We are, however, offered a suggestion that the quest may be complete:

> a cock stood on the rooftree
> Co co rico co co rico
> In a flash of lightning. Then a damp gust
> Bringing rain
>
> (391–94)

But even this intimation of an achieved goal is complicated by the cock-crow's possible allusion to an act of betrayal rather than one of attainment, and before the desert wastes can be refreshed the verse paragraph simply halts. There is no punctuation, no period; the ritual quest is arrested rather than concluded, and a *lacuna*, a typographical white space, intervenes before we read:

> Ganga was sunken, and the limp leaves
> Waited for rain, while the black clouds
> Gathered far distant, over Himavant.
> The jungle crouched, humped in silence.
> Then spoke the thunder
>
> (395–99)

We do not have a progression between lines 394 and 395 but rather a shift in place and time to an India where the rains have not yet come and where the thunder may well be the same moistureless thunder which accompanied the walk through the mountains (342). The thunder's sermon (or the protagonist's gloss of the thunder's commands) is not a promise of relief and release; its first two sections describe the surrender to selfish desires and the terrible isolation of the waste land dwellers, and the most hope it can offer the quester is that he could have had the capacity to construct a better existence had he submitted himself to a worthwhile authority (whether his own self-control or an external control is unclear): "your heart would have responded / Gaily, when invited, beating obedient / To controlling hands" (420–22). The past conditional of "would have" is the nearest to transcendent finality we are going to be given; at this point another typographical white space intervenes and returns us (again after no punctuation, no period) to the liminal condition of the quester:

> I sat upon the shore
> Fishing, with the arid plain behind me
> Shall I at least set my lands in order?
>
> (423–25)

The "arid plain" recalls to the reader the "endless plains" of the earlier nightmare visions [369]); have we indeed reached an end, or are we simply back where we started?

The discontinuities between the episodes of the grail chapel and the thunder sermon, and between the latter and the final, fragmentary ruminations of the poem are striking; we are brought to the verge of climax and then pulled back from it by movements of displacement or substitution until we are left in a more subdued threshold state where action is being contemplated, but has not been – and will not necessarily be – carried out. One suspects that Eliot is forcing us to disabuse ourselves of any idea that an orthodox teleology will be made manifest. The final lines of *The Waste Land* comprise a polyglot heaping together of various references to urban collapse, uncompleted purgation, metamorphosis, rape and madness – a short-hand compendium of the themes *The Waste Land* had so compulsively reiterated, constructed out of borrowings from other texts and other tongues. We then come to the ritual repetition of the thunder's imperative (432), and the triple "shantih" that forms the last line of the poem: is this the "spell" that will set one's lands in order? The commands to give, sympathize and control are followed by the threefold repetition of the word signifying a transcendent peace, as if obeying the former will result in the latter. Yet how convincing is this declaration of resolution? It is distanced linguistically from the reader by the barrier of a foreign tongue, by Eliot's informing us that his translation of "shantih" as "the Peace that passeth understanding" is but a "feeble translation" of the original Sanskrit,[25] and by the fact that in any case the notion in question defies comprehension. Readers may invest this untranslatable term for the inexpressible with whatever significance they desire, just as they might previously impose whatever significance they desired on the experiences in and beyond the hyacinth garden which could no longer be visualized or spoken of (38–40), or speculate about the imminent release of the waters, occluded by a poetic ellipsis. It is the narrating "I" – or at least one of the many "I"s of *The Waste Land* – who announces, "These fragments I have shored against my ruins" (430). But it is (as usual) up to us to resolve those fragments (which, rather than acting as stays against chaos, are always liable to turn out to be merely supplementary records of confusion) into a totalizing narrative – to discover the narrative "ends" that will permit us to articulate and synchronize our own significant design.

THE ENDS OF POETIC NARRATIVE

The Waste Land might well be termed a poetic anti-narrative. Narrative authority has been surrendered to fragmentary, often anonymous voices, which function less as would-be mediators or accommodators of vision than as helpless witnesses to repeated failures to plot its significance. Even as they bespeak the impossibility of representing contemporary experience according to any externally imposed and totalizing design, the poem's inconclusive diachronic unfolding is never quite countervailed by any local circumscription of a more synchronic vision. Nevertheless, the basic discursive strategies of *The Waste Land* are familiar enough, even if one cannot comfortably label the resultant work a poetic narrative. Reinvoking the forces which I identified in my introductory chapter as playing particularly significant roles in the production of poetic narratives, we may still trace their (somewhat modified) dynamics in *The Waste Land*.

Unlike the other works I have discussed, Eliot's poem does not so much incorporate within its plot the repeated small-scale pressures of poetic form as deploy various configurative schemata in an effort to contain and delimit its rebellious content. At the same time, *The Waste Land* partakes of their tendency towards heteromodality: Eliot simultaneously invokes the quest *mythos* of romance, lays claim to the scope and themes of epic (for he strives to voice the predicament and prophesy the fate of an entire civilization), and constructs a considerable portion of his work out of quasi-lyrical fragments. The poem's multiple quotations of and allusions to other works, quite apart from its explicit invocation of Jessie Weston and James Frazer, confirm its thoroughgoing intertextuality; furthermore, the author's repetitions – however inconclusive – of theme and motif, and his tongue-in-cheek, interpretive, self-augmentative glosses suggest an interest in what I have called "significant supplementation." Finally, *The Waste Land* manifests its own peculiar awareness of conventional strategies for authorizing the creation of poetic narrative – even if these are largely displaced into the marginal territory of the maker's endnotes.

Eliot toys with the fiction that Jessie Weston is the *auctour* whose writings connect his with an ancient, "true story"; in suggesting, moreover, that the poem as a whole articulates what is actually seen by Tiresias, he makes of that blind oracle a kind of muse.[26]

If we accept, then, that there are certain continuities between the dynamics of Eliot's "anti-narrative" and the forces at work in the other poems I have discussed (poetic fictions which have proved richly problematic in their own right), we may find that even *The Waste Land*'s quite striking narrative anomalies point the way towards some general conclusions about recurring phenomena in the works under consideration. One of the most conspicuous features of *The Waste Land* is its obsessive representation of thwarted epiphanies and its associated difficulties with finishing itself off. Even as the final *shantih* invites us to assume that a measure of peace and stasis has been achieved, we are wary of presupposing an end. It is not entirely clear how the poem "got there": after all, the ritual assertions of rest follow upon a supremely fragmentary verse paragraph which resists diachronic progression towards the closure of significance more than almost any other in the work. Chaucer, Spenser and Milton, by contrast, all make apocalypse part of their story: inscribing it within one's poetic fiction and simultaneously submitting that fiction to its transcendent perspective seems to constitute yet another strategy of authorization (as well as the ultimate "double plot").[27] In *Troilus and Criseyde*, the hero's ascent to the eighth sphere and subsequent epiphany initiate a more distanced and didactic narrative discourse that eventually generates the circumscriptive vision of the concluding Christian gloss; in Book I of *The Faerie Queene*, Redcrosse's glimpse of the New Jerusalem offers an exemplary vision of ending that the later books can never quite recapture (even the last stanzas of the *Mutabilitie Cantos* can only *yearn* for such a sight/site); in *Paradise Lost* the events of Eden are ultimately placed in the context of the Second Coming and the Last Judgment: the Book of Genesis is fused with (or collapsed into) the Book of Revelation.

Despite this preoccupation with transcendent endings, mere

narrative endings, last words, prove more problematic. Chaucer carefully and consciously dilates his source to hold off the unhappy conclusion of his fable and prolong the happiness of his lovers: even when he is committed to following the downward fortunes of Troilus he delays the final stanza announcing Troilus' death; even after Troilus has perished and he is supposed to be offering a summary moral, he finds it almost impossible to bid farewell to his work. In *The Faerie Queene*, successive books encounter increasing difficulties in articulating the successful completion of their quests, until, at the end of Book VI, the Blatant Beast escapes and the poet himself suggests that his own quest to write didactic epic will be abandoned. *Paradise Lost* is essentially open-ended: the final End has been revealed to Adam and to the reader, but Adam and Eve are left in a world of choice and uncertainty at its close. *The Waste Land* simply offers a more dramatic version of this inconclusiveness. If the arrival at the Grail Chapel offers intimations of revelation and rest, the poem does not end there: in its final verse paragraph the Fisher King/Quester faces the same kind of threshold of decision as Adam and Eve.

The formal configuration of poetic narrative may go some way to explaining why these works are at once fascinated with transcendent endings and liable to run into difficulties – or evince some degree of internal resistance – when they attempt to set a final limit upon their diachronic unfolding. The poem-as-narrative is constantly halting at a right hand margin determined by the externally imposed pressures of meter, a margin often reinforced by the artificial equations of rhyme. As lines are assembled into stanzas or verse paragraphs, the work incorporates hundreds of premature endings and new beginnings,[28] and the constant recurrence of interim (verse) endings may generate a certain narrative suspicion of merely artificial closure. These "premature endings," furthermore, inevitably complicate any diachronic plotting of a movement from beginning to end, and thus make it all the more tempting for the maker to inscribe and infold a consummate vision of finality which will put all these smaller, provisional endings in perspective. The poetic narrative must confront, it seems, both the

Scylla of the non-significant terminus and the Charybdis of the irredeemable middle – learning, on the one hand, to distrust endings that are all too likely to dissolve into reiterations; fearing, on the other, lest it articulate nothing but a meaningless mean time where the *telos* that will enable its reader to apprehend a synchronic whole will never be won.

The texts I have discussed resist the twin threats of the non-significant terminus and the irredeemable middle through rearguard actions of containment. Privileged *narrative* space – literally a counter-"plot" – is characteristically created by subordinating narrative progression to a hyperpoetic and schematic ordering of particularly imperilled (or subversive) matter. In *The Faerie Queene*, when Spenser, aware of the equivocations and the didactic inadequacies of the discourse of the quest, despairs of ever properly *narrating* courtesy, he creates, if not a lyric *per se*, then at least the patterned round dance of the Graces in which the songs of a lyric poet can accompany the vision of Courtesy-in-action. In Milton's Eden, the songs of Adam and Eve focus and exemplify the suspended bliss of Paradise and suggest its paradoxically dynamic stasis, its existence outside the context of postlapsarian linear time, its transcendence of belated, equivocal re-creations.[29] Even after the Fall, the lyrical and consolatory visions variously articulated by Adam, Eve, and Milton himself briefly resist the entropy of postlapsarian history and postlapsarian narrative. Books II and III of Chaucer's *Troilus and Criseyde* offer us celebrations of human desire, which include a paean to love's "sikernesse" and mutuality, set within the enclosed female domain of the heroine's garden and which climax in the songs of the lovers in Criseyde's bed. They challenge the progress towards loss and betrayal ordained by Chaucer's source, and their circumscription of earthly bliss remains in perpetual tension with that other circumscribing (and heavenly) perspective offered by the poem's final rejection of worldly loves.

The emergence of parallel plots, of "lyric alternatives," within these poetic narratives is often, although not invariably, coincident with a dynamics of dilation which actually privileges problematic narrative middle, elaborating upon and suspending a redeemed between-time. In a narrative which is recreating a previous text, such anti-teleological dilation almost inevitably functions as a reinterpretive gesture. I chose to emphasize this most forcibly in my meditations upon the radical expansions in *Troilus and Criseyde* of that portion of *Il Filostrato* which relates the earlier stages and the consummation of Troiolo and Criseida's affair. As we have seen, Chaucer's sympathetic narrator tries to enlarge upon the joys of his third book for as long as possible – banishing the turn of Fortune's wheel into the beginning of Book IV in order to prolong the lovers' bliss together, endeavoring, through lyrical recapitulations of their happiness, to defer the "necessary ending" furnished by his source. But Spenser's expansive pastoral interlude in Book VI of *The Faerie Queene* is equally end-resistant. In a radically self-revisionary move, the poet offers a context in which the previously heinous crime of sitting down in the middest of one's race suddenly becomes a significant alternative to the enfeebled repetitions and increasingly equivocal ends of the romance quest. The Arcadian experience circumscribes a lyricized revelation whose sustained envisioning might postpone for ever the questionable, even "infamous," pursuit of the Blatant Beast: had Calidore not interrupted the dance on Acidale, the Graces would circle indefinitely and the graces of Courtesy remain joyously suspended in the synchronic, unending pattern of the dance. We have yet another variation on the same theme in *Paradise Lost*'s description of the "enormous bliss" of Eden (which is punctuated by the circling lyricism of the songs of Eden). Milton's *copia* holds off the loss of Paradise: the fall into the seemingly endless mean time before the Second Coming is (paradoxically) delayed by the dilation of the middle time of *this* narrative. (One of the more dilatory passages in *The Waste Land*, by contrast, is the description of Belladonna's chamber at the beginning of "A Game of Chess": the artifice of the room, as I have already suggested, reifies and travesties the hyacinth garden which the reader was never permitted to see. The anti-narrative's false *hortus conclusus* is the nearest we get to the elaboration of Eden as a narrative stay against an unhappy end.)

When Chaucer, Spenser and Milton make use of highly wrought strategies of dilation (whether involving the local interpolation of lyric or the deployment of more expansive "lyric alternatives"), they invoke a poetic that supplements, and provides a counterpoint to, an overtly diachronic and goal-directed narrative agenda. The instances of interpretive supplementation I have mentioned above resist, respectively, a narrative progression towards the moment of Criseyde's betrayal of Troilus, a narrative progression towards Calidore's failure to muzzle Slander completely, and a narrative progression towards the fatal moment of "man's first disobedience." At the same time, our poets' – already sufficiently perplexed – relations with the proper end/s of narratives manifest even further complications. We have come to recognize that a poet's declared commitment to the authoritative realization of a "significant" narrative may meet resistance within his own text from matter which will not easily be subordinated to its grander designs. When a work is strongly didactic, its author is naturally highly conscious of his or her "ends," and less interested in suspended middles than in a rational and discursive progression towards specific goals; nevertheless, the very aspiration to offer narrative *sentence*, as well as *solaas*, can confound closure. The last thirteen stanzas of *Troilus and Criseyde* offer a multiplicity of morals, but none will happily *finish* the work: Chaucer can only terminate his text by surrendering it to the circumscription of the Trinity (v. 1863–69). Until the earthly maker abdicates poetic authority, none of his final glosses, it seems, can entirely subsume what has gone before: they cannot "circumscribe" it, only turn it into a different kind of narrative, substituting divine comedy for the curious hybrid of "tragedye" and romance that has been born out of Chaucer's reproduction of *Il Filostrato*. In *The Faerie Queene*, as each successive book attempts to recapitulate a *telos* that would totalize the aesthetic and didactic significance of its quest, the virtues under discussion become increasingly harder to contain within the discourse of that same quest: by the time we reach canto ix of Book VI, the narrative is actually engendering a return to former beginnings as Spenser strives to articulate a plenary vision of Courtesy. And when Milton sets out to justify the ways of God to men, and tries to rationalize the *lacunae* of scripture, his intervening narratives raise questions which require still further digressions in order to answer them: the ideal of the seamless Christian epic which would leave the reader wholly satisfied is always just out of reach.

When a poetic narrative seeks to make a commentary upon its story a part of that story, it engenders a doubleness of vision. (The egregious "doublespeak" of Spenser's allegorical narrative merely emphasizes this phenomenon.) And the poet who essays to bring didactic and fabulatory ends into harmony tends to end up confirming the duplicity of his narrative. In *The Faerie Queene*, for example, the didactic "end" of Book VI is achieved by way of the lyrical circumscription of a particularly vulnerable ideal within the Graces' dance. Nevertheless, the ritual and linear unfolding of the quest still has to be completed in order to fulfil the supposedly significant design of *The Faerie Queene* – even though the pursuit of the Blatant Beast, inextricably linked as it is to the ambiguous pursuit of a dubious worldly "grace," of a fame that is also infamy, has become emblematic of the vulnerability to misinterpretation of that same significant design. Calidore (briefly) achieves his "famous quest," but the lessons of canto x remain quite separate from his defeat of the enemy: the subsequent escape of Slander, Infamy and Misprision back into the world of the text and the world of the poet confirms the reader's conviction that the end of the quest has little to do with the higher end represented by the epiphany on Acidale.

The duplicitous designs of Chaucer, Spenser and Milton may embrace, then, not only a dialogue between the dynamics of linear, diachronic narrative and those of embedded and synchronic "lyric alternatives," but also an interplay between didactic and aesthetic narrative ends, as they tell – simultaneously – different stories in different voices. In my discussion of *Troilus and Criseyde*, I dissected out three narrative configurations: the dilatory romance narrative that challenges the fixed ending of *Il Filostrato* by expanding the upward movement of the love affair; the symmetrical and carefully balanced "tragedye," whose design reflects the rise and fall of Fortune's wheel; and the didactic "Boethian" narrative whose terminal gloss retrospectively reconfigures and deprivileges both of the other plots. The six complete books of *The Faerie Queene* display a gradual separation of increasingly circumscribed scenes of vision from the discourse and narration of the quest, until, in Book VI, the nominal hero of the quest of Courtesy is shown to be positively inimical to the vision of Courtesy: when he infringes its privileged but vulnerable space, its counter-"plot," the Graces vanish. And *Paradise Lost* offers us a profusion of double plots. Milton's discursive, logical justification of God's ways to men exists in tension with his synchronic/lyric strategies for sensuously reapprehending origin and redeeming fallen time; his poem incorporates an intricate interplay between redeemed and fallen literary kinds; his "higher argument" perpetually and perilously engages with Satanic counterplots of genesis, creativity and inspiration. Even the anti-narrative of *The Waste Land* proffers an idiosyncratic version of such parallel plotting: Eliot's hints that his poem encodes the linear representation of an archetypal – and achievable – quest compete with the text's relentless redescriptions of a barren existence that can hope for no amelioration, no illumination, no end.

Although the precise relations of the competing narratives in these duplicitous designs vary from work to work, each poetic fiction is capable of exploiting the hybrid nature of the poem-as-narrative to engender a productive tension between what we might call the "dynamics of the line" and "the dynamics of the circle." The former represents the goal-directed movement of conventional plotting, the diachronic progression towards a revelation or resolution that will impose a retrospective unity on the narrative experience. The latter represents a narrative configuration which prefers to order experience or insight in terms of closed, synchronic patterning rather than linear unfolding through time. Ideally, the "dynamics of the line" should eventually collapse into the "dynamics of the circle," in as much as a narrative that comes to a good end will offer the reader a retrospective apprehension of its synchronic design. As we have seen, however, the makers of poetic narratives are both enormously conscious of endings and enormously concerned lest their designs cannot be brought to a proper conclusion. Poets and poems are torn between various aesthetic and didactic criteria as to what constitutes a satisfactory "end"; poetic fictions are also quite likely to come to less than desirable ends (Milton cannot actually conclude Book XII of the story of the Fall with the Second Coming, for example). Consequently, they exploit the dynamics of the circle to foreclose upon a poetic space in which the errant narrative may be redeemed. This space may be encompassed *within* the narrative by circular *topoi* (the *hortus conclusus*, the round dance) which enclose and mediate privileged but vulnerable epiphanies; such moments of vision may be simultaneously or alternatively contained by semi-autonomous lyric passages which depart from a more linear, more conventionally teleological narrative discourse.

Chaucer's subversive dilation of the progression of *Il Filostrato* towards its unhappy conclusion includes, as we have seen, the lyrical episodes in the walled garden of Criseyde and secret nights of love in the private chamber in Pandarus' house that are celebrated in both the songs of the lovers and the joyful outbursts and apostrophes of the narrator. If the attempt to enclose and preserve the articulation of earthly desire must defer to the rise and fall of Fortune's wheel, Fortune's parallel plot, as I have already suggested, is not actually allowed to come full circle: the final description of the death of Troilus is delayed by the interpolation of several stanzas that begin to gloss *Troilus and Criseyde* as if it is already over (V. 1772–99). The diffusion of the emotional impact of Troilus' *quietus* through the author's remarks on the immediate significance and the putative transmission of his text; his revisionary account of the ascent of Troilus' spirit and subsequent reversal of the significance of Troilus' "double sorwe"; his repeated invocation of "ending" across a flurry of stanzas which attempt to close the work: all of these gestures transmute the narrative discourse of finality into a testament to perplexed dilatoriness. It is only when Chaucer reinvokes the synchronic and lyric paradigm, deferring to the transcendent design of the all-circumscribing eternal circle of Dante's Trinity (V. 1863–69), that all the stories told by *Troilus and Criseyde* can be closed – and even so, the paeans to earthly desire rehearsed in Books II and III are perhaps never completely subordinated to the containing strategies of that final stanza.

The dynamics of the circle are inscribed clearly enough within Book VI of *The Faerie Queene*. The abandonment of the goal-directed quest leads reader and quester to the circles of shepherds and Graces and the pastoral songs of Arcadia and Acidale. On Acidale, the circles of dancers collapse beginning into end and offer a tempting alternative to the perilously enfeebled and morally ambiguous unfolding of the quest. The *perpetuum mobile* of the dancing ladies moves them about numinous figures who represent the higher goods of civility and earthly grace: their round dance encloses a sacred space of perpetual dynamism, a refuge from non-significant sequence, equivocal goals, and unhappy endings. If its pivot, its cynosure, is unspeakable, ultimately unnarratable, she is at least safe from the slanderous misprisions which have assailed the (no longer privileged) "doublespeak" of the allegorical narrative of the quest.

In *Paradise Lost*, Eden is translated into the dynamics of the circle. It is watched over by the circling dance of the angels and the heavenly bodies; it is celebrated in the circling lyrics of Adam and Eve; it is an enclosed space in which the eternal and preternaturally dilated moment of bliss triumphs over linear chronology. On one side of it lies the linear quest of Satan; on the other, the linear projection of the damnable iterations of human history and the commencement of our grand parents' quest to find a place for themselves in postlapsarian narrative time. The journey of Satan from Hell to Eden is part of Milton's "rational" narrative of causality ("say first what cause / Moved our grand parents... to fall off... Who first seduced them?" [I. 27–31]); the final books offer the coolly logical extrapolation of all the consequences of humanity's lapse. The narrative redescription of Eden, by contrast, represents the sublime counterplot of *Paradise Lost* – the poet's "lyricized" and sensuous reapprehension of origin. At the last, Book XII has two "endings" to set against Edenic synchrony. One of them is represented by the threshold of human history upon which

Adam and Eve stand in the last lines of the poem, the other by Michael's revelation of the Incarnation and the Second Coming (XII. 359–465) – and this greater End is already anticipated in Book X's briefer but more resonant rendering of apocalypse (X. 183–92). But it is only Book X's half-buried vision, circumscribed in a kind of parenthesis between the Son's judgment of the serpent and his judgment of Eve, that partakes of – and reinvokes – the simultaneity of Eden, where beginnings and ends are collapsed into one glorious *now*.

The dynamics of the circle suffer characteristic modification in *The Waste Land*. We stay on the outside of Eliot's *hortus conclusus*, the hyacinth garden hedged on either side with fragments of Wagnerian lyrics that recount only loss (31–42). And although the "Death by Water" section of the poem offers a self-contained lyric in which the body of Phlebas is drawn into the circlings of the whirlpool (318), this is a lyric ordering of the unhappy ending of one avatar of the quester, an elaboration and containment of his failure to achieve enlightenment or a desired goal. Unless we declare this lyrical exercise to be a uniquely direct confrontation of the possibility of dissolution, and thus an essential preliminary to whatever resolution is achieved in the poem's final section (an interpretation I have already suggested to be a risky one), its presence is less a defense against narrative dissipation than a primary symptom of entropy. *This* lyric does not pre-empt or forestall an infelicitous end; it is a subversive premature end in itself.

The double plots of sophisticated poetic narratives tend to remain double to the last. The epiphany circumscribed by the secret space of Acidale survives Spenser's cursory and disillusioned winding up of the quest of Courtesy; neither the measured unfolding of the source-determined narrative of betrayal in *Troilus and Criseyde* nor Chaucer's concluding palinode can entirely do away with the rapturous celebration of earthly passion preserved in the suspended lyric moments of Book III. Eden is held perpetually unviolated in the celebratory songs of *Paradise Lost* IV and V, even as *Paradise Lost* moves on inexorably towards the narration of its loss; the final defeat of Satan, apocalyptically anticipated in Book x, which will set a period upon fallen time, is balanced against the beginning of postlapsarian history with which the poem actually concludes. Such double visions remain co-terminous in the reader's apprehension of the work: one design is not necessarily subordinated to another. Indeed, as I have already had cause to suggest, the very character of the highly wrought poetic narrative *as a literary kind* lends itself to the articulation of such unresolved doubleness, for a narrative poem is by definition the product of a perpetual conversation between two distinct – and unhierarchized – discursive strategies.

I remarked at the very beginning of this study that the intrinsic formal duplicity of the poetic narrative, the simple fact that it is *both* poem *and* narrative, makes it difficult to insert within those binary taxonomies which require one descriptive term of a pair (such as lyric/narrative; synchrony/diachrony) to be privileged over another at the moment of classification. My subsequent chapters have proposed that the very same constitutive doubleness, the suspension in simultaneity of "poetic" and "narrative" strategies of representation and redescription, may contribute *within* the text of a poetic fiction to its significant and signifying designs.[30] The local elaboration-cum-containment that narration in verse paragraphs or stanzas encourages on the small scale may become, within the fiction as a whole, a dynamic exerting a potentially revisionary pressure upon orthodox teleology. An author, consciously or unconsciously, may choose to exploit this counter-poetic to challenge the official conclusions of his or her narrative line, to infold alternative visions within lyrical or quasi-lyrical schemata, to invoke another discourse and tell another story.

My hypothesis that the inherent doubleness of the poetic narrative permits it to incorporate within its design the alternative dynamics – and the alternative epiphanies – of a lyric counterplot must needs be a tentative one, based as it is upon a limited sampling of texts which ignores, for example, the poetic narratives of the eighteenth and nineteenth centuries. I would nevertheless like to propose that the interior dialogue between configurative forces in the works I have examined – a dialogue which is further elaborated in their tendency to incorporate rival *modes* of storytelling – is indeed a constitutive characteristic of poetic narrative as a literary kind. I must thus take issue with Bakhtin's claims for "the single-voiced purity and unqualified directness that intentions possess in poetic discourse":[31] the "poetic discourse" of *these* texts has much more in common with the radical challenge to univocal, authoritative discourse which, for Bakhtin, characterizes the novel. I do not, however, find the multivocality of the poetic narrative wholly interchangeable with the multilayered and at times ironically displaced reproductions of language systems that interest Bakhtin. The relatively greater pressures exerted by form and genre in the poetic narrative play a major role in engendering its "polyglossia"; its competing voices are not, therefore, exactly like those produced, according to Bakhtin, by the novelist's *re*presentation – or construction – of the play of language systems. These formal and generic pressures, I would suggest, are especially crucial in differentiating the *structurally significant* – yet finite – polyglossia of the poetic narrative from the potentially interminable heteroglossia of the fiction which enters into an endless dialogue with the discourses of its historical moment.[32]

Bakhtin's suggestion that heteroglossia is *the* defining characteristic of the novel tellingly downplays (or ignores) the containing devices of plot. My account of the poetic narrative's polyglossia – and in particular, my discussion of the "counterplots" engendered by the lyric/synchronic voice – suggests that poetic fictions may infold alternative visions (and endings) which do not so much militate against the closure of significance as pre-empt its diachronic dissipation. In extended fictional narratives cast in verse, various formal pressures (for example, the "premature ends" of verse lines), source-related pressures (for example, a resisted but pre-authorized ending) and semantic pressures (for example, the complication of the configuration of closure by the desire to inscribe within the text an interpretive metanarrative) may inhibit the poetic narrative's ability to reach its desired conclusion. Readers may be frustrated in their attempts, *after* the work has officially ended, to reapprehend its diachronic unfolding as significant sequence. In selectively and significantly emphasizing the discourse associated with a more lyric/synchronic order, poetic fiction-makers can forestall this hermeneutic *impasse*. Their infolded counterplots somewhat defiantly circumscribe other imaginative possibilities, other visions, other stories – and allow us to come to conclusions that we might otherwise be denied.

Notes

1 INTRODUCTION: SOME STRATEGIES OF POETIC NARRATIVE

1 Robert Scholes and Robert Kellogg, *The Nature of Narrative* (New York: Oxford University Press, 1966), p. 4.

2 I am here borrowing Gérard Genette's definitions of the terms "narrative" and "story"; *Narrative Discourse: An Essay in Method*, trans. Jane E. Lewin (Ithaca: Cornell University Press, 1980), p. 27. Genette in his turn is making use of the *szujet/fabula* distinction of the Russian formalists (see note 17 below).

3 William Nelson, *Fact or Fiction: The Dilemma of the Renaissance Storyteller* (Cambridge, Mass.: Harvard University Press, 1973), p. 38. Twentieth-century taxonomic exclusiveness offers an interesting contrast to Philip Sidney's assertion that "poetry" embraces all imaginative makings, all fictions: for him, Plato's dialogues, More's *Utopia* or Heliodorus' *Aethiopica* are as much "poems" as the *Aeneid*. See *A Defence of Poetry*, ed. Jan Van Dorsten (Oxford: Oxford University Press, 1982), pp. 27, 33, 50.

4 Wayne C. Booth, *The Rhetoric of Fiction* (Chicago: University of Chicago Press, 1961). David Lodge, *The Language of Fiction* (New York: Columbia University Press, 1966). "The Nature and Modes of Narrative Fiction" appears in René Wellek and Austin Warren's *Theory of Literature*, 3rd edn. (New York: Harcourt, Brace & World, Inc., 1973).

5 See, for example, Wallace Martin, *Recent Theories of Narrative* (Ithaca: Cornell University Press, 1986) and Seymour Chatman, *Story and Discourse: Narrative Structure in Fiction and Film* (Ithaca: Cornell University Press, 1978).

6 Shlomith Rimmon-Kenan, *Narrative Fiction: Contemporary Poetics* (London: Methuen, 1983), p. 1.

7 Mieke Bal, *Narratology: Introduction to the Theory of Narrative*, trans. Christine van Boheemen (Toronto: University of Toronto Press, 1985), p. 9.

8 Northrop Frye, for one, further muddies the issue by using "fiction" to denote the broad category of *written* literature, sharply opposing it to the orally composed *epos* (comprising drama, epic and lyric), only to remove "the epic" and "narrative poetry" from *epos* later in his discussion, and relocate them rather closer to fiction than *epos* on an imaginary line stretching between the two. See *Anatomy of Criticism: Four Essays* (New York: Athenaeum, 1968), pp. 248–50. There is a useful account of these inconsistencies in Frye's work in Robert Scholes, *Structuralism in Literature: An Introduction* (New Haven: Yale University Press, 1974), pp. 124–26.

9 There are exceptions, of course, such as the study by Scholes and Kellogg (see note 1 above), and the criticism of Frank Kermode, which has been consistently sensitive to the fact that not all narrative fictions are novels. Indeed Kermode insists that the novel is not so much the most highly evolved product of our interest in creating narrative fictions as a "local and transient" manifestation of a constant (and complex) literary phenomenon. See his monograph *Novel and Narrative* (Glasgow: University of Glasgow Press, 1972), pp. 7–9.

10 Jonathan Culler, *Structuralist Poetics: Structuralism, Linguistics and the Study of Literature* (London: Routledge and Kegan Paul, 1975).

11 Michael J. Toolan, *Narrative: A Critical Linguistic Introduction* (London and New York: Routledge, 1988). One could offer similar examples *ad infinitum.* When the journal *Poetics Today* devoted two issues to articles on "Narratology," an editorial statement at the beginning of the first of these announced: "It is not clear why all works of fiction should be called 'narrative' (even if there are few narrative elements in them) in any sense which makes them essentially different from texts of poetry. What extent of dominance must a narrative structure have for the whole text to be called 'narrative'?" (*Poetics Today* 1, no. 3 [1980]: 6). The writer, while apparently protesting an artificial critical divide (in this case the assimilation of *all* prose fictions into the category of "narrative" and their separation from poetic texts), nevertheless considers "narrative works of fiction" and "texts of poetry" to be mutually exclusive forms; whatever features he suspects may be shared by the structures of poetry and those of "fiction," they are unlikely, in his view, to include the narrative element.

12 Chatman, *Story and Discourse*, p. 23.

13 Genette, *Narrative Discourse*, pp. 37–38. See also Tzvetan Todorov's essay "Primitive Narrative," a discussion of narrative in the *Odyssey*, in *The Poetics of Prose* (*sic*!), trans. Richard Howard (Ithaca: Cornell University Press, 1977). The early pages of Booth's *Rhetoric of Fiction* include references to Homer and Chaucer,

although Booth's account of "fiction" is thereafter wholly concerned with the novel.

14 Ben Jonson, *Timber*, ed. Felix C. Schelling (Boston: Ginn & Co., 1892), p. 73.

15 It would obviously be foolish to attempt to deal with *The Faerie Queene* in its entirety in the space of one chapter. I have chosen to focus upon Book VI because of the important questions it raises concerning closure (or the failure/impossibility of closure) in Spenser's poem, particularly since its striking parallels with Book I encourage us to look back to the groundplot of *The Faerie Queene* and consider what has become of it. I am convinced that Book VI, and not the appended Mutability Cantos, marks the actual end of *The Faerie Queene* (or at least the impossibility of continuing the allegorical poetic narrative); for an extended discussion of this issue see chapter 3, pp. 82–83; 118–21.

16 For narrative "grammar" see Tzvetan Todorov, *Grammaire du Décaméron* (The Hague: Mouton, 1969). For the five "codes" see Roland Barthes, *S/Z*, trans. Richard Miller (New York: Hill and Wang, 1974), pp. 18–20. For the Author...Reader series see Chatman, *Story and Discourse*, chapter 4. For "anachronies," see Genette, *Narrative Discourse*.

17 "Thematics," *Russian Formalist Criticism: Four Essays*, ed. Lee T. Lemon and Marion J. Reis (Lincoln: University of Nebraska Press, 1965), pp. 66–68. Wallace Martin offers a useful summary of later theorists' variations on the *fabula/szujet* opposition in *Recent Theories of Narrative*, p. 108.

18 Admittedly, the route taken towards this sense of narrative fulfillment and completion may not always be a straightforward one; its unfolding may be complicated by wanderings, repetitions and delays. For an interesting discussion of the relationship between the plenitude of meaning and satisfaction ideally won at the end of a narrative and the sometimes tortuous process of "getting there," see Peter Brooks, "Freud's Masterplot: A Model for Narrative," *Reading for the Plot: Design and Intention in Narrative* (New York: Vintage, 1985), pp. 90–112.

19 The phrase is borrowed from Roman Jakobson's essay, "The Dominant," *Readings in Russian Poetics: Formalist and Structuralist Views*, ed. L. Matejka and K. Pomorska (Cambridge, Mass.: MIT Press, 1971), p. 82.

20 *Anatomy of Criticism*, p. 271.

21 *Anatomy of Criticism*, p. 271.

22 *Anatomy of Criticism*, p. 272. Frye cites the "stanzaic epos" of medieval romance as an example of this.

23 Of related interest here is Shlomith Rimmon-Kenan's distinction between the atemporal synchrony of the non-narrative text (her example happens to be a lyric) and the necessary temporal succession – the linear chronology – in the story underpinning any narrative. See *Narrative Fiction: Contemporary Poetics*, p. 15.

24 I am here indebted to Thomas Greene's observations on the form of the Spenserian stanza and its effects on narrative in *The Descent From Heaven: A Study in Epic Continuity* (New Haven: Yale University Press, 1963), pp. 327ff.

25 For an extended discussion of the crucial role of the fifth line in shaping the form of the Spenserian stanza, see William Empson, *Seven Types of Ambiguity*, 3rd edn. (Cleveland: Meridian Books, 1964), pp. 40–41.

26 Roman Jakobson, "Linguistics and Poetics," in *Style in Language*, ed. Thomas A. Sebeok (Cambridge, Mass.: MIT Press, 1960), p. 358. And see also Jakobson's related study, "Two Aspects of Language and Two Types of Aphasic Disturbance," in Roman Jakobson and Morris Halle, *Fundamentals of Language*, 4th edn. (The Hague: Mouton, 1980), pp. 69–96. David Lodge offers an illuminating analysis, critique and extension of Jakobson's arguments in *The Modes of Modern Writing: Metaphor, Metonymy and the Typology of Modern Literature* (Ithaca: Cornell University Press, 1977), pp. 73–124. He makes the important observation that although Jakobson starts "Linguistics and Poetics" by announcing his intention of defining what constitutes "poetic" (that is, literary) language, he in fact comes up with a formula for poetry alone and does not advance a definition of literary prose. (In "Poetic Language, Poetics of Language," Gérard Genette, by contrast, *starts* by looking at the prose/poetry divide and works his way towards a definition of "poetic" language as a whole. See *Figures of Literary Discourse* [*Selections from Figures 1966–72*], trans. Alan Sheridan [New York: Columbia University Press, 1982], pp. 75–102.)

27 Jakobson, "Two Aspects of Language," p. 95.

28 "Linguistics and Poetics," p. 375. And see also Lodge, *The Modes of Modern Writing*, p. 81. I am aware, of course, that in recent years Jakobson's account of a binary system of master tropes has been variously challenged. On the one hand, we have such alternative tropologies as that of Kenneth Burke (since reappropriated by historiographer Hayden White). Burke proposes a system of four "master tropes": metaphor, metonymy, synecdoche and irony; see *A Grammar of Motives* (Berkeley and Los Angeles: University of California Press, 1969), pp. 503–17, and see also James M.

Mellard, *Doing Tropology: Analysis of Narrative Discourse* (Urbana: University of Illinois Press, 1987), pp. 13–36. On the other hand, we have Paul Ricoeur's arguments in *The Rule of Metaphor: Multidisciplinary Studies of the Creation of Meaning in Language*, trans. Robert Czerny *et al.* (Toronto: University of Toronto Press, 1977), that Jakobson offers a "false symmetry" (pp. 132–33) between metaphor and metonymy. According to Ricoeur, metonymy, in replacing one name with another, "remains a semiotic process, perhaps even the substitutive process *par excellence* in the realm of signs" (p. 198), while metaphor, as "unusual attribution," is a "semantic process" of mimetic redescription (p. 198). I have chosen to concentrate on the Jakobsonian schematics, however, because in this particular context they seem representative of a continuing tendency to oversimplify our apprehension of relations between poetic and prose literary texts.

29 Jakobson, "Two Aspects of Language," p. 91.

30 Lodge, *The Modes of Modern Writing*, p. 81.

31 The reductiveness of the metaphor/metonymy dyad and its tendency to collapse into a consideration of metaphor alone in the criticism of Jakobson and his followers is convincingly argued by Genette in "Rhetoric Restrained," *Figures of Literary Discourse*, pp. 103–26. See also Ricoeur, *The Rule of Metaphor*, pp. 178ff.

32 Lodge, *The Modes of Modern Writing*, p. 109.

33 Brooks, *Reading for the Plot*, p. 91. For Brooks, interestingly, the metonymical function in narrative is associated with sequence in the sense of wandering, repetition, delay – the transformative process of "getting there" – i.e. with phenomena that seem to correspond to some of the local manifestations of form acting on content in the narrative poem.

34 *Unpublished Letters of Samuel Taylor Coleridge*, Vol. II, ed. Earl Leslie Griggs (London: Constable and Company, Ltd., 1932), p. 128.

35 The discussion which follows is indebted to John Hollander's extremely suggestive *Melodious Guile: Fictive Pattern in Poetic Language* (New Haven: Yale University Press, 1988), pp. 1–17. I follow Hollander in challenging over-tidy distinctions between what he calls "the matter of verse" and the "matter of fiction" (p. 1); I do not go quite as far as him in arguing that all poetic scheme is a sort of self-consuming artifact, all pattern ultimately (or "ulteriorly") metaphor.

36 Paul J. Alpers, *The Poetry of The Faerie Queene* (Princeton: Princeton University Press, 1967), p. 36. Jonathan Goldberg advances similar views (translated into the critical vocabulary of deconstruction) on Spenser's subordination of coherent narrative rep-

resentation to rhetorical play in *Endlesse Worke: Spenser and the Structures of Discourse* (Baltimore: The Johns Hopkins University Press, 1981).

37 W. K. Wimsatt, Jr., "One Relation of Rhyme to Reason," in *The Verbal Icon: Studies in the Meaning of Poetry* (Lexington: University of Kentucky Press, 1954), pp. 153–66. For another interesting meditation on the relationship between rhyme and meaning see John Hollander, "Rhyme and the True Calling of Words," in *Vision and Resonance: Two Senses of Poetic Form* (New York: Oxford University Press, 1975), pp. 117–34.

38 For a suggestive discussion of this phenomenon see John Hollander, "'Sense Variously Drawn Out': Some Observations on English Enjambment" in *Literary Theory and Structure: Essays in Honor of William K. Wimsatt*, ed. Frank Brady *et al.* (New Haven: Yale University Press, 1973), pp. 201–25.

39 All references to and quotations from *Paradise Lost* are from John Milton, *Paradise Lost*, ed. Alastair Fowler (London: Longman, 1976). Fowler draws our attention to this metrically induced moment of double syntax in his note to Book I. 1.

40 See Lodge, *The Modes of Modern Writing*, p. 88.

41 Of course, the division of earlier poetic narratives into books, fits, etc. is frequently related to oral performance: the length of the segment is determined by its suitability for continuous delivery. The narrators of the works under consideration may on occasion refer to themselves as being in the process of composing or singing aloud, but this is a convention invoked by a fictive persona within a highly self-conscious *literary* performance, and I have discounted the oral aspect of narrative division in my discussion.

42 Graham Hough suggests that in the Italian tradition of epic-romance the book was thought to be the more formal and unified division, the canto a relatively casual slice of the narrative; see *A Preface to The Faerie Queene* (New York: W. W. Norton and Co., 1967), p. 85. We may note that in Spenser's simultaneous use of book and canto, the canto seems to be moving towards a much more carefully determined role in the plot as a whole.

43 For a concise overview of recent discussions of world/text relations, see Linda Hutcheon, *The Politics of Postmodernism* (London and New York: Routledge, 1989), pp. 47–61.

44 The term is borrowed from Maureen Quilligan's terminology in *The Language of Allegory: Defining the Genre* (Ithaca: Cornell University Press, 1979). Quilligan describes it as "the text that the narrative comments on by re-enacting, as well as the claim the narrative makes to be a fiction *not* built upon another text"

(pp. 97–98). In appropriating the term I would prefer to contrast the poetic narrative's overt invocation of a source which becomes the "pretext" for the creative act with the more fleeting, silent, yet equally hermeneutically loaded exploitation of a prior text through paraphrase or indirect allusion.

45 For Chaucer's classification of his narrative see Book v, line 1786. The text of *Troilus and Criseyde* referred to here and (parenthetically) in all subsequent citations is that of *The Riverside Chaucer*, ed. Larry D. Benson *et al.* 3rd rev. edition (Boston: Houghton Mifflin Co., 1987). For a comprehensive summary of most of the critical positions on the genre of the *Troilus* see Alice R. Kaminsky, *Chaucer's Troilus and Criseyde and the Critics* (Athens, Ohio: Ohio University Press, 1980), pp. 74–83.

46 C. S. Lewis remarks that, in fashioning *The Faerie Queene*, Spenser "allegorized the romantic epic." See *The Allegory of Love: A Study in Medieval Tradition* 1936 (New York: Oxford University Press, 1958), p. 310.

47 For a discussion of the wide range of genres invoked and exploited by Milton in *Paradise Lost* see Barbara K. Lewalski, *Paradise Lost and the Rhetoric of Literary Forms* (Princeton: Princeton University Press, 1985).

48 E. D. Hirsch Jr. notes this drawback of elaborate genre systems in *Validity in Interpretation* (New Haven: Yale University Press, 1967), pp. 110–11. The problem is, of course, a variation on the "hermeneutic circle" paradox. For an interesting revisionary defense of the deductive, "constitutive" genre system, see Adena Rosmarin, *The Power of Genre* (Minneapolis: University of Minnesota Press, 1985), pp. 23–51.

49 The term "romance," for example, may mean for one reader the relatively narrow class of texts comprised by medieval narratives concerned with aristocratic love, chivalry, and magic, written in the vernacular and often, although by no means exclusively, in verse. In the critical vocabulary of another it may cover a much larger group of works, which, while sharing certain narrative traits, are neither limited to a specific form nor to a particular epoch.

50 Paul Hernadi argues for a multi-dimensional, "polycentric" theory of genre in *Beyond Genre: New Directions in Literary Classification* (Ithaca: Cornell University Press, 1972), pp. 152–53. It is telling that, while generic distinctions can be, and have been, made on the basis of both form *and* content, many schemes of classification do not incorporate even this modest polycentrism; it is only fairly recently that Fredric Jameson proposed that every

grouping of texts which is to qualify as a "genre" should be capable of two distinct formulations: a "semantic" (content-based) definition which gives us genre-as-*mode*, and a "syntactic" (structure-based) definition which gives us genre-as-*model*. See *The Political Unconscious: Narrative as a Socially Symbolic Act* (Ithaca: Cornell University Press, 1981), pp. 107–10. Jameson's dual categories are perhaps anticipated by Hernadi's discussion of the possibility of classifying a text according to both "mimetic" and "structural" principles (pp. 54–113). Alastair Fowler's excellent study, *Kinds of Literature: An Introduction to the Theory of Genres and Modes* (Cambridge, Mass.: Harvard University Press, 1982) outlines a flexible and "polycentric" system for describing literary texts without ever quite coming to grips with the constitutive form versus constitutive content issue.

51 Jonathan Monroe, *A Poverty of Objects: The Prose Poem and the Politics of Genre* (Ithaca: Cornell University Press, 1987), p. 15. Monroe argues that such texts become disputed territory where dialogic and dialectical relations between "socio-aesthetic oppositions" are played out (pp. 17–19).

52 Of related interest here is Hans Robert Jauss' theory of the "aesthetics of reception." Jauss posits an interplay between (a) the form and content of a new work and (b) readerly expectations about familiar rules of genre which may conclude in the redrawing of generic boundaries. See "Literary History as a Challenge to Literary Theory," *NLH* 2 (1970): 7–37; in particular, pp. 12–13.

53 Goldberg argues that any recourse to allusion in narrative brings with it self-obliteration: the author is letting someone else write his text – indeed his text is already "written" (*Endlesse Worke*, p. 31). But the process presumably works in both directions: the secondary imposition of a new form and an (explicit or implicit) reinterpretation upon a prior text results in at least a momentary appropriation of it by the later poet.

54 *Reading for the Plot*, pp. 101–8.

55 See Frank Kermode, *The Genesis of Secrecy: On the Interpretation of Narrative* (Cambridge, Mass.: Harvard University Press, 1979), chapter 4. Gerald L. Bruns makes a similar point to myself in *Inventions: Writing, Textuality and Understanding in Literary History* (New Haven: Yale University Press, 1982), p. 55; see also Eugène Vinaver's remarks on progressive self-supplementation as exegesis in romance narrative in *The Rise of Romance* (Oxford: Clarendon Press, 1971), pp. 17–22.

56 For a detailed discussion of the relationship between sacred, "inspired" texts and the secular imagination, see John Guillory,

Poetic Authority: Spenser, Milton and Literary History (New York: Columbia University Press, 1983).

57 Patricia A. Parker identifies the multiplication-as-diminution problem as a characteristic of the romance mode which is an exaggerated form of the desire to "stray" common to all fictions. See *Inescapable Romance: Studies in the Poetics of a Mode* (Princeton: Princeton University Press, 1979), pp. 40–43.

58 Terence Cave, *The Cornucopian Text: Problems of Writing in the French Renaissance* (Oxford: Clarendon Press, 1979), p. 75.

59 Parker's discussion of the tension between narrative dilation and apocalyptic *telos* is of relevance here; see *Inescapable Romance*, pp. 4–5, 158. Her dilation/*telos* dyad has obvious connections with Peter Brooks' reworking of the metonymy/metaphor opposition.

60 *A Defence of Poetry*, p. 48.

61 *Defence of Poetry*, p. 53. This claim is of course developed from Sidney's celebrated statement that the poet "nothing affirms, and therefore never lieth" (p. 52) and can be compared with Edward Said's theory of "contingent authority" (see note 66 below).

62 *Defence of Poetry*, p. 23. For an account of the early history of the *topos* of the *deus artifex* (which originates in Plato's *Timaeus*), see Ernst Robert Curtius, *European Literature and the Latin Middle Ages*, trans. Willard R. Trask (Princeton: Princeton University Press, 1973), pp. 544–46.

63 Torquato Tasso, *Discourses on the Heroic Poem*, trans. and annotated by Mariella Cavalchini and Irene Samuel (Oxford: Clarendon Press, 1973), p. 78.

64 Cf. Edward W. Said's suggestion that in all sophisticated fictions "There is derivation, begetting, continuity, augmentation – and also a nagging molesting awareness that beyond these there is something more authentic, to which fiction is secondary." "Molestation and Authority in Narrative Fiction," *Aspects of Narrative: Selected Papers from the English Institute*, ed. J. Hillis Miller (New York: Columbia University Press, 1971), p. 50.

65 George Puttenham, *The Arte of English Poesie* in *Elizabethan Critical Essays*, Vol. II, ed. G. Gregory Smith (Oxford: Clarendon Press, 1904), pp. 3–4. We might contrast the rhetorical impasse we find in Puttenham with the dynamic interplay between the three translations Sidney offers for Aristotle's *mimesis*: "counterfeiting," "representing," and "figuring forth" (*Defence of Poetry*, p. 25).

66 That is, does such a work of seemingly "pure" imagination lack even what Said calls "contingent authority" to provide "a quite satisfactory transitory alternative to the absolute truth" in a literary structure "whose absolute authority is radically nil." "Molestation and Authority," p. 53.

67 *Paradise Lost* I. 27–31; *The Faerie Queene* I. Proem 2. All references to and citations of the latter work are from Edmund Spenser, *The Faerie Queene*, ed. Thomas P. Roche and C. Patrick O'Donnell, Jr. (New Haven: Yale University Press, 1981).

68 Of related interest here is Robert O. Payne's account of the representation of "auctoritee" in medieval texts as, in effect, the remaking of past experience in living artifice: *The Key of Remembrance: A Study of Chaucer's Poetics* (New Haven: Yale University Press, 1963), p. 65.

69 Robert Kellogg has suggested that an artist at work during an epoch when narratives are beginning to be produced as texts rather than oral performances is particularly likely to provide himself with a narrator who will not only create the illusion of a unique performance of the poem *within* the poem, but will also set up a creative dynamic between narrative and sources through the narrator's explicit relationship with his authorities. See "Oral Narrative, Written Books," *Genre* 10 (1977): 664–65.

70 M. M. Bakhtin, "Discourse in the Novel," in *The Dialogic Imagination*, ed. Michael Holquist, trans. Caryl Emerson and M. Holquist (Austin and London: University of Texas Press, 1981), pp. 259–422; p. 314.

71 Bakhtin, "Discourse in the Novel," p. 330.

72 My main quarrel with Bakhtin's definition of the novel arises from the unresolved tension between his obvious desire to make "the poetic" and "the novelistic" polar opposites (as in a Jakobsonian dyad) and the fact that his actual definition of what constitutes "novelistic" discourse is equally applicable to many poetic narratives.

2 DILATION, DESIGN AND DIDACTICISM IN *TROILUS AND CRISEYDE*

1 In addition to Stephen A. Barney's text of *Troilus and Criseyde* in *The Riverside Chaucer*, I have also consulted Geoffrey Chaucer, *Troilus and Criseyde*, ed. B. A. Windeatt (London & New York: Longman, 1984). All references to and citations of *Il Filostrato* (hereafter marked by book and stanza number) are taken from the parallel text of the Italian poem in Windeatt's edition; the English translations are based (with some variations) upon *The Filostrato of Giovanni Boccaccio*, trans. and ed. Nathaniel E. Griffin and Arthur B. Myrick (Philadelphia: University of Pennsylvania Press, 1929). Chaucer was familiar with Benoît de Sainte-Maure's *Roman de Troie* where the story of Troilus and Criseyde was first told, and occasionally (especially in the *Troilus* IV and V) follows it in

preference to *Il Filostrato*. (Boccaccio himself knew Benoît's work through its Latin prose redaction, Guido delle Colonne's *Historia Trojana*.) The *Filostrato* was translated into French prose by one Beauveau, and Chaucer almost certainly read this work; there are instances where his narrative is closer to the *Roman de Troyle et de Criseide* than to Boccaccio's Italian. See Stephen A. Barney's Introduction to *Troilus and Criseyde*, pp. 471–72, and his notes pp. 1021–22 in the *Riverside Chaucer*. My own discussion of the poem, however, assumes that the *Troilus/Filostrato* relationship is the substantial one as regards Chaucer's overall narrative strategy; in this I differ from Winthrop Wetherbee, who argues, in *Chaucer and the Poets: an Essay on Troilus and Criseyde* (Ithaca: Cornell University Press, 1984), that the *Troilus* displays its narrator's growing engagement, first with such pagan *poetae* as Virgil, Ovid, and Statius, and eventually with the model Christian poet, Dante; for Wetherbee, Chaucer's revision of the Boccaccian narrative merely provides the *occasion* for the telling of a very different story.

2 The line counts are those of Sanford B. Meech, *Design in Chaucer's Troilus* (Syracuse: Syracuse University Press, 1959), p. 433 (note 13). Meech gives 1462·5 as the equivalent figure for Troilus.

3 The comparative lengths (number of lines) of corresponding books of *Il Filostrato* and the *Troilus* are as follows:

Filostrato		*Troilus*	
I	46	I	1092
II	1144	II	1757
III	752	III	1820
IV	1336	IV	1701
V	568		
VI	272		
VII	848	V	1869
VIII	264		
IX	64		
	5704 total		8239 total

The narrative of Book I of *Il Filostrato* is covered by lines 1–546 of Book I of the *Troilus*; the remainder of the latter takes us up to II. 34 in *Il Filostrato*.

4 Indeed, one Renaissance reader succumbed to this temptation: the "J. S.," who composed a verse paraphrase of Chaucer's poem in the 1630s refused to "translate" beyond Book III. See *A Seventeenth-Century Modernization of the First Three Books of Chaucer's Troilus and Criseyde*, ed. H. G. Wright (Bern: Francke Verlag, 1960).

5 Extrapolating the relative proportions of rising (Books I–II), consummatory (III) and falling (IV–V) action from the number of lines of poetic narrative devoted to each movement, we arrive at ratios of 1·7:1·1:2·2 for the *Troilus* – ratios which deviate far less

from the ideal symmetry of 2 : 1 : 2 than the corresponding ratios of Books I–II, III, and IV–IX of *Il Filostrato*, which stand at 1·4:0·65: 2·95. For a suggestive discussion of structural parallels in the poem, see in particular Alice S. Miskimin, *The Renaissance Chaucer* (New Haven: Yale University Press, 1975), p. 199.

6 Gerry Brenner, in "Narrative Structure in Chaucer's *Troilus and Criseyde*," *Annuale Mediaevale*, 6 (1965): 5–18 also identifies a double narrative strategy in the poem, but Brenner chooses to contrast "the surface harmony that narrative repetition creates" with "the underlying chaos that inverted parallels, ironic foreshadowing, and multiple points of view wreak upon it" (p. 13). He associates the former with the conventions of romance narrative, the latter with Chaucer's subversion and "transcendence" of those conventions (p. 8). My discussion, by contrast, associates the dilatory and additive construction of "mere" repetition with the subversive delays and desires of romance, and the web of often disturbing inverted/ironic parallels in *Troilus and Criseyde* with Chaucer's refining of orthodox *de casibus* tragedy through the use of mimetic form.

7 Few critics of the *Troilus* do not have something to say about Chaucer's narrative strategies, and the following catalogue is necessarily selective. The most detailed study of the *Troilus/Filostrato* relationship is perhaps Sanford B. Meech's *Design in Chaucer's Troilus*, which catalogues differences and similarities in plot, characterization, imagery, etc. between the two works, without, however, drawing many interpretive conclusions from the material amassed. Barry Windeatt's "Chaucer and the *Filostrato*" offers a brief but suggestive comparison of the poems, focusing in particular on Chaucer's finely tuned "translations and transvaluations" – small-scale modulations in content and emphasis in passages of close paraphrase; see *Chaucer and the Italian Trecento*, ed. Piero Boitani (Cambridge: Cambridge University Press, 1983), pp. 163–83. Books and articles of more general scope whose insights into the re-production aspect of the creation of *Troilus and Criseyde* I have found useful include Morton W. Bloomfield, "Distance and Predestination in *Troilus and Criseyde*," *PMLA* 72 (1957): 14–26; G. T. Shepherd, "*Troilus and Criseyde*" in *Chaucer and Chaucerians: Critical Studies in Middle English Literature*, ed. D. S. Brewer (University, Alabama: University of Alabama Press, 1966), pp. 65–87; Robert O. Payne's chapter on *Troilus and Criseyde* in *The Key of Remembrance*; and Eugene Vance, "'Mervelous Signals': Sign Theory and the Politics of Metaphor in Chaucer's *Troilus and Criseyde*" in *Mervelous Signals: Poetics and*

Sign Theory in the Middle Ages (Lincoln: University of Nebraska Press, 1986), pp. 256–310. Piero Boitani's *English Medieval Narrative in the Thirteenth and Fourteenth Centuries*, trans. Joan K. Hall (Cambridge: Cambridge University Press, 1982) has a useful chapter on the *Troilus* (pp. 193–226); Robert M. Jordan's "The Narrator in Chaucer's *Troilus*," *ELH* 25 (1958): 237–57, and his chapter on the *Troilus* in *Chaucer and the Shape of Creation: The Aesthetic Possibilities of Inorganic Structure* (Cambridge, Mass.: Harvard University Press, 1967) discuss dilation and repetition in Chaucerian narrative. Structural(ist) readings of the *Troilus* narrative tend towards the descriptive rather than the interpretive and include William Provost, *The Structure of Chaucer's Troilus and Criseyde* (Copenhagen: Rosenkilde and Bagger, 1974) and Stephenie Yearwood, "The Rhetoric of Narrative Rendering in Chaucer's *Troilus*," *ChauR* 12 (1977): 27–37.

8 In the immediate context of my discussion of Chaucer's subversive augmentation of Boccaccio, "the narrator" refers to the loquacious and somewhat naive persona invented by the poet to voice a sympathetic engagement with his characters and to chafe at the ending ordained by his sources: in the larger context of my reading of the *Troilus* as a network of multiple designs and plural voices, however, "the narrator" is something of an enabling fiction. *This* narrator has the most idiosyncratic voice in the poem, but he does not represent the totality of its designs upon us.

9 *Troilus and Criseyde* is, of course, some 2535 lines longer than *Il Filostrato*, and Chaucer only appropriated directly about 2730 lines of the Italian.

10 Little has been written about the role of the rhyme royal stanza in shaping the narrative of the *Troilus*. A. C. Spearing refers briefly to its "patterning" pressure in *Criticism and Medieval Poetry* (New York: Barnes & Noble, 1964), p. 98. Paull F. Baum has a few words to say on its recurring rhymes and occasional double syntax in *Chaucer's Verse* (Durham, N.C.: Duke University Press, 1961), pp. 44; 85–86. A suggestive early article by G. H. Cowling identifies the repeated appearance of a "volta" in the stanza (most frequently after its fourth line) followed by amplification or restatement, but Cowling only uses this observation to advance a theory of dating for the *Troilus* and other Chaucerian rhyme royal narratives. See "A Note on Chaucer's Stanza," *RES* 2 (1926): 311–17.

11 In Book 1 of the *Troilus*, for example, 57 (out of 156) stanzas offer clear examples of "floating" fourth or fifth lines while a further 26 offer somewhat less elegant, but nevertheless workable ones – a

total frequency of 54·8 percent. The "dilatory," centrally elaborative stanzas begin at the following lines (I have asterisked the less perfect ones and indicated whether the "floating" line is the fourth or fifth in the stanza):
1(4)*; 15(5); 36(5); 43(5); 50(5)*; 57(5); 85(5); 92(4); 106(4); 113(4)*; 120(4); 141(4)*; 148(5)*; 155(4); 169(5); 176(5); 190(5); 197(5); 204(4)*; 211(4); 248(5)*; 253(4); 260(5)*; 267(4); 274(4)*; 295(5)*; 309(5); 323(5); 330(5); 337(5)*; 344(4)*; 379(4)*; 386(5)*; 407(4); 414(5); 421(4); 442(4); 449(4); 491(4); 498(5); 505(5); 512(4); 519(5)*; 526(4); 547(4)*; 554(4)*; 561(4); 568(4); 631(5); 666(4)*; 708(4); 715(4); 722(4); 736(4)*; 743(4)*; 750(5); 757(4)*; 778(5); 785(4); 792(5)*; 799(5); 813(5)*; 841(4)*; 855(5); 862(4); 869(4); 876(4); 890(5)*; 925(5)*; 932(4); 939(4); 946(5); 953(4); 967(4); 981(4); 1002(4); 1009(5); 1023(4); 1037(5); 1044(4); 1058(4); 1065(4); 1072(4).

12 Compare *Il Filostrato* I.25. The use of proverbs and sententiae is much increased in Chaucer's narrative: Bartlett J. Whiting counts 5 proverbs and 21 sententiae in *Il Filostrato* as compared with 61 proverbs and 67 sententiae in the *Troilus*. See *Chaucer's Use of Proverbs* (Cambridge, Mass.: Harvard University Press, 1934).

13 Nor is this phenomenon entirely limited to the rising action. Diomede, who has only one chance to press his suit in Boccaccio, does so twice (on the ride from Troy and later in the Greek camp) in Book v of the *Troilus*.

14 I am indebted to Jordan, *Chaucer and the Shape of Creation* (p. 78), for this observation. Jordan also offers an extended account of the dilation through repetition of Book III's consummation scene (pp. 91–92).

15 See also Charles A. Owen, Jr., "Mimetic Form in the Central Love Scene of *Troilus and Criseyde*," *MP* 67 (1969): 125–32. We might note also that Pandarus visits each of the lovers the morning after their night together, while in *Il Filostrato* Pandaro visits only Troiolo.

16 Davis Taylor has identified certain general affinities of the hero's discourse with the lyric mode, in particular Troilus' use of superlatives and absolute commitments, and his addiction to the monologue. See "The Terms of Love: A Study of Troilus' Style," in *Chaucer's Troilus: Essays in Criticism*, ed. Stephen A. Barney (Hamden: Archon Books, 1980), pp. 231–56. See also A. C. Spearing, *Chaucer: Troilus and Criseyde* (London: E. Arnold, 1976), pp. 20; 41.

17 Boccaccio gives Troiolo such lengthy formal complaints that the

actual *amount* of embedded lyric in the *Troilus* seems no greater than in the Italian poem, but its interpenetration of Criseyde's (and the narrator's) universe ensures that the lyric mode infiltrates, even saturates, Chaucer's narrative in a more generalized manner.

18 G. L. Kittredge argued that Guillaume de Machaut's lay *Le Paradis D'Amour* was the source for Antigone's song; more recently James I. Wimsatt has suggested a more generalized Machauvian influence upon the song's themes and diction. See G. L. Kittredge, "Chaucer's *Troilus* and Guillaume de Machaut," *MLN* 30 (1915): 69; James I. Wimsatt, "Guillaume de Machaut and Chaucer's *Troilus and Criseyde*," *Medium Aevum* 45 (1976): 277–93.

19 These are articulated by both narrator and protagonists and I offer a tentative list (tentative because the line between narrative and lyric is so tenuous in this episode) of their occurrences in the consummation scene: III. 1226–46 (narrator); 1254–74 (Troilus); 1353–58 (Troilus' brief lyric address to Criseyde's eyes); 1422–42 (Criseyde's *aubade*); 1454–70 (Troilus' *aubade*). Most of this material is original to Chaucer, although Troilus' *aubade* does appear in a much shorter form in Boccaccio (*Fil.* III. 45–46) as does a less elaborate version of the address to Criseyde's eyes (*Fil.* III. 36). In his chapter on the *Troilus* in *Style and Consciousness in Middle English Narrative* (Princeton: Princeton University Press, 1983), John M. Ganim argues that the world with which Book III ends is the emphatically *lyric* universe of the *alba* (pp. 93–94).

20 Robert Payne, for example, counts ten (*The Key of Remembrance*, p. 185), William Provost identifies thirteen (*Structure of Chaucer's Troilus and Criseyde*, p. 100), while in "The French Lyric Element in *Troilus and Criseyde*," *YES* 15 (1985): 18–32, James I. Wimsatt's catalogue of "developed lyric passages" in *Troilus* runs to fifty-six (Wimsatt is arguing that the structure of the *Troilus* is heavily influenced by the overwhelming lyricality of the fourteenth-century *dit amoreux*). See also Boitani, *English Medieval Narrative*, p. 220.

21 "Mervelous Signals," p. 270. Vance identifies certain lyrical "cores" in the poem, which he perceives as marking the main "stations" in the progress of passion (271). He is more interested, however, in constructing a Jakobsonian dyad contrasting the "exclamatory" and "paradigmatic" axis of lyric with the "constitutive" and "syntagmatic" axis of narrative (274), than in the possibility that the embedded lyric may have a special function in plotting the extended poetic narrative.

22 *Troilus* I. 547–875; *Il Filostrato* II. 1–20.

23 Criseyde also engages in rhetorical delaying actions – far more

than Boccaccio's Criseida. Her speeches during Pandarus' first attempt to secure her love for Troilus add over a hundred lines to the corresponding scene in *Il Filostrato* (*Troilus* II. 220–595; *Fil.* II. 35–67). In Book III, when she is faced with the suggestion that Troilus thinks her unfaithful, she launches into several stanzas in the high style on the transitoriness of earthly happiness (III. 812–40).

24 It is not my purpose here to offer an exhaustive analysis of Chaucer's web of allusion/textual appropriation in the *Troilus*; I refer the reader to Barney's detailed notes in *The Riverside Chaucer*; Wetherbee's *Chaucer and the Poets* (which offers some particularly fresh insights on *Troilus and Criseyde*'s relations with the *Metamorphoses* and the *Roman de la Rose*); Howard H. Schless, *Chaucer and Dante: A Revaluation* (Norman, Oklahoma: Pilgrim Books, 1984), pp. 101–47; Karla Taylor, *Chaucer Reads The Divine Comedy* (Stanford: Stanford University Press, 1989); John M. Fyler, *Chaucer and Ovid* (New Haven: Yale University Press, 1979); Wimsatt, "Guillaume de Machaut and Chaucer's *Troilus and Criseyde*," and, for Chaucer and Boethius, Ida L. Gordon, *The Double Sorrow of Troilus: A Study of Ambiguities in Troilus and Criseyde* (Oxford: Clarendon Press, 1970).

25 On the use of proverbs in the *Troilus* see Whiting, *Chaucer's Use of Proverbs*, and also Karla Taylor's fine essay "Proverbs and the Authentication of Convention in *Troilus and Criseyde*," in Barney, *Chaucer's Troilus: Essays in Criticism*, pp. 277–96.

26 The equivalent passage in *Il Filostrato* is II. 10 (= *Troilus* I. 624–30); II. 11 of *Il Filostrato* is taken up at I. 666 of the *Troilus*.

27 The terminology is that of Karla Taylor, "Proverbs and the Authentication of Convention," p. 285.

28 Chaucer has his own narrator discuss the "in-eching" of supplementary narrative detail at III. 1329. Windeatt borrows the term in his discussion of Chaucer's textual "thickening" of Boccaccio; see the introduction to his edition of *Troilus and Criseyde*, p. 5ff., and "Chaucer and the *Filostrato*."

29 Indeed James I. Wimsatt suggests that, while the ambiguities of the *Troilus* manage to subvert any possibility of the narrative's absolute allegiance to the ideals of Dantean epic, Machauvian romance, or Boethian demonstration, its striking "realism" is never undercut: "Realism in *Troilus and Criseyde* and the *Roman de la Rose*," *Chaucer Studies III: Essays on Troilus and Criseyde*, ed. Mary Salu (Totowa: Rowman and Littlefield, 1979), pp. 43–56. Charles Muscatine discusses the "realism" in the *Troilus* in relation to Chaucer's use of the "bourgeois" style in portraying Pandarus

and Criseyde in *Chaucer and the French Tradition: A Study in Style and Meaning* (Berkeley and Los Angeles: University of California Press, 1957), p. 131ff.

30 Boccaccio's characters can shift from point A to point B within a couple of lines: Pandaro leaves Troiolo at *Il Filostrato* II. 34.3 and is "where Criseida dwelt" by line 4. When Pandarus leaves his friend at the close of Book I of the *Troilus*, he first spends at least one night at home (II. 62–3); the next morning he has to get up (II. 71), make his way "unto his neces palays ther biside" (II. 76), enquire of the servants her whereabouts (II. 79), actually enter the building (II. 80), and penetrate further to a "paved parlour" (II. 82) before he finally sits down beside her on a bench (II. 91). In the scenes which follow in *Il Filostrato*, Pandaro and Criseida seek out a more secluded "loggia" (*Fil.* II. 34) where they remain until he departs. Criseida then retires to her room (II. 68) and is still there when the narrator returns to Troiolo at II. 84. In Chaucer's narrative, by contrast, after the conversation between Pandarus and Criseyde the lady goes to her closet (II. 599), from whose window she peers out when Troilus rides by – only to bring her head back in hastily (II. 857). Following her meditations on love, she goes downstairs to her garden (II. 813–14), whose general layout we learn (II. 820–22). When night falls she re-enters the house (II. 910) and then retires to her bedroom (II. 914). Chaucer, moreover, pays more attention to material surroundings and possessions: chimney pieces and candles (III. 1141), furred cloaks (III. 738) and cushions (III. 964); sanded paths (II. 822), benches (II. 91; 822), books (II. 86; 95; III. 980) and bedstands (III. 954). We are told, too, what people are doing with their bodies: when they sit down and stand up, or stroll around, or cast their eyes down (II. 142) or catch somebody by the corner of his garment (II. 448; III. 792).

31 So that (in view of Boccaccio's longer stanzaic unit) there is perhaps in some cases simultaneous condensation and expansion of the source.

32 For a discussion of Chaucer's manipulation of Boethian borrowings for potentially ironic ends, see Gordon, *Double Sorrow of Troilus*, pp. 40–60.

33 For a concise but remarkably rich discussion of the poem's complicated relationship and negotiations with pre-existing generic categories, see Barry Windeatt, "Classical and Medieval Elements in Chaucer's *Troilus*," in *The European Tragedy of Troilus*, ed. Piero Boitani (Oxford: Clarendon Press, 1989), pp. 111–31.

34 Barbara Nolan, in *Chaucer and the Tradition of the Roman Antique* (Cambridge: Cambridge University Press, 1992), argues that

Boccaccio conceived *Il Filostrato* as a poem in the tradition of learned "Ovidian" *artes* and *remedia amoris.*

35 For a discussion of the epic aspects of the *Troilus*, see John P. McCall, "The Trojan Scene in Chaucer's *Troilus*," *ELH* 29 (1962): 263–75; also Bloomfield, "Distance and Predestination," pp. 16–17. Christopher C. Baswell and Paul B. Taylor, in "The 'Faire Queene Eleyne' in Chaucer's *Troilus*," *Speculum* 63 (1988): 293–311, argue that "...the genre of the *Troilus* shifts brilliantly but troublingly between public and private, epic and romance, shuttling the reader's attention from the invocation of the muses to lengthy and nuanced psychological analysis, from civic council to emotional crisis, from battlefield to bedchamber" (p. 293).

36 This phenomenon is also evident in the (non-Boccaccian) comparison of Troilus' state, once he is finally in his lady's arms, to the rewards of the patient Christian brought to heaven after "sondry peynes" (III. 1204). (We have a similar conflation of the sacred and secular vocabularies when Chrétien de Troyes' Lancelot genuflects before Guinevere in her bedroom as if he were in the shrine of a saint.)

37 A useful tabulation of instances of the narrator's overt interference may be found in Appendix A of Bernard F. Huppé's "The Unlikely Narrator: Narrative Strategy in the *Troilus*," *Signs and Symbols in Chaucer's Poetry*, ed. J. P. Hermann and John J. Burke, Jr. (University: University of Alabama Press, 1981), pp. 179–94.

38 E. Talbot Donaldson, "Criseyde and Her Narrator," *Speaking of Chaucer* (New York: Norton, 1970), pp. 65–83.

39 The figures are those of Meech, *Design in Chaucer's Troilus*, p. 433, note 15.

40 Pandarus' relationship with the narrator of the *Troilus* has been widely discussed, although relatively little has been said about the relationship between Pandarus' "makings" and the amplificatory designs of *Troilus and Criseyde* or about the fabulation vacuum left in the poem by his regression back into his Boccaccian role after Book III. I am, however, indebted to the observations of Boitani, *Medieval English Narrative*, pp. 195; 216–17; Evan Carton, "Complicity and Responsibility in Pandarus's Bed and Chaucer's Art," *PMLA* 94 (1979): 47–61; E. Talbot Donaldson, "Chaucer's Three 'P''s: Pandarus, Pardoner and Poet," *Michigan Quarterly Review* 14 (1975): 282–301; Fyler, *Chaucer and Ovid*, pp. 128–38; Adrienne Lockhart, "Semantic, Moral and Aesthetic Degeneration in *Troilus and Criseyde*," *ChauR* 8 (1973): 100–18; Alice S. Miskimin, *The Renaissance Chaucer*, p. 173ff.; Spearing, *Chaucer: Troilus and Criseyde*, p. 46; Karla Taylor, *Chaucer Reads The Divine Comedy*,

pp. 51–53; Thomas A. Van, "Chaucer's Pandarus as an Earthly Maker," *Southern Humanities Review* 12 (1978): 89–97; Vance, "'Mervelous Signals,'" pp. 281; 298; Richard Waswo, "The Narrator of *Troilus and Criseyde*," *ELH* 50 (1983): 1–25; Rose A. Zimbardo, "Creator and Created: The Generic Perspective of Chaucer's *Troilus and Criseyde*," *ChauR* 11 (1977): 283–98, in particular 292ff.

41 The go-between's ties with the narrator are reinforced by telling parallels between their diction; compare, for example the narrator at I. 19–21 and Pandarus at I. 1042–43, and see Karla Taylor, "Proverbs and the Authentication of Convention," p. 290. Many readers have noted that the role of Pandarus as alternative maker is further suggested by his association with the poetic practices recommended by Geoffroi de Vinsauf, a passage from whose *Poetria Nova* Chaucer closely translates at I. 1065–71 and puts into the mouth of his go-between. (For the original, see *Les Arts Poétiques du xiie et du xiiie Siècle*, ed. Edmond Faral [Paris: E. Champion, 1924], p. 194.)

42 For a discussion of Pandarus as a maker of romance who in effect "counterfeits" Criseyde by making her a character in his fictions, see R. Allen Shoaf, "Dante's *Commedia* and Chaucer's Theory of Mediation: A Preliminary Sketch," *New Perspectives in Chaucer Criticism*, ed. Donald M. Rose (Norman: Pilgrim Books Inc., 1981), pp. 96–98; 101–2. Pandaro offers only one really concentrated stanza on the "pitiless beauty" theme in his first meeting with Criseida (*Fil.* II. 64); Pandarus dilates upon the subject for some thirty lines.

43 By the end of the poem, Pandarus' propensity for treating the love affair as a kind of text will have proved contagious. Troilus says that, as far as his suffering at Love's hands is concerned, "Men myght a book make of it, lik a storie" (V. 585). Criseyde sadly anticipates that her betrayal of Troilus will be the subject of songs and books (V. 1058–61). Neither of their remarks are in Boccaccio.

44 See, for example, Troilus' remarks at I. 835–50, Pandarus' at I. 851–54, and Criseyde's at III. 813ff.

45 For an extended discussion of the parallels between the condition of Troy and that of the lovers, see McCall, "The Trojan Scene."

46 See Shepherd, "Troilus and Criseyde," p. 82 – but see also pp. 64–65 of this chapter, where I argue that this attractive formula must eventually be modified.

47 But see Nolan, *Chaucer and the Tradition of the Roman Antique*, for an argument that *Il Filostrato* has its own symmetries.

48 Noted by Monica E. McAlpine, *The Genre of Troilus and Criseyde* (Ithaca: Cornell University Press, 1978), p. 157.

49 Vance briefly addresses the "manifest destiny" of certain "rhyme equivalences" in the *Troilus* – in particular the pairing *joye/Troye* – in "'Mervelous Signals,'" p. 278.

50 The *routhe/trouthe* rhyme appears at I. 582–84; I. 769–70; II. 349–50; II. 489–90; II. 664–65; II. 1138–39; II. 1280–81; II. 1502–3; III. 120–22; III. 1511–1512; IV. 1476–77; IV. 1490–91; IV. 1609–10; IV. 1672–73; V. 1000–1; V. 1098–99; V. 1385–86; V. 1586–87; V. 1686–87. *Rewe/trewe* occurs at II. 786–89; II. 1609–10; III. 114–17; III. 1770–71; IV. 1528–31; V. 706–7; V. 1070–71; V. 1364–65.

51 The various connotations which Chaucer gives the word *trouthe* in *The Franklin's Tale* and the "Balade de Bon Conseyl" (which modern editors give the alternative title "Truth") suggest its semantic range in his *oeuvre*. We should note, though, that some of the territory covered by the modern "truth" would be divided with "sooth" or "sothe" in Middle English. See also Spearing, *Chaucer: Troilus and Criseyde*, pp. 37–38, and Vance, "'Mervelous Signals,'" pp. 333–35.

52 The corresponding "Why I gave you my love speech" in *Il Filostrato*, interestingly, is spoken by Troiolo – who mentions neither Criseida's fidelity nor her pity, but mainly praises her noble manners.

53 *Herte/smerte* rhymes occur at I. 792–94; II. 930–31; II. 1096–97; II. 1287–88; III. 146–47; III. 904–6; III. 947–50; III. 1000–1; III. 1182–83; IV. 240–43; IV. 426–27; IV. 1140–41; IV. 1184–86; IV. 1448–49; IV. 1618–20; V. 62–63; V. 132–33; V. 198–201; V. 722–24; V. 1049–50; V. 1224–25; V. 1324–26; V. 1420–21. *Troye/joye* rhymes occur at I. 2–4; I. 118–19; I. 608–9; II. 139–40; II. 643–44; II. 748–49; II. 881–82; III. 356–57; III. 790–91; III. 874–75; III. 1441–42; III. 1450–52; III. 1714–15; IV. 55–56; IV. 90–91; IV. 274–76; IV. 335–36; IV. 1441–42; IV. 1630–31; V. 27–28; V. 118–19; V. 393–95; V. 426–27; V. 608–9; V. 615–16; V. 729–31; V. 779–81; V. 930–31; V. 1380–82; V. 1546–47.

54 Compare Troilus' first conversation with his lady, in which he avows he will "with good herte al holly youre talent / Receyven wel, how sore that me smerte; / Lo this mene I, myn owen swete herte" (III. 145–47).

55 Meech (*Design in Chaucer's Troilus*, pp. 158–65) observes Chaucer's introduction of many new references to death in the *Troilus*, but draws no interpretive conclusions therefrom. See also Windeatt, "Chaucer and the *Filostrato*," pp. 171–72. The "death references" in Book III occur at (and this is a conservative list) lines 63; 103; 110; 112; 118–19; 379ff.; 798; 805; 904–5; 1049; 1071; 1171; 1292; 1483; 1499–1503; 1614; 1697.

56 Of related interest here is Eugene Vance's notion of "figurativity

as primal violence" in *Troilus and Criseyde*; "'Mervelous Signals,'" p. 284.

57 Pandarus' long speech at II. 316–85, telling Criseyde of Troilus' love for her and imploring her to pity him, contains no less than fourteen death references. In Troilus' first speech to his lady he refers three times (III. 103; 110; 112) to the possibility of death in her service. Criseyde's immediate response to Pandarus' fiction of Troilus' jealousy is to claim that she has lived too long (III. 805).

58 Recent discussion of the ending of *Troilus and Criseyde* has tended to suggest that the final voice of the poem represents (a) Chaucer the Poet finally taking over from his unreliable and all too partial narrator, or (b) a merging of the poet's voice with the narrator's as the latter belatedly realizes what his story has *really* been about. (For view [a] see, for example, Gordon, *The Double Sorrow of Troilus*; for view [b] see, for example, E. F. Dyck, "Ethos, Pathos and Logos in *Troilus and Criseyde*," *ChauR* 20 [1986]: 176 and Stephen Manning, "*Troilus*, Book V: Invention and the Poem as Process," *ChauR* 188 [1984]: 288–303.) It will already be clear that my own reading of the poem assumes a more complex polyphony of narrative voices – a polyphony in which the final privileging of any one "narrator" or "poet" may be much more problematic.

59 *S/Z*, p. 76.

60 Of the many critics who have tangled with the ending of the *Troilus* I have found the following particularly helpful: Robert B. Burlin, *Chaucerian Fiction* (Princeton: Princeton University Press, 1977), p. 132ff; Donaldson, "The Ending of Chaucer's *Troilus*" in *Speaking of Chaucer*, pp. 84–101; Manning, "*Troilus*, Book V"; McAlpine, *The Genre of Troilus and Criseyde*, pp. 139–43 (I am indebted to her for the point about the non-sequitur nature of Troilus' death at Achilles' hands); A. C. Spearing, "Narrative Closure: the End of *Troilus and Criseyde*," *Readings in Medieval Poetry* (Cambridge: Cambridge University Press, 1987), pp. 107–33; John M. Steadman, *Disembodied Laughter: Troilus and the Apotheosis Tradition* (Berkeley & Los Angeles: University of California Press, 1972); Karla Taylor, *Chaucer Reads the Divine Comedy*, pp. 187–209; Waswo, "The Narrator of *Troilus and Criseyde*," pp. 18–21; Wetherbee, *Chaucer and the Poets*, pp. 224–43.

61 Cf. Waswo, "The Narrator of *Troilus and Criseyde*," p. 12.

62 Huppé, "The Unlikely Narrator," p. 179. And see also Dyck, "Ethos, Pathos and Logos," p. 176.

63 *Paradiso* 14. 28–30.

64 See Kaminsky, *Chaucer's Troilus and Criseyde and the Critics*, for the critical battle over the genre of *Troilus and Criseyde*, and also

Windeatt, "Classical and Medieval Elements in Chaucer's *Troilus*." Several critics discuss the play of literary kinds within the poem. Andrea Clough, in "Medieval Tragedy and the Genre of *Troilus and Criseyde*," *Medievalia et Humanistica* ns 11 (1982): 211–27, argues that it offers an example of "romance tragedy," uniting the "imaginative empathy" of romance with the "moral objectivity" of *de casibus* tragedy (p. 219). McAlpine (*The Genre of Troilus and Criseyde*) presents a detailed and useful analysis of the interwoven dynamics of *de casibus* tragedy and Boethian comedy in the poem. Muscatine (*Chaucer and the French Tradition*) discusses the relationship between Troilus's secular idealism, articulated in the "high style" of courtly romance, Pandarus' pragmatism, with its pull towards bourgeois "realism," and the poet's more complex, synthesizing vision. Zimbardo ("Creator and Created") associates the creator/created disjunction in the work with the struggle between the genres of tragedy and romance for control over its interpretation.

65 Northrop Frye, in *The Secular Scripture: A Study of the Structure of Romance* (Cambridge, Mass.: Harvard University Press, 1976), describes romance as the "and then" narrative mode of addition and supplementation (p. 47); see also Parker, *Inescapable Romance.*

66 A. C. Spearing remarks that "poetry has the advantage over philosophy of being able to say different things, and even contradictory things, at the same time." See "Narrative Closure: the End of *Troilus and Criseyde*," p. 133.

67 Cf. Zimbardo, "Creator and Created," p. 288.

68 See *The Riverside Chaucer*, p. 328; lines 1084–85. Steadman (*Disembodied Laughter*, p. 154) observes that the language Chaucer uses to condemn "wordly vanities" at the close of the *Troilus* (v. 1837) is turned against the *Troilus* itself (along with other works) in the Retraction following the *Canterbury Tales*.

3 THE END OF QUESTING, THE QUEST FOR AN ENDING: CIRCUMSCRIBED VISION IN *THE FAERIE QUEENE*, BOOK VI

1 See Spenser's "Letter to Raleigh" (first printed after the 1590 edition of Books I–III), reprinted in *The Faerie Queene*, ed. Thomas P. Roche, Jr. *et al.* (New Haven: Yale University Press, 1981), p. 15.

2 This chapter's account of the perplexed relations between the diachronic narrative of quest and the synchronic poetry of vision in *The Faerie Queene* takes up some issues raised by Kenneth Gross in

Spenserian Poetics: Idolatry, Iconoclasm and Magic (Ithaca: Cornell University Press, 1985), especially his discussion of the "tenuous" and "oblique" relations between the poem's "most potent visions of harmony and restitution" and the progression of its various quests (p. 15).

3 "Letter to Raleigh," Roche, p. 16.

4 For a contrary view see Jan Karel Kouwenhoven, *Apparent Narrative as Thematic Metaphor: The Organization of The Faerie Queene* (Oxford: Clarendon Press, 1983). Kouwenhoven insists that the poem offers only the "illusion of narrative," (p. 10) but never quite explains why Spenser expends so much energy in creating this illusion, and in embedding within his poem the many allusions and parallels that invite us to read it in the context of other narrative works. Unwilling to abandon the mediating term "fiction" (e.g. p. 10, p. 30) to describe whatever it is that constitutes the vehicle for Spenserian allegory, Kouwenhoven nevertheless does not inform us why it is safer to use *this* potentially loaded term rather than "narrative" when one argues that *The Faerie Queene* does not represent or redescribe truth within the context of fallen time and fallen narrative but fulfills it by imitating a time already redeemed, a time which transcends narrative.

5 Susanne Lindgren Wofford, in "Britomart's Petrarchan Lament: Allegory and Narrative in *The Faerie Queene* III, iv," *Comparative Literature* 39 (1987): 28–57, argues that *The Faerie Queene*'s narrative line is in perpetual and resonant flux: alternately privileging "narrative" and "allegorical" significance, its "overdetermined images" produce a poetic discourse underpinned by "a logic of both [narrative]/and [allegory]" (42). Although Wofford does not explicitly address Kouwenhoven's polemic, her essay in effect offers a rebuttal to his view of the poem.

6 Angus Fletcher in *The Prophetic Moment: An Essay on Spenser* (Chicago: University of Chicago Press, 1971) identifies five "matrices" – Biblical, Virgilian, Ovidian, Galfridian and Hermetic – which generate in various ways the narrative of *The Faerie Queene.* My own reading of the poem, however, centers on my identification of its self-generated "matrix" which substantially subsumes or modifies the influence of other texts.

7 James Nohrnberg offers a copious discussion of the way consecutive books and opposing books (i.e. 1/6, 2/5) illuminate each other in *The Analogy of The Faerie Queene* (Princeton: Princeton University Press, 1976), and see also Fletcher, *The Prophetic Moment*, p. 57ff. My own interests, however, center upon the revisionary *narrative* recapitulation evident when all six books are superimposed on

each other. The nearest approximation to my own practice is perhaps A. Bartlett Giamatti's account of the total design of the poem in *Play of Double Senses: Spenser's Faerie Queene* (Englewood Cliffs: Prentice-Hall, 1975), pp. 67–77.

8 Joanne Field Holland, "The Cantos of Mutabilitie and the Form of *The Faerie Queene*," *ELH* 35 (1968): 27.

9 Patricia Parker, *Inescapable Romance*, p. 76. And see also Maureen Quilligan, *Milton's Spenser: The Politics of Reading* (Ithaca: Cornell University Press, 1983), p. 168.

10 All references to and quotations from *The Faerie Queene* will be noted parenthetically by book, canto and stanza number, except during extended discussions of Book VI, when only canto and stanza number will be given.

11 Spenser makes it clear from the outset that he desires to offer "solaas" as well as "sentence" in his work: he excuses the overlay of romance and of allegorical conceit upon his moral epic by announcing that he is complying with "the vse of these dayes, seeing all things accounted by their showes, and nothing esteemed of, that is not delightfull and pleasing to commune sence" ("Letter to Raleigh," Roche, p. 16). As A. C. Hamilton suggests in *The Structure of Allegory in The Faerie Queene* (Oxford: Clarendon Press, 1961) Spenser is here playing with the fiction that his matter is a crowd-pleasing romance (p. 42). But by the close of Book VI, our author has become aware that any attempt to communicate "sentence" through poetry may be mutilated by uncharitable and malicious misreading: satisfying the cruder pleasures of inadequate readers is now not a means to a higher end but the only safe "end" of the poet.

12 I am here indebted to Kenneth Gross, "'Each Heav'nly Close': Mythologies and Metrics in Spenser and the Early Poetry of Milton," *PMLA* 98 (1983): 21–36.

13 William Nelson notes the "ambiguous note which characterizes the endings of... legends of *The Faerie Queene*, a compromise between the storyteller's demand for a resolution and the moralist's conviction that the world stands irresolute still." *The Poetry of Edmund Spenser: A Study* (New York: Columbia University Press, 1963), p. 294. I would argue that Book VI's ending bears witness to the disillusionment of both moralist *and* storyteller.

14 Goldberg, *Endlesse Worke*, p. xiv.

15 Parker, *Inescapable Romance*, p. 80: "apocalyptic movement towards revelation is countered by a movement towards multiplication and refraction." Harry Berger, Jr. hypothesizes, by contrast, that it is Redcrosse's frailty which rubs off on the poet as

he continues his work; "The Prospect of Imagination: Spenser and the Limits of Poetry," *SEL* 1 (1961): 97. But although Redcrosse falls badly, he also learns and recovers more than any other hero; he is, moreover, better able to remake the fallen world in his own purged and cleansed image than the later questers.

16 It might be argued that my "Fable" is simply the quest mythos common to many cultures in many eras. I shall suggest, however, that Book I's attempt to redeem the perpetual *in medias res* of the postlapsarian quest fiction renders Spenser's Fable a particularly complex and idiosyncratic version of this persistent narrative design.

17 For an interesting meditation on Spenserian "middle," see Debra Fried, "Spenser's Caesura," *ELR* 11 (1981): 261–80; in particular 278ff. Wofford (p. 55) argues that Spenser's poetry is "anti-apocalyptic"; while agreeing that *The Faerie Queene* unfolds in the middle time of fallen humanity, I would argue that its ability to achieve its narrative and didactic ends is dependent on its capacity to reinvoke, however briefly, beginnings and ends which transcend those of its "secular scripture."

18 John Guillory remarks that "[t]he closure of Book I, unlike the closure of Revelation... is broken by the continued wandering of the Redcrosse Knight," and proposes that as Spenser's narrative itself "wanders" farther and farther from Book I it gets drawn deeper into the ambiguities and duplicities of romance. *Poetic Authority*, p. 27.

19 On betrothal in *The Faerie Queene* see Fletcher, *The Prophetic Moment*, pp. 20–23.

20 See Ludovico Ariosto, *Orlando Furioso*, trans. Barbara Reynolds, (Harmondsworth: Penguin, 1975) canto iii; compare *The Faerie Queene* II. vii. 35–36 and III. iii. 9.

21 Goldberg, *Endlesse Worke*, p. 63.

22 Giamatti, *Play of Double Senses* p. 44, notes the sight/site pun.

23 The best piece of critical writing on Book VI is still Harry Berger Jr.'s essay "A Secret Discipline: *The Faerie Queene* Book VI," *Form and Convention in the Poetry of Edmund Spenser*, ed. William Nelson (New York: Columbia University Press, 1961), pp. 33–75. I am indebted to Berger throughout this chapter. I have also found the following studies of Book VI helpful: Richard Neuse, "Book VI as Conclusion to *The Faerie Queene*," *ELH* 35 (1968): 329–53; Arnold Williams, *Flower on a Lowly Stalk: The Sixth Book of The Faerie Queene* (East Lansing: Michigan State University Press, 1967); Humphrey Tonkin, *Spenser's Courteous Pastoral: Book VI of The Faerie Queene* (Oxford: Clarendon Press, 1972). Critics who offer

illuminating briefer treatments of the Legend of Courtesy include Isabel G. MacCaffrey, *Spenser's Allegory: The Anatomy of Imagination* (Princeton: Princeton University Press, 1976), pp. 343–402; Patricia Parker, *Inescapable Romance*, pp. 101–113; Nohrnberg, *The Analogy of The Faerie Queene*, pp. 656–733; Gary Waller, *English Poetry of the Sixteenth Century* (London and New York: Longman, 1986), pp. 194–205; Donald Cheney, *Spenser's Image of Nature: Wild Man and Shepherd in The Faerie Queene* (New Haven: Yale University Press, 1966); and Guillory, *Poetic Authority*, pp. 23–45.

24 *The Poetry of The Faerie Queene*, p. 22.

25 Of related interest here is Berger's account of the tensions between the poet's representation of the inner poetic journey and his experience of the outside world in Books v and vi; see "A Secret Discipline," pp. 36–37, and also Neuse, "Book vi as Conclusion," p. 331.

26 I am here indebted to Roger Sale, *Reading Spenser: An Introduction to The Faerie Queene* (New York; Random House, 1968), pp. 164–65; see also Berger, "The Prospect of Imagination," p. 107.

27 *Spenser's Allegory*, pp. 55–57. In *Poetic License: Authority and Authorship in Medieval and Renaissance Contexts* (New York and Oxford: Oxford University Press, 1986), Jacqueline T. Miller argues that, while a poetic fiction may seek to authorize its representation of the ideal by exploiting allegory's apparent rejection of the terms and structures of the fallen "real" world, it is always caught in the double bind that demands that it persuade its readers by way of a familiar – and fallen – discourse (pp. 73–87).

28 The titular virtues appear in their respective books as follows:

Holiness:	Arg.i and Arg.x.
Temperance:	Proem 5; i.31; i.58; iv.2; iv.33; v.1; Arg.ix; Arg.xi; xii.1.
Chastity:	Proem 1; Proem 5; iv.3; v.8; v.53; v.54; v.55; vi.2; vii.59; vii.60; viii.29; viii.42; viii.43; xi.6.
Friendship:	i.40; ii.12; ii.13; ii.18; ii.24; ii.29; iii.50; iv.1; iv.11; vi.46; ix.2; ix.3; x.27; x.34.
Justice:	Proem 3; Proem 9; Proem 10; Proem 11; i.2 (twice); i.3; i.5 (twice); i.6; i.30; ii.26 (twice); ii.36; iv.1 (three times); iv.2; vii.1; vii.2; vii.3; vii.4; vii.42; viii.20; viii.44; ix.36; ix.44; ix.49 (twice); x.1; x.3; xi.1; xii.26; xii.27; xii.40.
Courtesy:	Proem 4; Proem 5; Proem 6; i.1; i.26; i.27; i.41; i.45; ii.1; iii.9; iii.15; iii.21; iii.31; iii.39; iii.40; iii.41; iv.39; v.36; ix.18; ix.44; ix.45; x.23; x.27; xii.2.

29 For an extended discussion of linguistic play as a constitutive characteristic of Spenserian allegory see Quilligan, *The Language of Allegory*.

30 Waller discusses the tensions and contradictions which characterize Spenser's repeated attempts to define courtesy in *English Poetry of the Sixteenth Century*, p. 198.

31 Northrop Frye, "The Structure of Imagery in *The Faerie Queene*," *Fables of Identity: Studies in Poetic Mythology* (New York: Harcourt, Brace & World, 1963), p. 86. See also Giamatti, *Play of Double Senses*, p. 98, on courtesy at its best as a "secular sacrament." Tonkin (*Spenser's Courteous Pastoral*, pp. 226–37) offers a particularly rich discussion of the relationship of grace and the Graces, and Kenneth Gross's account of VI. x includes an interesting meditation on the overdetermined yet elusive quality of "grace" in a context where it becomes "simultaneously an agent, a quality, and a mode of action" (*Spenserian Poetics*, pp. 214–15).

32 Nohrnberg remarks that the "civill conversation" of VI.i.1 is the secular equivalent of the *Logos* underpinning Book I's Christian epic (*Analogy of The Faerie Queene*, p. 676).

33 Roger Ascham, *The Schoolmaster*, ed. Lawrence V. Ryan, (Charlottesville: University Press of Virginia, 1974), p. 42.

34 Ascham, *The Schoolmaster*, p. 43.

35 Patricia Parker (*Inescapable Romance*, p. 106) offers an interesting discussion of the tension between the fact that divine grace is by definition beyond any human control and the fact that human "grace" may be reduced to the art of control. Of course, the popularity of courtesy books in Renaissance Europe suggests that Spenser's contemporaries thought of courtesy as an acquirable art; at their most reductive, these manuals look like "how-to" books for social climbers. In Book I of Castiglione's emphatically elitist *Il Cortegiano*, it is suggested that, although one may polish and refine one's social graces, these must exist in embryo in one's nature. However, Castiglione's Count Lewis insists that grace should never appear less than spontaneous – one should "use in everye thing a certaine disgracing to cover arte withall" ("usar in ogni cosa una certa sprezzatura, che nasconda l'arte"). (See Baldassare Castiglione, *The Book of the Courtier*, trans. Sir Thomas Hoby [London; J. M. Dent and Sons, 1974], p. 46; Hoby's translation was first published in 1561.) Revealingly, the Count is less interested in the likelihood that too much superficial and artificial grace will make it impossible to discern inner gracefulness of spirit than in the fact that an overt show of artfulness may be unprofitable in the courtly world "for in case it be open it looseth credit cleane and maketh a man little set by" (Hoby translation,

p. 46: in the original, "perchè se è scoperta, leva in tutto il credito, e fa l'omo poco estimato"). He offers the sophisticated art of *sprezzatura*, of "disgracing" one's acquired graces, as a profitable substitute for an ideal of grace naturally integrated into the virtuous behavior of the individual. In "*Grazia, Sprezzatura, Affettazione* in *The Courtier*," *Castiglione: The Ideal and the Real in Renaissance Culture*, ed. Robert W. Hanning and David Rosand (New Haven: Yale University Press, 1983), pp. 45–67, Eduardo Saccone makes some suggestive remarks about the ironic nature of *sprezzatura*, and its function as a touchstone of "courtliness" (59–60). See also Daniel Javitch's discussion of the relations between grace and art in Castiglione and Spenser in *Poetry and Courtliness in Renaissance England* (Princeton: Princeton University Press, 1978).

36 Stefano Guazzo, *The Civile Conversation*, trans. George Pettie (New York: Alfred A. Knopf, 1925), Volumes I and II, p. 121.

37 This is the first time that the "despoyling" of a corpse has been normative behavior in *The Faerie Queene*: compare Arthur's defense in II. viii. 26–52 of Guyon's lifeless body and armor.

38 Cf. Cheney, *Spenser's Image of Nature*, p. 182.

39 *The Yale Edition of the Shorter Poems of Edmund Spenser*, ed. William A. Oram *et al.*, (New Haven: Yale University Press, 1989), p. 12, line 5 and p. 526.

40 Elizabeth J. Bellamy suggests that the Beast is "Babel itself, the diaspora of the logocentric word, the most serious threat yet in *The Faerie Queene* to the potential union of signifier and signified." "The Vocative and the Vocational: The Unreadability of Elizabeth in *The Faerie Queene*," *ELH* 54 (1987): 13. See also Gross, *Spenserian Poetics*, p. 229.

41 In the first canto of Book II, Redcrosse *is* congratulated for the "euerlasting fame" he has won, but it is the Palmer, not Guyon, who speaks, and he speaks only of the "heauenly Registers" where the hero's name is "enrolled": this fame is bestowed by God, not by the world (II. i. 32).

42 Greene, *The Descent From Heaven*, p. 228.

43 By my estimate, the total occurrences in II, III, IV and V are, respectively, 39, 45, 41, 37. Various critics have noted the role of fortune in Book VI (e.g. Tonkin, *Spenser's Courteous Pastoral*, p. 35; Cheney, *Spenser's Image of Nature*, p. 188); the methods (and thus the final totals) of those who actually carry out word counts differ from my own, but their results are consonant with my findings: see MacCaffrey, *Spenser's Allegory*, p. 371, note 1, and Michael F. N. Dixon, "Fairy Tale, Fortune and Boethian Wonder: Rhetorical Structure in Book VI of *The Faerie Queene*," *UTQ* 44 (1975): 145.

44 See Book I.i.29; ii.12; ii.25; ii.40; iii.5; v.10; vi.22; vi.27; vii.29; vii.47; vii.50; viii.19; ix.27; xi.29; xi.45.
Book II.i.5; i.35; i.51; ii.7; iii.6; iv.3; vi.47.
Book III.ii.22; v.18; vi.11; vii.27; vii.29; viii.11; viii.15; viii.29; ix.12; x.6; x.37.
Book IV.i.38; ii.30; iv.30; vi.19; vii.23; vii.42; viii.3; viii.6; viii.19; viii.51; xii.4.
Book V.ii.2; iii.29; iv.4; iv.10; iv.21; vi.19; viii.4; xi.10; xi.13; xii.4.
Book VI. i.4; i.11; ii.9; ii.15; ii.16; ii.33; iii.20; iii.21; iii.29; iii.46; iii.51; iv.2; iv.19; iv.25; iv.26; v.10; vi.19; viii.34; viii.36; viii.46; ix.2; ix.5; x.5; x.34; x.38; x.39; xi.3; xi.9; xi.27; xi.36; xi.51. (I have included within my computations instances of chance-generated incidents in stories-within-stories.)

45 See, for example, MacCaffrey, *Spenser's Allegory*, p. 388.

46 J. C. Maxwell notes the dislocation of the relationship between the typical vice and the central virtue of Book VI; the Beast attacks not those who *fail* to be courteous but those who *are* courteous. See "The Truancy of Calidore," *ELH* 19 (1952): 148. The characters we encounter in Book VI are fully aware of the instability of their universe; see Calidore's remarks at i.41 and Aldus's Boethian lament at iii.5.

47 Berger offers an excellent account of such narrative entropy in "A Secret Discipline," pp. 38–9.

48 Stefano Guazzo, ever pragmatic, is quite clear on this point: "[T]he wife must know, that to fulfill the law which she is bound to, it is not sufficient to be honest and innocent indeed, if she does not likewise avoyde all suspicion of dishonesty... she shall finde small difference (in respect of the world) betweene being naughte and being thoughte naughte" *The Civile Conversation*, trans. George Pettie and Bartholomew Young (New York: Alfred A. Knopf, 1925), Volumes III and IV, p. 31.

49 Arnold Williams discusses the mixing of the metaphorical and the literal in this episode in *Flower on a Lowly Stalk*, p. 53.

50 The term is borrowed from David Lee Miller, *The Poem's Two Bodies: The Poetics of the 1590 Faerie Queene* (Princeton: Princeton University Press, 1988), p. 16.

51 I am here adapting for my own purposes terms used by Bellamy in "The Vocative and the Vocational," p. 13.

52 Tonkin (*Spenser's Courteous Pastoral*, p. 102) points out that, although salvage society will not countenance the rape of Serena, "its 'civilized' way of behaving is simply to consume, to destroy Beauty."

53 Cheney, *Spenser's Image of Nature*, p. 108.

54 Renato Poggioli, in *The Oaten Flute: Essays on Pastoral Poetry and the Pastoral Ideal* (Cambridge, Mass.: Harvard University Press, 1975), suggests that pastoral is a characteristically lyric mode: "the pastoral romance is not narrative" (p. 39).

55 J. C. Maxwell long ago pointed out the equivocal nature of Calidore's sojourn among the shepherds: it is at once an act of truancy from the quest and offers, in the graces of Arcadia, the most impressive exemplifications of the central virtue directing the quest. "The Truancy of Calidore," pp. 146ff.

56 Cf. Gordon Teskey's assertion that "narrative is always erroneous, always in drift through the interstices of any motionless pattern with which commentary strives to equate it." "From Allegory to Dialectic: Imagining Error in Spenser and Milton," *PMLA*, 101 (1986): 13. In *Narrative and Its Discontents: Problems of Closure in The Traditional Novel* (Princeton: Princeton University Press, 1981), D. A. Miller offers an interesting discussion of the potential tensions between the impulse to narrate (or the very possibility of narration, given that narratability is so often a function of errancy, the breakdown of communication, the instability of our systems of signification, etc.) and our requirement that fictions *end* in some sort of aesthetically and/or ideologically pleasing manner. "Like language itself, narrative intrinsically tends to subvert the categories of the whole, the irreplaceable, the authentic: fragmentation is a consequence of its syntagmatic nature, substitution a part of its logic of expansion, and mediation is its central figure. Narrative is thus a domain in which the absoluteness of value is *risked*, where nothing can be got whole or all at once" (pp. 150–51). While Miller is specifically discussing the nineteenth-century novel, his arguments may equally well be applied to the attempt of Spenserian allegorical narrative to unite two "ends" – the satisfactory closure of a quest narrative *and* the weaving into a resonant and unequivocal totality of the host of other meanings released by *The Faerie Queene*'s knowing doublespeak.

57 See Waller, *English Poetry of the Sixteenth Century*, p. 203. Critics have been uneasy about Calidore's behavior to Coridon ever since Thomas Warton remarked that it was hardly courteous of the hero to detach Pastorella so efficiently from her former suitor; see *Observations on The Faerie Queene of Spenser* (London, 1762) Volume II, p. 19.

58 Guazzo, *The Civile Conversation*, I. 192.

59 We should note, however, that Coridon's point of view regarding Calidore's "marring" of his market does hint that the values of the marketplace may have already infected Arcadia.

60 Javitch, *Poetry and Courtliness*, p. 147.

61 The earlier cantos of Book VI are noticeably much more intra- than inter-textual, but in cantos ix and x, and particularly in the Acidalian vision, Spenser invokes multiple pretexts. Calidore's welcome into the green world recalls Erminia's in Book VII of Tasso's *Gerusalemma Liberata*; Pastorella's captivity among the Brigands may be likened to Isabella's imprisonment and near enslavement in canto xiii of the *Orlando Furioso*. Dorothy Woodward Culp has discussed canto ix and canto x's relations with Greek romance narrative in "Courtesy and Fortune's Chance in Book VI of *The Faerie Queene*," *MP* 68 (1971): 255. Renaissance mythographies and iconographies inform the treatment of the Graces in canto x (cf. Edgar Wind, *Pagan Mysteries in the Renaissance*, revised edn. [New York: W. W. Norton and Co., 1968], pp. 26–35 and 117ff.) – as do E. K.'s glosses to "Aprill" in *The Shepheardes Calender* (a work which also gives us Colin Clout).

62 "Aprill," lines 109–17.

63 On circles and garlands in Book VI, see Nohrnberg, *Analogy of The Faerie Queene*, p. 661, Parker, *Inescapable Romance*, p. 104 and also Berger, "A Secret Discipline," p. 40. One should note that the triumphant comparison of the dancers to Ariadne's crown is self-subverting. Spenser conflates the myth of Theseus and his abandoned mistress with the battle of the Centaurs and Lapiths at the wedding of Pirithoos, in a stanza which recalls one of Ate's monuments to discord (IV. i. 23). The "bloody fray" evoked by the simile reinvokes the violence of the Cannibals and anticipates the destruction of the green world by the Brigands; even as Spenser draws our attention to the beauty of the vision, he offers a subtextual counternarrative pointing to its fragility.

64 Spenser is living dangerously. True courtesy has detached itself from the pursuit of courtly favor (x. 3) and the "painted showes" of the court – yet Gloriana/Elizabeth remains at the center of the court. The poet resorts to the parenthesizing strategies of x. 4 to emphasize her separateness from debased, worldly courtesy, but he nevertheless cannot admit her to the core of his vision of courtesy in action. On the "disappearance" of Elizabeth from Book VI, see Waller, *English Poetry of the Sixteenth Century*, p. 195 and also Bellamy, "The Vocative and the Vocational," pp. 15ff.

65 Tonkin, *Spenser's Courteous Pastoral*, p. 138.

66 Berger, "A Secret Discipline," pp. 70–72.

67 C. S. Lewis, *The Allegory of Love*, p. 351.

68 David R. Shore, *Spenser and the Poetics of Pastoral* (Kingston & Montreal: McGill-Queen's University Press, 1985), p. 159; and also 143ff.

69 Patricia Parker urges that in Book VI "the cynosure is always at least potentially a visual gluttony or embowered fix" (*Inescapable Romance*, p. 104); certainly, Calidore fails to become a true "seer" at this point because he is too busy being a voyeur (on seers and voyeurs in the poem compare Giamatti, *Play of Double Senses*, pp. 91; 102). See also Gross, *Spenserian Poetics*, p. 213.

70 Cf. Proem 4; Proem 5; v. 38; ix. 22; ix. 27; x. 3; x. 4.

71 Harry Berger suggests that Spenser's dissolution of the Acidalian vision is less a helpless testimony to the poet's loss of control over his supreme fiction than a manifestation of "the controlled surrender whereby [the 'secret discipline' of the imagination] acknowledges the limits of artifice." The poet triumphs in bringing into being his "second nature," but his greater triumph is to show how "it must yield to reality at last" ("A Secret Discipline," pp. 74–75). It seems to me, however, that Colin's frustrated response to the shattering of the vision, the violence with which the green world is subsequently ripped apart by the Brigands' raid, and the disillusioned tone of canto xii's concluding stanzas conspire to countervail the idea that Spenser is serenely reinscribing and accepting the limitations of the poetry of vision within his didactic epic.

72 Their nakedness (and wordlessness) also reminds us of canto iv's good Salvage: what is merely primitive ignorance in him is a refined and original innocence in them.

73 Many critics of Book VI have tangled with Spenser's idiosyncratic iconography of the Graces: for a concise account of the various readings and the traditions behind them, see Roche's edition of *The Faerie Queene*, pp. 1227–28.

74 This reading is also supported by the eccentricities of Spenserian orthography, which make it quite likely that the "then" of the alexandrine may be "than" in the sense of "rather than."

75 Cf. Tonkin: "Calidore is in a sense Colin's public, his imperfect understanding reflecting the imperfections of every poet's public in every age" (*Spenser's Courteous Pastoral*, p. 302).

76 This ambiguous passage is the more remarkable because the love plot has already been "closed." In ix. 46, before his visit to Acidale, we read that Calidore stayed among the shepherds "To winne the loue of the faire Pastorell; / Which hauing got, he used without crime / Or blamefull blot, but menaged so well, / That he of all the rest, which there did dwell, / Was fauored, and to her grace commended." Did Calidore keep their love spotless, or did he merely "menage" matters so that no "blamefull blot" of slander accrued to Pastorella? Tellingly, the two episodes of

possible defilement/deflowering frame the scene on Mount Acidale which offers another destructive "penetration" by Calidore of an idyllic world.

77 MacCaffrey (*Spenser's Allegory*, p. 421) notes that canto x gives us an odd sense of an elided causal link between Calidore's absence on Acidale and the Brigands' raid. She is not alone in her impression – whoever composed the introductory Argument to canto x states that Calidore sees the Graces dance "the whiles his Pastorell is led, / Into captiuity." One begins to suspect that Calidore's "fall" on Acidale, his need to know that shatters the vision, combines with his possession and "knowledge" of Pastorella to bring about the destruction of the green world's Eden. See also Parker, *Inescapable Romance*, p. 105, and Stanley Stewart, "Sir Calidore and 'Closure,'" *SEL* 24 (1984): 77.

78 On Pastorella/Proserpina see, for example, Alice Fox Blitch, "Proserpina Preserved: Book VI of *The Faerie Queene*," *SEL* 13 (1973): 15–30.

79 Cf. Tonkin, *Spenser's Courteous Pastoral*, p. 279.

80 Berger, "A Secret Discipline," p. 43.

81 Lila Gella, "The Acidalian Vision: Spenser's Graces in Book VI of *The Faerie Queene*" *RES* ns 23 (1972): 271–2. For E. K. on the Graces, see *The Yale Edition of the Shorter Poems*, pp. 81–82.

82 On "infolding" and the Graces see Wind, *Pagan Mysteries*, pp. 240ff., and Gerald Snare, "The Poetics of Vision: Patterns of Grace and Courtesy in *The Faerie Queene*, VI," *Renaissance Papers* (1974): 1–8.

83 Book VI's concluding measure/threasure rhyme also occurs at two earlier moments when particularly threatening extra-textual forces seem to be embodied within the narrative; see viii. 43 (Serena and the Cannibals) and xi. 14 (Pastorella and the Brigands).

84 In *The Promised End: Romance Closure in the Gawain-poet, Malory, Spenser and Shakespeare* (New York and Berne: Peter Lang, 1986), Joseph M. Lenz suggests (p. 59) that Spenser achieves closure in his poem "by exchanging narrative for spatial order" (he is thinking in particular of the enclosed space of pastoral); Lenz does not, however, pursue the implications of the fact that this "closure" fails to coincide with the actual narrative *ending* of the work.

85 The slippery orthography of VII. viii. 2 in the 1609 text of the poem has generated many discussions of the first two meanings of Sabbaoth/Sabaoth which I have cited; see, for example, Harry Berger, Jr., "The *Mutabilitie Cantos*: Archaism and Evolution in Retrospect," in *Spenser: A Collection of Critical Essays*, ed. Harry Berger, Jr. (Englewood Cliffs: Prentice-Hall, 1968), p. 172. The

pun on Elizabeth Tudor's name is noted by A. C. Hamilton, who also points out that Elizabeth's name was glossed (from the Hebrew) by contemporary scholars as "Peace of the Lord"; see "Our New Poet: Spenser, 'Well of English undefyled,'" *Theatre for Spenserians*, ed. Judith M. Kennedy and James A. Reither (Toronto: University of Toronto Press, 1973), p. 110. Elizabeth J. Bellamy pursues this trace of Elizabeth to some interesting and very different conclusions in "Vocative and Vocational," pp. 23–24.

4 INSPIRED DUPLICITY: THE MULTIPLE DESIGNS OF *PARADISE LOST*

1 Although Spenser's retellings of Book 1's Fable in *The Faerie Queene* are ultimately versions of the biblical pre-text of the Legend of Holiness, the Book of Revelation, Spenser makes no explicit claim to be producing a sacred text, inspired by a Heavenly Muse, that will "assert eternal providence" and thus – at least in the early stages of *The Faerie Queene* – maintains a less anxiety-provoking relationship with Scripture.

2 Erich Auerbach, *Mimesis: The Representation of Reality in Western Literature*, trans. Willard Trask (Garden City: Doubleday Anchor, 1953), p. 9. In his fine study, *The Art of Biblical Narrative* (New York: Basic Books, 1981), Robert Alter suggests that Auerbach's account of the nature of scriptural narrative is not sufficiently attuned to the different *kinds* of narrative within the Bible (pp. 17; 114); nevertheless, the summary I have quoted seems to me apposite and applicable to Genesis 1–3.

3 J. M. Evans' *Paradise Lost and the Genesis Tradition* (Oxford: Clarendon Press, 1968) briefly discusses the implications of questioning the *lacunae* in Genesis and filling them in with narrative commentary. It will be evident in what follows that I do not agree with the more sanguine attitude of (for example) James H. Sims, who celebrates Milton's *via media* between a "firm anchoring in the text of Scripture and free sailing before the breath of the Spirit Muse"; see "The Miltonic Narrator and Scriptural Tradition: An Afterword," *Milton and Scriptural Tradition: The Bible into Poetry*, ed. James H. Sims and Leland Ryken (Columbia: University of Missouri Press, 1984), p. 204.

4 C. S. Lewis, *A Preface to Paradise Lost* (New York: Oxford University Press, 1942), p. 92.

5 I am drawing here upon Paul Ricoeur's thesis that *mimesis* should be understood as "redescription" rather than as "copy." See *The Rule of Metaphor*, pp. 244–45.

6 Frank Kermode, *The Genesis of Secrecy*, p. 81. See also *Midrash and Literature*, ed. Geoffrey H. Hartman and Sanford Budick (New Haven: Yale University Press, 1986).

7 Kermode, *The Genesis of Secrecy*, p. 82.

8 On *Paradise Lost* and the Jewish tradition of commentary upon Genesis see, for example, Harold Fisch, "Hebraic Style and Motifs in *Paradise Lost*," in *Language and Style in Milton: A Symposium in Honor of the Tercentenary of Paradise Lost*, ed. R. D. Emma and John T. Shawcross (New York: Frederick Ungar Publishing Co., 1967), pp. 30–64. Opinions concerning Milton's *direct* knowledge of rabbinical commentaries vary. Golda Werman has recently argued that his familiarity with *midrash* was almost entirely mediated by Renaissance translations and compendia. See her article "Milton's Use of Rabbinical Material," *Milton Studies* 21 (1985): 34–47; and also Jason P. Rosenblatt, "Milton's Chief Rabbi," *Milton Studies* 24 (1988): 43–71. On the poem's relations with Christian commentaries on Genesis see Evans, *Paradise Lost and the Genesis Tradition*, Arnold Williams, *The Common Expositor; An Account of the Commentaries upon Genesis 1527–1633* (Chapel Hill: University of North Carolina Press, 1948) and Sanford Budick, "Milton and the Scene of Interpretation: from Typology toward Midrash," in Hartman and Budick, eds., *Midrash and Literature*, pp. 195–212.

9 Evans (*Paradise Lost and the Genesis Tradition*, p. 219) mentions the huge generic variety within earlier commentaries on Genesis, and George K. Hunter's *Paradise Lost* (London: George Allen & Unwin, 1980) is particularly interesting on the poem's hetero-modality (pp. 1–13). John M. Steadman's less adventurous *Epic and Tragic Structure in Paradise Lost* (Chicago: University of Chicago Press, 1976) offers a discussion of the work's "mixed modes" (pp. 20–28). See also Lewalski, *Paradise Lost and the Rhetoric of Literary Forms*.

10 See also Fowler's note to this passage, pp. 253–54.

11 For a suggestive meditation on the interweaving of beginnings and ends in the poem see Regina M. Schwartz, *Remembering and Repeating: Biblical Creation in Paradise Lost* (Cambridge: Cambridge University Press, 1988), pp. 1–6; p. 74; p. 110. See also Mary Nyquist, "The Father's Word/Satan's Wrath," *PMLA* 100 (1985): 187 and Rosalie L. Colie, "Time and Eternity: Paradox and Structure in *Paradise Lost*," *Journal of the Warburg and Courtauld Institutes*, 23 (1960): 127–38.

12 According to the citations in *A Concordance to Milton's English Poetry*, ed. William Ingram and Kathleen Swaim (Oxford: Clarendon Press, 1972), "Author" appears fourteen times in *Paradise Lost*.

This is especially significant as the collators only count one other appearance of this word in the remainder of his poetic *oeuvre*. Its occurrences are at II. 381; II. 864; III. 374; IV. 635; V. 73; V. 188; V. 397; VI. 262; VII. 591; VIII. 317; VIII. 360; IX. 771; X. 236; X. 356.

13 *Narrative Discourse*, p. 46. For an interesting but rather confused exploration of this topic, see Edward W. Said, *Beginnings: Intention and Method* (New York: Basic Books, 1975). Said specifically addresses Milton's relations with origins and Genesis at pp. 212–13.

14 See also William Kerrigan, *The Sacred Complex: On the Psychogenesis of Paradise Lost* (Cambridge, Mass.: Harvard University Press, 1983), p. 158.

15 "The Father's Word/Satan's Wrath," p. 195.

16 The "necessary yet superfluous" aspect of Milton's pre-texts is discussed by Joan Malory Webber, *Milton and His Epic Tradition* (Seattle: University of Washington Press, 1979), p. 89. Francis C. Blessington, in *Paradise Lost and the Classical Epic* (Boston and London: Routledge and Kegan Paul, 1979) offers another useful account of *Paradise Lost*'s relations with pagan epic, and see also Hunter, *Paradise Lost*, p. 2 and Donald F. Bouchard, *Milton: A Structural Reading* (Montreal: McGill-Queens University Press, 1974), p. 112. My discussion in this chapter of Milton's engagement with pre-existing generic models shares some common ground with Lewalski's *Paradise Lost and the Rhetoric of Literary Forms*, but I am not convinced by her argument that the integrity of the heroic genres is not put into question by their treatment within the Christian epic (p. 78).

17 For an extended and richly suggestive account of the Sin/Error relationship, see Maureen Quilligan, *Milton's Spenser: The Politics of Reading* (Ithaca: Cornell University Press, 1983), pp. 79–128.

18 Eve's celebration of Adam at IV. 541–56, for example, asks to be re-examined and reappreciated in the light of Satan's celebration of Eve in her dream (V. 38–47); see also pp. 213–14 below.

19 See also Robert Crosman, *Reading Paradise Lost* (Bloomington: Indiana University Press, 1980), p. 85, Schwartz, *Remembering and Repeating*, p. 49, and John R. Mulder, "The Lyric Dimension of *Paradise Lost*," *Milton Studies* 23 (1987): 147.

20 An anomaly within this hierarchy might seem to be Sin, whose account of her own genesis is never questioned within the poem. But her precise ontological status in *Paradise Lost* is so hazy that it is difficult to decide whether she is actually "fallen" or whether she simply represents, in her person and her discourse, the allegorical *sign* and mediating "true fiction" of what it is to be fallen.

21 In *Milton's Epic Voice: The Narrator in Paradise Lost* (Cambridge,

Mass.: Harvard University Press, 1963), Anne Davidson Ferry proposes that Milton-the-poet is to be distinguished from the "blind bard" whose mediating voice speaks (or hears and retells) the events of *Paradise Lost*, (p. 45). I share Guillory's view (*Poetic Authority*, p. 104) that Ferry's argument does not adequately address Milton's "habitual stance, both in his poetry and his prose" of presenting himself "as he is, or believes himself to be."

22 See Marshall Grossman, "*Authors to Themselves*"*: Milton and the Revelation of History* (Cambridge: Cambridge University Press, 1987), pp. 127–30, for a particularly incisive discussion of the classical "closet drama" of Book IX.

23 On suspense and delay in Book IX, see Arnold Stein, *The Art of Presence: The Poet and Paradise Lost* (Berkeley and Los Angeles: University of California Press, 1977), pp. 108–09.

24 For an illuminating discussion of suspense and delay in the central books of *Paradise Lost*, see Parker, *Inescapable Romance*, p. 143ff. and also Mary Nyquist, "Reading the Fall: Discourse and Drama in *Paradise Lost*," *ELR* 14 (1984): 200.

25 On day 22 out of 33 days; see Fowler's edition of *Paradise Lost*, p. 26.

26 Milton's complicated entanglement of the story of the Fall with that of the Redemption is exhaustively explored in Grossman, "*Authors to Themselves.*"

27 The dramatic outlines are reprinted in Fowler's edition of *Paradise Lost*, pp. 3–5.

28 For a discussion of seventeenth-century views on the fall of speech after the fall of man, see Beverley Sherry, "Speech in *Paradise Lost*," *Milton Studies* 8 (1975): 249–51. On the problem of speaking and narrating the ineffable, see Quilligan, *Milton's Spenser*, p. 129ff.

29 For other discussions of the "layering" of acts of accommodation in *Paradise Lost* see, for example, Said, *Beginnings*, p. 280 and Crosman, *Reading Paradise Lost*, pp. 120–21.

30 Mark A. Wollaeger discusses Raphael's "Apocryphal" status and authority in "Apocryphal Narration: Milton, Raphael and the Book of Tobit," *Milton Studies* 21 (1985): 137–56.

31 See Davis P. Harding, *The Club of Hercules* (Urbana: University of Illinois Press, 1962), pp. 102–3. On Raphael, Hermes and Mercury, see also Greene, *The Descent From Heaven*, p. 374ff. and Blessington, *Paradise Lost and the Classical Epic*, pp. 25–27.

32 The phrase is Marshall Grossman's: "*Authors to Themselves*," p. 112.

33 Geoffrey H. Hartman, "Adam on the Grass With Balsamum," *ELH* 36 (1969): 178.

34 "*Authors to Themselves*," pp. 98–101.

35 J. B. Broadbent, *Some Graver Subject: An Essay on Paradise Lost* (London: Chatto and Windus, 1960), p. 146. On God's speeches see also Jackson I. Cope, *The Metaphoric Structure of Paradise Lost* (Baltimore: The Johns Hopkins University Press, 1962), pp. 169–76. In "The Language of Milton's Heaven," *MP* 74 (1976–77): 357, Michael Murrin argues that Books V and VI also show us a hermetic and self-referential world, but, as I have already indicated, I feel that the earthly models Milton has introjected into Raphael's discourse obscure and deny the mystery they seek to communicate rather than being informed or transcended by it.

36 E.g. the exaltation of the Son as the cause of the war in heaven and the Son's active role in the defeat of the rebels. See Stella P. Revard, *The War in Heaven: Paradise Lost and the Tradition of Satan's Rebellion* (Ithaca: Cornell University Press, 1980), pp. 175ff. and 195. (Interestingly, Milton has almost nothing to say about the war in heaven in *Of Christian Doctrine* – indeed, he there asserts that "Anyone who asks what God did before the creation of the world is a fool, and anyone who answers him is not much wiser." See *The Complete Prose Works of John Milton*, ed. Maurice Kelley [New Haven: Yale University Press, 1973], Vol. IV, p. 299.)

37 Fowler's edition of *Paradise Lost*, p. 26.

38 On Milton's manipulation of such temporal dislocations, see also Leopold Damrosch, Jr., *God's Plot and Man's Stories: Studies in the Fictional Imagination from Milton to Fielding* (Chicago: University of Chicago Press, 1985), p. 117.

39 James Whaler calculates that nearly 60% of the lines in the poem are enjambed; see *Counterpoint and Symbol: An Inquiry into the Rhythm of Milton's Epic Style* (Copenhagen: Rosenkilde and Bagger, 1956), pp. 13–14. Stanley E. Fish offers a more guarded version of the "synchronicity" argument in *Surprised By Sin: The Reader In Paradise Lost* (Berkeley and Los Angeles: University of California Press, 1971), p. 35. I am also indebted here to Parker's discussion of syntactic suspension and Miltonic "feints" at line endings; *Inescapable Romance*, p. 126 and 144–45. For a recent and revisionary discussion of Milton's "signifying aporia," however, see Richard Bradford, "Milton's Graphic Poetics," in *Re-Membering Milton: Essays on the Texts and Traditions*, ed. Mary Nyquist and Margaret W. Ferguson (New York and London: Methuen, 1987), pp. 179–96.

40 F. T. Prince has some observations on this phenomenon in *The Italian Element in Milton's Verse* (Oxford: Clarendon Press, 1954), p. 122.

41 For catalogues of rhymes in the poem see John S. Diekhoff, "Rhyme in *Paradise Lost*" *PMLA* 49 (1934): 539–45 and J. M. Purcell, "Rime in *Paradise Lost*," *MLN* 59 (1944): 171–72.

42 Eve's entrances and exits in *Paradise Lost* are often accompanied by an efflorescence of lyricism; cf. VIII. 59–63, IX. 385ff. and IX. 425ff. William Kerrigan and Gordon Braden offer a provocative discussion of Milton's representation of Eve in relation to the Petrarchan tradition in "Milton's Coy Eve: *Paradise Lost* and Renaissance Love Poetry", *ELH* 53 (1986): 27–51.

43 Crosman, *Reading Paradise Lost*, p. 100 (and see also pp. 99–116). A number of critics have discussed the "lyric dimension" of *Paradise Lost*. On the lyric space of Eden see Grossman, "*Authors to Themselves*," p. 68. Schwartz's account of the "re-creative" function of human and sacred song in the poem is particularly interesting (*Remembering and Repeating*, pp. 60–90), and see also Lewalski, *Paradise Lost and the Rhetoric of Literary Kinds*, pp. 183–95 and 200–5 and Francis C. Blessington, "'That Undisturbed Song of Pure Concent': *Paradise Lost* and the Epic-Hymn," in *Renaissance Genres: Essays on Theory, History and Interpretation*, ed. Barbara K. Lewalski (Cambridge, Mass.: Harvard University Press, 1986), pp. 468–95. Mulder, in "The Lyric Dimension of *Paradise Lost*," discusses only the invocations of Books I, III and VII; other readers have been sidetracked into a hunt for embedded "sonnets" in the poem; cf. Lee M. Johnson, "Milton's Blank Verse Sonnets," *Milton Studies* V (1973): 129–53 and also Peggy Samuels, "Milton's Use of Sonnet Form in *Paradise Lost*", *Milton Studies* 24 (1988): 141–54; Samuels does offer, however, an insightful discussion of Eve's praise song in Book IV (pp. 143–44), to which I am indebted.

44 In *The Muse's Method: An Introduction to Paradise Lost* (New York; W. W. Norton and Co., 1968), Joseph H. Summers draws attention to the "strophic" nature of the Morning Hymn (pp. 76–77). For John Hollander's account of the generation of refrain in the hymn, see *The Figure of Echo: A Mode of Allusion in Milton and After* (Los Angeles and Berkeley: University of California Press, 1981), p. 37.

45 As Leslie Brisman notes in *Milton's Poetry of Choice and its Romantic Heirs* (Ithaca: Cornell University Press, 1973), p. 124.

46 See Fish, *Surprised By Sin*, pp. 316–17 and Hunter, *Paradise Lost*, p. 35.

47 On time/space relations in *Paradise Lost*, see Isabel G. MacCaffrey, *Paradise Lost as "Myth"* (Cambridge, Mass.: Harvard University Press, 1959), pp. 47; 53–4; also Galbraith M. Crump, *The Mystical Design of Paradise Lost* (Lewisburg: Bucknell University Press, 1975), pp. 148–81.

48 Milton's accretion of clause upon clause in his apparently infinitely extendable sentences seems to be the result of his maintaining a strong counterpoint between his enjambed clauses of irregular length and his tireless generation of lines of blank verse through the purely formal reiteration of five stresses (or, more likely, roughly ten syllables) per line: the submerged metrical structure maintains the syntactic impetus. If *Paradise Lost* is "translated" into prose, it immediately acquires more sentence divisions: see, for example, the French prose rendering of Francois René de Châteaubriand, *Le Paradis Perdu de Milton* (Paris, 1836), in which I. 1–16 becomes three sentences.

49 Donald Davie, "Syntax and Music in *Paradise Lost*," in *The Living Milton*, ed. Frank Kermode (London: Routledge & Kegan Paul, 1960), p. 76.

50 Brisman discusses at length Milton's techniques for recapturing and representing the "presentness of the moment of choice" (p. 58) in *Milton's Poetry of Choice*, and see also Virginia R. Mollenkott, "Milton's Technique of Multiple Choice," *Milton Studies* 6 (1975): 101–11. Kerrigan, in a somewhat different context, remarks that "the subtlest way to postpone unwanted choice is to multiply alternatives" (*Sacred Complex*, p. 133) – an observation that may speak interestingly to Milton's representation of Eden before the fatal choice of the Fall.

51 For a useful overview of Milton's representations of pagan myth in the poem, see Jonathan Collett, "Milton's Use of Classical Mythology in *Paradise Lost*," *PMLA*, 85 (1970): 88–96.

52 Guillory, *Poetic Authority*, p. 130.

53 Frank Kermode, "Adam Unparadised," *The Living Milton*, p. 89.

54 The seminal essay on proleptic allusion in *Paradise Lost* is James Whaler's "The Miltonic Simile", *PMLA* 46 (1931): 1034–74. In *Milton's Grand Style* (Oxford: Clarendon Press, 1963), Christopher Ricks asserts that "prolepsis is surely the key figure throughout *Paradise Lost*" (p. 105). Linda Gregerson offers a rather different account of the Miltonic simile's powers of transformation and "translation" in "The Limbs of Truth: Milton's Use of Simile in *Paradise Lost*," *Milton Studies* 14 (1980): 132–52.

55 On *chronos* and *kairos* – and on questions of temporality in *Paradise Lost* in general – see Edward W. Tayler, *Milton's Poetry: Its Development in Time* (Pittsburgh: Duquesne University Press, 1979), pp. 17; 60–124.

56 For Lewis' remark, see *A Preface to Paradise Lost*, p. 129. For rehabilitations of XI and XII, see, for example, Fowler's note to XII. 466 (*Paradise Lost*, pp. 631–2); F. T. Prince, "On the Last Two

Books of *Paradise Lost*," *Essays and Studies* 11 (1958): 38–52; Barbara K. Lewalski, "Structure and the Symbolism of Vision in Michael's Prophecy: *Paradise Lost* Books XI–XII," *PQ* 42 (1963): 25–35; H. R. MacCallum, "Milton and Sacred History: Books XI and XII of *Paradise Lost*," in *Essays in English Literature from the Renaissance to the Victorian Age*, ed. Millar MacLure and F. W. Watt (Toronto: University of Toronto Press, 1964) pp. 149–68.

57 "*Authors to Themselves*," p. 165.

58 In his discussion of the competing "tragic" and "comic" visions of history represented in Book XII, David Loewenstein notes that Michael's discourse of apocalypse "interrupts, without cancelling out, Adam's severe history lessons." See *Milton and the Drama of History: Historical Vision. Iconoclasm, and the Literary Imagination* (Cambridge: Cambridge University Press, 1990), p. 120.

59 Arthur O. Lovejoy offers a history of the idea of the *felix culpa* (which appears in Christian theology as early as the seventh century) in "Milton and the Paradox of the Fortunate Fall," *Journal of English Literary History* 4 (1937): 161–79.

60 See also Hollander, *The Figure of Echo*, p. 40. Schwartz (*Remembering and Repeating*, pp. 91–110) offers a related, and quite brilliant, meditation upon the differences between recreative, willed, unfallen repetition and demonic, pathological iteration in *Paradise Lost*.

61 Milton's practice in *Paradise Lost* might seem to be at variance with the Protestant belief that individual faith and faith-filled perusal of the Logos could bring every Christian to a personal understanding of Divine Truth. Milton himself writes in the introductory epistle attached to *Of Christian Doctrine* that his readers should ultimately test the writer's assertions against Scripture itself (*Complete Prose Works of John Milton*, IV: 121). But the assertions of Milton the Protestant apologist and propagandist upon this subject should perhaps be viewed as something quite apart from the desire of Milton the creative artist to offer a universalized and definitive refashioning of the Genesis narrative which would be immediately intelligible to the contemporary reader. This last produces what Thomas M. Greene, in another context, calls the "creative imitation" of a canonical text, a practice which entails "a happy fall from the primary to the secondary, a civilized violence, a loving sacrilege" – see *The Light in Troy: Imitation and Discovery in Renaissance Poetry* (New Haven: Yale University Press, 1982), pp. 38–9. Perhaps some of the tensions within the narrative strategies of *Paradise Lost* spring from its author's refusal to admit his connivance in this knowing and happy lapse.

62 On Milton as *deus artifex* see John T. Shawcross, "The Rhetor as Creator in *Paradise Lost*," *Milton Studies* 8 (1975): 209–19.

63 *Surprised by Sin*, p. 240. Fish is here addressing the representation of the Fall in IX; he seems to have forgotten this much earlier sequence of causal substitution.

64 Cf. Crosman, *Reading Paradise Lost*, p. 25.

65 See Fish, *Surprised by Sin*, p. 233, for dissenting view.

66 This aspect of the poem is extensively explored in Dennis H. Burden's *The Logical Epic: A Study of the Argument of Paradise Lost* (Cambridge, Mass.: Harvard University Press, 1967).

67 Various critics have uncovered a "double plot" in *Paradise Lost*: its nature tends to vary with the reader. Parker identifies a governing duality within the fragile Miltonic "suspense," which may either collapse into a reductive and fallen goal-directedness or alternatively dilate a perpetual threshold time before Apocalypse (*Inescapable Romance*, p. 158). Grossman ("*Authors of Themselves*," p. 178) suggests that Milton's narrative conflates the "temporal, empirical, mimetic" story of "man's first disobedience" with the "eternal, revelatory" story of "one greater Man." Mary Nyquist discusses the relationship of the Satanic plot to the prelapsarian eternal moment in "Reading the Fall." And see also Geoffrey H. Hartman, "Milton's Counterplot," *ELH* 25 (1958): 1–12.

68 See, for example, IV. 42–61, where Satan admits the injustice of his rebellion, only to undercut his insight with "Yet why not?" Jun Harada discusses soliloquy as a mode of fallen discourse in "Self and Language in the Fall," *Milton Studies* 5 (1973): 213–14; see also Schwartz, *Remembering and Repeating*, p. 104.

69 When Dryden turned *Paradise Lost* into *The State of Innocence*, he foregrounded this feature of his source by having the fiend tempt Eve in human, not reptilian, form; see *The Dramatic Works*, ed. Montague Summers (London: Nonesuch Press, 1932) Vol. III. On "Satanic" and postlapsarian literary values see Ferry, *Milton's Epic Voice*, p. 140ff.; William Kerrigan, *The Prophetic Milton* (Charlottesville: University Press of Virginia, 1974), p. 136 and William G. Riggs, "The Poet and Satan in *Paradise Lost*," *Milton Studies* 2 (1970): 59–82.

70 Cf. Guillory, *Poetic Authority*, p. 108.

71 Kerrigan, *The Prophetic Milton*, p. 143.

72 Compare III, 38–39; VII. 3; VII. 28–29.

73 Mary Nyquist argues that Book IX does not in fact commence with a formal Invocation of the Muse; see "The Father's Word," p. 195. In "Creation and the Place of the Poet in *Paradise Lost*," in *The Author in His Work: Essays on a Problem in Criticism*, ed. Louis L.

Martz and Aubrey Williams (New Haven: Yale University Press, 1978), pp. 51–69, Janet Adelman offers an interesting account of the tension between self-assertion and self-denial in the poem.

74 Kerrigan (*The Prophetic Milton*, p. 187) sees this refusal to disallow the possibility that the poem is indeed a Satanic fiction as evidence of the inspired poet's integrity; he also argues that the multiple personae and methods of the Muse entertained by Milton open up the poem to all possible kinds of inspiration (p. 139). I am less sanguine about Milton's claim to literal inspiration: for all his serious and complex attempts to locate the Muse's acts of inspiration within the poem that she has supposedly inspired, I believe that *Paradise Lost* inevitably contains and narrates an abiding tension between, or incomplete synthesis of, prophecy and poetic fiction-making. On this tension, and on the difficulty of bridging the gap between the poetic and prophetic calling to produce a sacred text, see Guillory, *Poetic Authority*, p. 106.

75 MacCaffrey, *Paradise Lost as "Myth,"* p. 42.

76 MacCaffrey, *Paradise Lost as "Myth,"* p. 44.

77 Rosenblatt describes a fascinating instance of the poem being cited in support of the arguments of a commentator on Genesis as early as 1683; see "Milton's Chief Rabbi": 43–44.

78 Kermode, *The Sense of an Ending: Studies in the Theory of Fiction* (New York: Oxford University Press, 1967), p. 39.

79 On *Paradise Lost* as a "true fiction," see Crosman, *Reading Paradise Lost*, p. 135.

80 And, like Genesis, *Paradise Lost* becomes subject to other writers' attempts to penetrate its secrets, to repossess, gloss, or "save" it. Thus we have Dryden's transformation of the poem into *The State of Innocence*, Richard Bentley's Enlightenment cuts and emendations, and, more recently, *Paradise Lost by John Milton: A Prose Rendition*, ed. Robert Shepherd (New York: Seabury Press, 1983), which does not merely "translate" *Paradise Lost* into prose but also glosses it through omission: the editor, for example, considers most of Books XI and XII, and nearly every classical allusion in the poem, irrelevant to the "real story."

81 Cf. Lee M. Johnson, "Milton's Blank Verse Sonnets," pp. 143–44.

82 Fish, *Surprised By Sin*, p. 329.

83 Although the narrative conclusion of *Paradise Lost* is utterly unlike the lyric "simultaneity" of this apocalyptic glimpse of another ending, I do not believe that this means that the lyric mode is eventually and completely subordinated to narrative discourse in the poem (as Earl Miner has argued in "The Reign of Narrative in *Paradise Lost*," *Milton Studies* 17 [1983]: 3–25). At moments such

as this, the synchronic vision seems to break free, for a moment, from its discursive, narrative frame.

5 THE ENDS OF POETIC NARRATIVE

1 Denis Donoghue, "The Word Within a Word," *The Waste Land in Different Voices*, ed. A. D. Moody (London: Edward Arnold, 1974), p. 194.

2 M. L. Rosenthal, "*The Waste Land* as an Open Structure," *Mosaic* 6 (1972): 189. Rosenthal and his co-author Sally M. Gall further develop this account of the poem in *The Modern Poetic Sequence: The Genius of Modern Poetry* (New York: Oxford University Press, 1983), pp. 156–64.

3 Rosenthal and Gall, *The Modern Poetic Sequence*, p. 6. Margaret Dickie argues that Eliot himself is not immune to the desire to create a totalizing narrative; she contrasts his poem's "internal tendency toward discontinuity" with its author's "rigid plan for continuity imposed late and tentatively," See *On the Modernist Long Poem* (Iowa City: University of Iowa Press, 1986), p. 34. And see also John Xiros Cooper, *T. S. Eliot and the Politics of Voice: The Argument of The Waste Land* (Ann Arbor: UMI Research Press, 1987), p. 58.

4 "*Ulysses*, Order and Myth," reprinted in *James Joyce, The Critical Heritage*, ed. Robert H. Deming, (London: Routledge & Kegan Paul, 1970) Vol. 1, p. 271.

5 Weston notes that the unredacted Grail Legend is "a congeries of widely different elements... which at first sight appear hopelessly incongruous." See *From Ritual to Romance* (Garden City: Doubleday Anchor, 1957), p. 2.

6 All references to *The Tempest* are from William Shakespeare, *The Tempest*, ed. Robert Langbaum (New York: New American Library, Inc., 1964).

7 Lines 46–48 and line 125. All references to and citations of *The Waste Land* – hereafter indicated by line numbers within the body of the text – are from T. S. Eliot, *Collected Poems 1909–1962* (London: Faber & Faber Ltd., 1970).

8 Calvin Bedient, *He Do The Police in Different Voices: The Waste Land and Its Protagonist* (Chicago: Chicago University Press, 1986), p. 160.

9 Roland Barthes defines the "writerly" text in *S/Z*, pp. 4–6.

10 For discussions of *The Waste Land* as a "sibylline" text, see Helen Williams, *T. S. Eliot: The Waste Land* (London: Edward Arnold, 1968), p. 17; Hugh Kenner, *The Invisible Poet: T. S. Eliot* (London:

Methuen and Co., 1965), p. 137; and also Donoghue, "The Word Within a Word," p. 191.

11 See T. S. Eliot, *The Waste Land: A Facsimile and Transcript of the Original Drafts*, ed. Valerie Eliot (London: Faber and Faber, 1971), p. 81. Subsequent citations of the original drafts will be noted in the body of the text.

12 Cf. Helen Gardner, *The Art of T. S. Eliot* (New York: E. P. Dutton and Co., 1959), p. 87.

13 In a letter to Eliot, 24 December, 1921. See *The Letters of Ezra Pound 1907–1941*, ed. D. D. Paige (New York: Harcourt, Brace, 1950), p. 169.

14 Cf. F. R. Leavis, "*The Waste Land*," in *T. S. Eliot: A Collection of Critical Essays*, ed. Hugh Kenner (Englewood Cliffs: Prentice-Hall, Inc., 1962), p. 99.

15 Nancy K. Lawlor hypothesizes that certain formal poetic schemes have particular semantic or emotional resonance in *The Waste Land*; see "Eliot's Use of Rhyming Quatrains in *The Waste Land*," *Poet and Critic* 4 (1967): 36. Ann P. Brady argues that the poem's embedded lyrics embrace "a measure of emotion against which the emotionless can be judged" in *Lyricism in the Poetry of T. S. Eliot* (Port Washington: Kennikat Press, 1978), pp. 32–43. As my own discussion of poetic scheme in *The Waste Land* will indicate, I am less certain that such "lyrical" moments are invested with a clear significance.

16 A. D. Moody argues that the three speeches of the Thames Daughters actually constitute a sonnet, but his uneasy "sonnet" of two quatrains and an unconvincing sestet is achieved at the expense of three, more regular quatrains. See *Thomas Stearns Eliot: Poet* (Cambridge: Cambridge University Press, 1979), p. 95. For other discussions of the structure of the Thames nymphs' songs see Brady, *Lyricism in the Poetry of T. S. Eliot*, pp. 38–39; Bedient, *He Do the Police in Different Voices*, p. 151; and Cooper, *T. S. Eliot and the Politics of Voice*, p. 45.

17 William M. Gibson, "Sonnets in T. S. Eliot's *The Waste Land*," *American Literature* 32 (1961): 465–66. In fact, the "couplet" is really the first two lines of a quatrain, cropped in the process of revision. See *The Waste Land: A Facsimile*, p. 47.

18 Bedient (*He Do The Police in Different Voices*, pp. 134–35) argues that the apparent orderliness of the quatrains describing the Typist/Clerk encounter is subverted by their actual circumscription of syntactic and semantic disorder (in this context he offers a particularly interesting reading of lines 224–27).

19 "The Word Within a Word," p. 191.

20 See "The Frontiers of Criticism," *On Poetry and Poets* (New York: Farrar, Strauss and Cudahy, 1957), p. 109.

21 On Eliot's selective citation, see also John Hollander, *The Figure of Echo*, p. 103, and Ruth Nevo, "*The Waste Land*: Ur-text of Deconstruction," *NLH* 13 (1982): 459.

22 On echoes of Old Testament prophets in *The Waste Land*, see Florence Jones, "T. S. Eliot Among the Prophets," *American Literature* 38 (1966): 285–302; Helen Williams, *T. S. Eliot: The Waste Land*, pp. 67ff., and Anne C. Bolgan, *What the Thunder Really Said: A Retrospective Essay on the Making of The Waste Land* (Montreal and London: McGill-Queen's University Press, 1973), p. 157.

23 Robert J. Andreach, "Paradise Lost and the Christian Configuration of *The Waste Land*," *PLL* 5 (1969): 299–300.

24 Compare Revelation 16:18.

25 See Eliot's note on "shantih" in the 1922 edition of *The Waste Land*, reprinted in *The Waste Land: A Facsimile*, p. 149; the qualification was suppressed in later editions of the poem.

26 This last is emphasized by Eliot's insistence (in his note to line 218) that Tiresias is not a "character" in the poem. It has, of course, irritated many critics that the *ex post facto* glosses of the "Notes" reconstruct Tiresias as a far more unified point of view, and a far more authoritative presiding presence, than the actual text of the poem might suggest.

27 My discussion of ending and apocalypse in this chapter is indebted to Frank Kermode, *The Sense of an Ending*, in particular pp. 7–8, and also to Patricia Parker's *Inescapable Romance*. Where the latter, however, finds complicated – and ambivalent – representations of ending to be a defining characteristic of the romance *mode*, I am more interested in associating them with the embracing *formal* category of poetic narrative.

28 Cf. Harold Toliver's *Animate Illusions: Explorations of Narrative Structure* (Lincoln: University of Nebraska Press, 1974), pp. 168–89, and especially pp. 169–71. Toliver, in one of the very few studies of narrative which addresses narrative in verse, notes the potential "tension between the rhythm of formal recurrence and the psychology of narrative forwarding" (p. 170), and contrasts units of prose narration which "are more or less naturalized as segments of meaning" with the "microcosmic" and "artificial" aspects of poetic measure (p. 169).

29 The phenomenon I address here and in what follows is not unrelated to what Kerrigan calls the "enfolded sublime" (*Sacred Complex*, pp. 231–32). Kerrigan, however, considers it to be a uniquely Miltonic achievement: "Spenser was unable to arrest the

spin of narrative in still points of enfolded sublimity." He argues that, even when the author of *The Faerie Queene* offers comparably vatic moments, such as "Redcrosse surveying the world in Book I, Colin's interrupted vision in Book VI," they "are not able to ingest the bulk of the poem with sufficient elegance. Too much redounds" (232). As my arguments here and in Chapter III suggest, I would contest Kerrigan's claim that Milton alone can achieve such effects.

30 Frank Kermode has argued that in some novels the ending is "supplemented in advance" by "end-effects in the text" – discussing *Middlemarch*, he cites Dorothea's epiphanies during her Roman journey and the insights Bulstrode attains when he confronts his past. See "Sensing Endings," *Nineteenth-Century Fiction* 33 (1978): 155. My examples of containment-before-the-end differ from Kermode's in offering alternatives, as well as supplements, to the official ending; these alternatives, moreover, tend to invoke alternative principles of formal construction.

31 Bakhtin, *The Dialogic Imagination*, p. 331.

32 Bakhtin, to be sure, valorizes the novel's redescriptions of the multivalent discourses of "reality" without, perhaps, recognizing that all redescriptions may actually be ideologically loaded and socially-constitutive *reinscriptions*. (For a detailed presentation of this latter view of the workings of fiction, see Jameson's *Political Unconscious*.)

Bibliography

Adelman, Janet. "Creation and the Place of the Poet in *Paradise Lost.*" *The Author in His Work: Essays on a Problem in Criticism*. Ed. Louis L. Martz and Aubrey Williams. New Haven: Yale University Press, 1978. 51–69

Alpers, Paul J. *The Poetry of The Faerie Queene*. Princeton: Princeton University Press, 1967

Alter, Robert. *The Art of Biblical Narrative*. New York: Basic Books, 1981

Andreach, Robert J. "*Paradise Lost* and the Christian Configuration of *The Waste Land.*" *PLL* 5 (1969): 296–309

Ariosto, Ludovico. *Orlando Furioso*. Trans. Barbara Reynolds. Harmondsworth: Penguin, 1975

Ascham, Roger. *The Schoolmaster*. Ed. Lawrence V. Ryan. Charlottesville: University Press of Virginia, 1974

Auerbach, Erich. *Mimesis: the Representation of Reality in Western Literature*. Trans. Willard Trask. Garden City: Doubleday Anchor, 1953

Bakhtin, M. M. *The Dialogic Imagination*. Trans. Caryl Emerson and Michael Holquist. Ed. Michael Holquist. Austin and London: University of Texas Press, 1981

Bal, Mieke. *Narratology: Introduction to the Theory of Narrative*. Trans. Christine van Boheemen. Toronto: University of Toronto Press, 1985

Barthes, Roland. *S/Z*. Trans. Richard Miller. New York: Hill and Wang, 1974

Baswell, Christopher C. and Paul B. Taylor. "The 'Faire Queene Eleyne' in Chaucer's *Troilus.*" *Speculum* 63 (1988): 293–311

Baum, Paull F. *Chaucer's Verse*. Durham, N.C.: Duke University Press, 1961

Bedient, Calvin. *He Do the Police in Different Voices: The Waste Land And Its Protagonist*. Chicago: Chicago University Press, 1986

Bellamy, Elizabeth J. "The Vocative and the Vocational: The

Unreadability of Elizabeth in *The Faerie Queene*." *ELH* 54 (1987): 1–30

Berger, Harry, Jr. "The *Mutabilitie Cantos*: Archaism and Evolution in Retrospect." *Spenser: A Collection of Critical Essays*. Englewood Cliffs: Prentice Hall, 1968. 146–76

"The Prospect of Imagination: Spenser and the Limits of Poetry." *SEL* 1 (1961): 93–120

"A Secret Discipline: *The Faerie Queene* Book VI." *Form and Convention in the Poetry of Edmund Spenser*. Ed. William Nelson. New York: Columbia University Press, 1961. 33–75

Blessington: Francis C. *Paradise Lost and the Classical Epic*. Boston and London: Routledge and Kegan Paul, 1979

"'That Undisturbed Song of Pure Concent': *Paradise Lost* and the Epic Hymn." *Renaissance Genres: Essays on Theory, History and Interpretation*. Ed. Barbara Kiefer Lewalski. Cambridge, Mass.: Harvard University Press, 1986. 468–95

Blitch, Alice Fox. "Proserpina Preserved: Book VI of *The Faerie Queene*." *SEL* 13 (1973): 15–30

Bloomfield, Morton W. "Distance and Predestination in *Troilus and Criseyde*." *PMLA* 72 (1957): 14–26

Boccaccio, Giovanni. *The Filostrato of Giovanni Boccaccio*. Trans. and ed. Nathaniel E. Griffin and Arthur B. Myrick. Philadelphia: University of Pennsylvania Press, 1929

Boitani, Piero. *English Medieval Narrative in the Thirteenth and Fourteenth Centuries*. Trans. Joan K. Hall. Cambridge: Cambridge University Press, 1982

Bolgan, Anne C. *What the Thunder Really Said: A Retrospective Essay on the Making of The Waste Land*. Montreal and London: McGill-Queen's University Press, 1973

Booth, Wayne C. *The Rhetoric of Fiction*. Chicago: University of Chicago Press, 1961

Bouchard, Donald F. *Milton: A Structural Reading*. Montreal: McGill-Queens University Press, 1974

Bradford, Richard. "Milton's Graphic Poetics." *Re-Membering Milton: Essays on the Texts and Traditions*. Ed. Mary Nyquist and Margaret W. Ferguson. New York and London: Methuen, 1987. 179–96

Brady, Ann P. *Lyricism in the Poetry of T. S. Eliot*. Port Washington: Kennikat Press, 1978

Brenner, Gerry. "Narrative Structure in Chaucer's *Troilus and Criseyde*." *Annuale Mediaevale* 6 (1965): 5–18

Brisman, Leslie. *Milton's Poetry of Choice and Its Romantic Heirs*. Ithaca: Cornell University Press, 1973

Broadbent, J. B. *Some Graver Subject: An Essay on Paradise Lost*. London: Chatto and Windus, 1960

Brooks, Peter. *Reading for the Plot: Design and Intention in Narrative*. New York: Vintage, 1985

Bruns, Gerald L. *Inventions: Writing, Textuality and Understanding in Literary History*. New Haven: Yale University Press, 1982

Burden, Dennis H. *The Logical Epic: A Study of the Argument of Paradise Lost*. Cambridge, Mass.: Harvard University Press, 1967

Burke, Kenneth. *A Grammar of Motives*. 1945. Berkeley and Los Angeles: University of California Press, 1969

Burlin, Robert B. *Chaucerian Fiction*. Princeton: Princeton University Press, 1977

Carton, Evan. "Complicity and Responsibility in Pandarus's Bed and Chaucer's Art." *PMLA* 94 (1979): 47–61

Castiglione, Baldassare. *The Book of the Courtier*. Trans. Sir Thomas Hoby. London: J. M. Dent and Sons, 1974

Cave, Terence. *The Cornucopian Text: Problems of Writing in the French Renaissance*. Oxford: Clarendon Press, 1979

Châteaubriand, Francois René de (trans.). *Le Paradis Perdu de Milton*. Paris, 1836

Chatman, Seymour. *Story and Discourse: Narrative Structure in Fiction and Film*. Ithaca: Cornell University Press, 1978

Chaucer, Geoffrey. *Troilus and Criseyde*. Ed. B. A. Windeatt. London and New York: Longman, 1984

Troilus and Criseyde. Ed. Stephen A. Barney. *The Riverside Chaucer*. Ed. Larry D. Benson *et al.* 3rd rev. edition. Boston: Houghton Mifflin and Co., 1987

Cheney, Donald. *Spenser's Image of Nature: Wild Man and Shepherd in The Faerie Queene*. New Haven: Yale University Press, 1966

Clough, Andrea. "Medieval Tragedy and the Genre of *Troilus and Criseyde*." *Medievalia et Humanistica* ns 11 (1982): 211–27

Colie, Rosalie L. "Time and Eternity: Paradox and Structure in *Paradise Lost*." *Journal of the Warburg and Courtauld Institutes* 23 (1960): 127–38

Collett, Jonathan. "Milton's Use of Classical Mythology in *Paradise Lost*." *PMLA* 85 (1970): 88–96

Cooper, John Xiros. *T. S. Eliot and the Politics of Voice: The Argument of The Waste Land*. Ann Arbor: UMI Research Press, 1987

Cope, Jackson I. *The Metaphoric Structure of Paradise Lost*. Baltimore: The Johns Hopkins University Press, 1962

Cowling, G. H. "A Note on Chaucer's Stanza." *RES* 2 (1926): 311–17

Crosman, Robert. *Reading Paradise Lost*. Bloomington: Indiana University Press, 1980

Crump, Galbraith M. *The Mystical Design of Paradise Lost*. Lewisburg: Bucknell University Press, 1975

Culler, Jonathan. *Structuralist Poetics: Structuralism, Linguistics and the Study of Literature.* London: Routledge and Kegan Paul, 1975

Culp, Dorothy Woodward. "Courtesy and Fortune's Chance in Book VI of *The Faerie Queene.*" *MP* 68 (1971): 254–59

Curtius, Ernst Robert. *European Literature and the Latin Middle Ages.* Trans. Willard R. Trask. Princeton: Princeton University Press, 1973

Damrosch, Leopold, Jr. *God's Plot and Man's Stories: Studies in the Fictional Imagination from Milton to Fielding.* Chicago: University of Chicago Press, 1985

Davie, Donald. "Syntax and Music in *Paradise Lost.*" *The Living Milton.* Ed. Frank Kermode. London: Routledge and Kegan Paul, 1960. 70–84

Dickie, Margaret. *On the Modernist Long Poem.* Iowa City: University of Iowa Press, 1986

Diekhoff, John S. "Rhyme in *Paradise Lost.*" *PMLA* 49 (1934): 539–43

Dixon, Michael F. N. "Fairy Tale, Fortune and Boethian Wonder: Rhetorical Structure in Book VI of *The Faerie Queene.*" *UTQ* 44 (1975): 141–65

Donaldson, E. Talbot "Chaucer's Three 'P's: Pandarus, Pardoner and Poet." *Michigan Quarterly Review* 14 (1975): 282–301

Speaking of Chaucer. New York: Norton, 1970

Donoghue, Denis. "The Word Within a Word." *The Waste Land in Different Voices.* Ed. A. D. Moody. London: Edward Arnold, 1974

Dryden, John. *The State of Innocence. Dramatic Works.* Ed. Montague Summers. London: Nonesuch Press, 1932. Volume III

Dyck, E. F. "Ethos, Pathos and Logos in *Troilus and Criseyde.*" *ChauR* 20 (1986): 169–82

Eliot, T. S. *Collected Poems 1909–1962.* London: Faber & Faber Ltd., 1970

"The Frontiers of Criticism." *On Poetry and Poets.* New York: Farrar, Strauss & Cudahy, 1957. 103–18

"*Ulysses*, Order and Myth." *James Joyce: The Critical Heritage.* Ed. Robert H. Deming. London: Routledge and Kegan Paul, 1970. Volume I. 268–71

The Waste Land: A Facsimile and Transcript of the Original Drafts. Ed. Valerie Eliot. London: Faber and Faber, 1971

Empson, William. *Seven Types of Ambiguity.* 3rd edition. Cleveland: Meridian Books, 1964

Evans, J. M. *Paradise Lost and the Genesis Tradition.* Oxford: Clarendon Press, 1968

Faral, Edmond. *Les Arts Poétiques du xiie et du xiiie Siècle.* Paris: E. Champion, 1924

Ferry, Anne Davidson. *Milton's Epic Voice: The Narrator in Paradise Lost.* Cambridge, Mass.: Harvard University Press, 1963

Fisch, Harold. "Hebraic Style and Motifs in Paradise Lost." *Language and Style in Milton: A Symposium in Honor of the Tercentenary of Paradise Lost.* Ed. R. D. Emma and John T. Shawcross. New York: Frederick Ungar Publishing Co., 1967. 30–64

Fish, Stanley E. *Surprised By Sin: The Reader in Paradise Lost.* 1967. Berkeley and Los Angeles: University of California Press, 1971

Fletcher, Angus. *The Prophetic Moment: An Essay on Spenser.* Chicago: University of Chicago Press, 1971

Fowler, Alastair. *Kinds of Literature: An Introduction to the Theory of Genres and Modes.* Cambridge, Mass.: Harvard University Press, 1982

Fried, Debra. "Spenser's Caesura." *ELR* 11 (1981): 261–80

Frye, Northrop. *Anatomy of Criticism: Four Essays.* 1957. New York: Athenaeum, 1968

The Secular Scripture: A Study of the Structure of Romance. Cambridge, Mass.: Harvard University Press, 1976

"The Structure of Imagery in *The Faerie Queene.*" *Fables of Identity: Studies in Poetic Mythology.* New York: Harcourt, Brace & World, 1963. 69–87

Fyler, John M. *Chaucer and Ovid.* New Haven: Yale University Press, 1979

Ganim, John M. *Style and Consciousness in Middle English Narrative.* Princeton: Princeton University Press, 1983

Gardner, Helen. *The Art of T. S. Eliot.* New York: E. P. Dutton and Co., 1959

Gella, Lila. "The Acidalian Vision: Spenser's Graces in Book VI of *The Faerie Queene.*" *RES* ns 23 (1972): 267–77

Genette, Gérard. *Figures of Literary Discourse (Selections from Figures 1966–72).* Trans. Alan Sheridan. New York: Columbia University Press, 1982

Narrative Discourse: An Essay In Method. Trans. Jane E. Lewin. Ithaca: Cornell University Press, 1980

Giamatti, A. Bartlett. *Play of Double Senses: Spenser's Faerie Queene.* Englewood Cliffs: Prentice Hall, 1975

Gibson, William M. "Sonnets in T. S. Eliot's *The Waste Land.*" *American Literature* 32 (1961): 465–66

Goldberg, Jonathan. *Endlesse Worke: Spenser and the Structures of Discourse.* Baltimore: The Johns Hopkins University Press, 1981

Gordon, Ida L. *The Double Sorrow of Troilus: A Study of Ambiguities in Troilus and Criseyde.* Oxford: Clarendon Press, 1970

Greene, Thomas M. *The Descent from Heaven: A Study in Epic Continuity.* New Haven: Yale University Press, 1963

The Light in Troy: Imitation and Discovery in Renaissance Poetry. New Haven: Yale University Press, 1982

Gregerson, Linda. "The Limbs of Truth: Milton's Use of Simile in *Paradise Lost*." *Milton Studies* 14 (1980): 135–52

Griggs, Earl Leslie (ed.). *Unpublished Letters of Samuel Taylor Coleridge*. London: Constable and Company, 1932. Volume II

Gross, Kenneth. "'Each Heav'nly Close': Mythology and Metrics in Spenser and the Early Poetry of Milton." *PMLA* 98 (1983): 21–36

Spenserian Poetics: Idolatry, Iconoclasm and Magic. Ithaca: Cornell University Press, 1985

Grossman, Marshall. "*Authors to Themselves*": *Milton and the Revelation of History*. Cambridge: Cambridge University Press, 1987

Guazzo, Stefano. *The Civile Conversation*. Trans. George Pettie. New York: Alfred A. Knopf, 1925. Volumes I and II

The Civile Conversation. Trans. George Pettie and Bartholomew Young. New York: Alfred A. Knopf, 1925. Volumes III and IV

Guillory, John. *Poetic Authority: Spenser, Milton and Literary History*. New York: Columbia University Press, 1983

Hamilton, A. C. "Our New Poet: Spenser, 'Well of English undefyled.'" *Theatre for Spenserians*. Ed. Judith M. Kennedy and James A. Reither. Toronto: University of Toronto Press, 1973. 101–23

The Structure of Allegory in The Faerie Queene. Oxford: Clarendon Press, 1961

Harada, Jun. "Self and Language in the Fall." *Milton Studies* 5 (1973): 213–28

Harding, Davis P. *The Club of Hercules*. Urbana: University of Illinois Press, 1962

Hartman, Geoffrey H. "Adam on the Grass with Balsamum." *ELH* 36 (1969): 168–92

"Milton's Counterplot." *ELH* 25 (1958): 1–12

Hartman, Geoffrey H. and Sanford Budick (eds.) *Midrash and Literature*. New Haven: Yale University Press, 1986

Hernadi, Paul. *Beyond Genre: New Directions in Literary Classification*. Ithaca: Cornell University Press, 1972

Hirsch, E. D., Jr. *Validity in Interpretation*. New Haven: Yale University Press, 1967

Holland, Joanne Field. "The Cantos of Mutabilitie and the Form of *The Faerie Queene*." *ELH* 35 (1968): 21–31

Hollander, John. *The Figure of Echo: A Mode of Allusion in Milton and After*. Los Angeles and Berkeley: Univ. of California Press, 1981

Melodious Guile: Fictive Pattern in Poetic Language. New Haven: Yale University Press, 1988

"'Sense Variously Drawn Out': Some Observations on English Enjambment." *Literary Theory and Structure: Essays in Honor of William K. Wimsatt*. Ed. Frank Brady *et al.* New Haven: Yale University Press, 1973. 201–25

Vision and Resonance: Two Senses of Poetic Form. New York: Oxford University Press, 1975

Homer. *Iliad*. 2 vols. Trans. A. T. Murray. Rev. edn. The Loeb Classical Library. Cambridge, Mass.: Harvard University Press, 1971

Hough, Graham. *A Preface to The Faerie Queene*. New York: W. W. Norton and Co., 1967

Hunter, George K. *Paradise Lost*. London: George Allen & Unwin, 1980

Huppé, Bernard F. "The Unlikely Narrator: Narrative Strategy in the *Troilus*." *Signs and Symbols in Chaucer's Poetry*. Ed. J. P. Hermann and John J. Burke. University: University of Alabama Press, 1981. 179–94

Hutcheon, Linda. *The Politics of Postmodernism*. London and New York: Routledge, 1989

Ingram, William and Kathleen Swaim (eds.). *A Concordance to Milton's English Poetry*. Oxford: Clarendon Press, 1972

Jakobson, Roman. "The Dominant." *Readings in Russian Poetics: Formalist and Structuralist Views*, ed. L. Matejka and K. Pomorska. Cambridge, Mass.: M.I.T. Press, 1971. 82–87

"Linguistics and Poetics." *Style in Language*. Ed. Thomas A. Sebeok. Cambridge, Mass.: M.I.T. Press, 1960. 350–77

"Two Aspects of Language and Two Types of Aphasic Disturbance." Roman Jakobson and Morris Halle. *Fundamentals of Language*. 4th edition. The Hague: Mouton, 1980. 89–96

Jameson, Fredric. *The Political Unconscious: Narrative as a Socially Symbolic Act*. Ithaca: Cornell University Press, 1981

Jauss, Hans Robert. "Literary History as a Challenge to Literary Theory." *NLH* 2 (1970): 7–37

Javitch, Daniel. *Poetry and Courtliness in Renaissance England*. Princeton: Princeton University Press, 1978

Johnson, Lee M. "Milton's Blank Verse Sonnets." *Milton Studies* v (1973): 129–53

Jones, Florence. "T. S. Eliot Among the Prophets." *American Literature* 38 (1966); 285–302

Jonson, Ben. *Timber*. Ed. Felix C. Schelling. Boston, 1892

Jordan, Robert M. *Chaucer and the Shape of Creation: The Aesthetic Possibilities of Inorganic Structure*. Cambridge, Mass.: Harvard University Press, 1967

"The Narrator in Chaucer's *Troilus*." *ELH* 25 (1958): 237–57

Kaminsky, Alice R. *Chaucer's Troilus and Criseyde and the Critics*. Athens, Ohio: Ohio University Press, 1980

Kellogg, Robert. "Oral Narrative, Written Books." *Genre* 10 (1977): 655–65

Kenner, Hugh. *The Invisible Poet: T. S. Eliot*. London: Methuen and Co., 1965

Kermode, Frank. "Adam Unparadised." *The Living Milton*, ed. Frank Kermode. London: Routledge and Kegan Paul, 1960, pp. 85–123

The Genesis of Secrecy: On the Interpretation of Narrative. Cambridge, Mass.: Harvard University Press, 1979

Novel and Narrative. Glasgow: University of Glasgow Press, 1972

The Sense of an Ending: Studies in the Theory of Fiction. 1967. New York: Oxford University Press, 1981

"Sensing Endings." *Nineteenth Century Fiction* 33 (1978): 144–158

Kerrigan, William. *The Prophetic Milton*. Charlottesville: University Press of Virginia, 1974

The Sacred Complex: On the Psychogenesis of Paradise Lost. Cambridge, Mass.: Harvard University Press, 1983

Kerrigan, William and Gordon Braden. "Milton's Coy Eve: *Paradise Lost* and Renaissance Love Poetry." *ELH* 53 (1986): 27–51

Kittredge, G. L. "Chaucer's *Troilus* and Guillaume de Machaut." *MLN* 30 (1915): 69

Kouwenhoven, Jan Karel. *Apparent Narrative as Thematic Metaphor: The Organization of The Faerie Queene*. Oxford: Clarendon Press, 1983

Lawlor, Nancy K. "Eliot's Use of Rhyming Quatrains in *The Waste Land*." *Poet and Critic* 4 (1967): 29–37

Leavis, F. R. "*The Waste Land*." *T. S. Eliot: A Collection of Critical Essays*. Ed. Hugh Kenner. Englewood Cliffs: Prentice-Hall, Inc., 1962. 89–103

Lenz, Joseph M. *The Promised End: Romance Closure in the Gawain Poet, Malory, Spenser and Shakespeare*. New York and Berne: Peter Lang, 1986

Lewalski, Barbara Kiefer. *Paradise Lost and the Rhetoric of Literary Forms*. Princeton: Princeton University Press, 1985

"Structure and the Symbolism of Vision in Michael's Prophecy: *Paradise Lost* Books XI–XII." *PQ* 42 (1963): 38–52

Lewis, C. S. *The Allegory of Love: A Study in Medieval Tradition*. 1936. New York: Oxford University Press, 1958

A Preface to Paradise Lost. New York: Oxford University Press, 1942

Lockhart, Adrienne. "Semantic, Moral and Aesthetic Degeneration in *Troilus and Criseyde*." *ChauR* 8 (1973): 100–18

Lodge, David. *The Language of Fiction.* New York: Columbia University Press, 1966

The Modes of Modern Writing: Metaphor, Metonymy and the Typology of Modern Literature. Ithaca: Cornell University Press, 1977

Loewenstein, David. *Milton and the Drama of History: Historical Vision, Iconoclasm, and the Literary Imagination.* Cambridge: Cambridge University Press, 1990

Lovejoy, Arthur O. "Milton and the Paradox of the Fortunate Fall." *Journal of English Literary History* 4 (1937): 161–79

McAlpine, Monica E. *The Genre of Troilus and Criseyde.* Ithaca: Cornell University Press, 1978

MacCaffrey, Isabel G. *Paradise Lost as "Myth."* Cambridge, Mass.: Harvard University Press, 1959

Spenser's Allegory: The Anatomy of Imagination. Princeton: Princeton University Press, 1976

McCall, John C. "The Trojan Scene in Chaucer's *Troilus.*" *ELH* 29 (1962): 263–75

MacCallum, H. R. "Milton and Sacred History: Books XI and XII of *Paradise Lost.*" *Essays in English Literature from the Renaissance to the Victorian Age.* Ed. Millar MacLure and F. W. Watt. Toronto: University of Toronto Press, 1964. 149–68

Manning, Stephen. "*Troilus*, Book V: Invention and the Poem as Process." *ChauR* 18 (1984): 288–303

Martin, Wallace. *Recent Theories of Narrative.* Ithaca: Cornell University Press, 1986

Maxwell, J. C. "The Truancy of Calidore." *ELH* 19 (1952): 143–49

Meech, Sanford B. *Design in Chaucer's Troilus.* Syracuse: Syracuse University Press, 1959

Mellard, James M. *Doing Tropology: Analysis of Narrative Discourse.* Urbana: University of Illinois Press, 1987

Miller, D. A. *Narrative and Its Discontents: Problems of Closure in The Traditional Novel.* Princeton: Princeton University Press, 1981

Miller, David Lee. *The Poem's Two Bodies: The Poetics of the 1590 Faerie Queene.* Princeton: Princeton University Press, 1988

Miller, Jacqueline T. *Poetic License: Authority and Authorship in Medieval and Renaissance Contexts.* New York and Oxford: Oxford University Press, 1986

Milton, John. *The Complete Prose Works.* Ed. Maurice Kelley. New Haven: Yale University Press, 1973. Vol. IV

Paradise Lost. Ed. Alastair Fowler. London: Longman, 1976

Miner, Earl. "The Reign of Narrative in *Paradise Lost.*" *Milton Studies* 17 (1983): 3–25

Miskimin, Alice. *The Renaissance Chaucer*. New Haven: Yale University Press, 1975
Mollenkott, Virginia R. "Milton's Technique of Multiple Choice." *Milton Studies* 6 (1975): 101–11
Monroe, Jonathan. *A Poverty of Objects: The Prose Poem and the Politics of Genre*. Ithaca: Cornell University Press, 1987
Moody, A. D. *Thomas Stearns Eliot: Poet*. Cambridge: Cambridge University Press, 1979
Mulder, John R. "The Lyric Dimension of *Paradise Lost*." *Milton Studies* 23 (1987): 145–63
Murrin, Michael. "The Language of Milton's Heaven." *MP* 74 (1977): 350–65
Muscatine, Charles. *Chaucer and the French Tradition: A Study in Style and Meaning*. Berkeley and Los Angeles: University of California Press, 1957
Nelson, William. *Fact or Fiction: The Dilemma of the Renaissance Storyteller*. Cambridge, Mass.: Harvard University Press, 1973
The Poetry of Edmund Spenser: A Study. New York: Columbia University Press, 1963
Neuse, Richard. "Book VI as Conclusion to *The Faerie Queene*." *ELH* 35 (1968): 329–53
Nevo, Ruth. "*The Waste Land*: Ur-Text of Deconstruction." *NLH* 13 (1982): 453–61
Nohrnberg, James. *The Analogy of The Faerie Queene*. Princeton: Princeton University Press, 1976
Nolan, Barbara. *Chaucer and the Tradition of the Roman Antique*. Cambridge: Cambridge University Press, 1992.
Nyquist, Mary. "The Father's Word/Satan's Wrath." *PMLA* 100 (1985): 187–202
"Reading the Fall: Discourse and Drama in *Paradise Lost*." *ELR* 14 (1984): 199–229
Ovid. *Metamorphoses*. 2 vols. Trans. Frank Justus Miller. 3rd edn., rev. G. P. Goold. The Loeb Classical Library. Cambridge, Mass.: Harvard University Press, 1977
Owen, Charles A., Jr. "Mimetic Form in the Central Love Scene of *Troilus and Criseyde*." *MP* 67 (1969): 125–32
Paige, D. D. (ed). *The Letters of Ezra Pound 1907–1941*. New York: Harcourt, Brace, 1950
Parker, Patricia A. *Inescapable Romance: Studies in the Poetics of a Mode*. Princeton: Princeton University Press, 1979
Payne, Robert O. *The Key of Remembrance: A Study of Chaucer's Poetics*. New Haven: Yale University Press, 1963
Poggioli, Renato. *The Oaten Flute: Essays on Pastoral Poetry and the*

Pastoral Ideal. Cambridge, Mass.: Harvard University Press, 1975

Prince, F. T. *The Italian Element in Milton's Verse.* Oxford: Clarendon Press, 1954

"On the Last Two Books of *Paradise Lost.*" *Essays and Studies* 11 (1958): 38–52

Provost, William. *The Structure of Chaucer's Troilus and Criseyde.* Copenhagen: Rosenkilde and Bagger, 1974

Purcell, J. M. "Rime in *Paradise Lost.*" *MLN* 59 (1944): 171–72

Puttenham, George. *The Arte of English Poesie. Elizabethan Critical Essays.* Ed. G. Gregory Smith. Oxford: Clarendon Press, 1904. Volume II

Quilligan, Maureen. *The Language of Allegory: Defining the Genre.* Ithaca: Cornell University Press, 1979

Milton's Spenser: The Politics of Reading. Ithaca: Cornell University Press, 1983

Revard, Stella P. *The War in Heaven: Paradise Lost and the Tradition of Satan's Rebellion.* Ithaca: Cornell University Press, 1980

Ricks, Christopher. *Milton's Grand Style.* Oxford: Clarendon Press, 1963

Ricoeur, Paul. *The Rule of Metaphor: Multidisciplinary Studies of the Creation of Meaning in Language.* Trans. Robert Czerny *et al.* Toronto: University of Toronto Press, 1977

Riggs, William G. "The Poet and Satan in *Paradise Lost.*" *Milton Studies* 2 (1970): 59–82

Rimmon-Kenan, Shlomith. *Narrative Fiction: Contemporary Poetics.* London: Methuen, 1983

Rosenblatt, Jason P. "Milton's Chief Rabbi." *Milton Studies* 24 (1988): 43–71

Rosenthal, M. L. "*The Waste Land* as an Open Structure." *Mosaic* 6 (1972): 181–89

Rosenthal, M. L. and Sally M. Gall. *The Modern Poetic Sequence: The Genius of Modern Poetry.* New York: Oxford University Press, 1983

Rosmarin, Adena. *The Power of Genre.* Minneapolis: University of Minnesota Press, 1985

Saccone, Eduardo. "*Grazia, Sprezzatura, Affettazione* in *The Courtier.*" *Castiglione: The Ideal and the Real in Renaissance Culture.* Ed. Robert W. Hanning and David Rosand. New Haven: Yale University Press, 1983

Said, Edward W. *Beginnings: Intention and Method.* New York: Basic Books, 1975

"Molestation and Authority in Narrative Fiction." *Aspects of Narrative: Selected Papers from the English Institute.* Ed. J. Hillis Miller. New York: Columbia University Press, 1971. 47–68

Sale, Roger. *Reading Spenser: An Introduction to The Faerie Queene*. New York: Random House, 1968

Samuels, Peggy. "Milton's Use of Sonnet Form in *Paradise Lost*." *Milton Studies* 24 (1988): 141–54

Schless, Howard H. *Chaucer and Dante: A Revaluation*. Norman, Oklahoma: Pilgrim Books, 1984

Scholes, Robert. *Structuralism in Literature: An Introduction*. New Haven: Yale University Press, 1974

Scholes, Robert and Robert Kellogg. *The Nature of Narrative*. New York: Oxford University Press, 1966

Schwartz, Regina M. *Remembering and Repeating: Biblical Creation in Paradise Lost*. Cambridge: Cambridge University Press, 1988

Shakespeare, William. *The Tempest*. Ed. Robert Langbaum. New York: New American Library, Inc., 1964

Shawcross, John T. "The Rhetor as Creator in *Paradise Lost*." *Milton Studies* 8 (1975): 209–19

Shepherd, G. T. "*Troilus and Criseyde*." *Chaucer and Chaucerians: Critical Studies in Middle English Literature*. Ed. D. S. Brewer. University, Alabama: University of Alabama Press, 1966. 65–87

Shepherd, Robert (ed.). *Paradise Lost by John Milton: A Prose Rendition*. New York: Seabury Press, 1983

Sherry, Beverly. "Speech in *Paradise Lost*." *Milton Studies* 8 (1975): 247–66

Shoaf, R. Allen. "Dante's *Commedia* and Chaucer's Theory of Mediation: A Preliminary Sketch." *New Perspectives in Chaucer Criticism*. Ed. Donald M. Rose. Norman: Pilgrim Books, 1981. 83–103

Shore, David R. *Spenser and the Poetics of Pastoral*. Kingston & Montreal: McGill-Queen's University Press, 1985

Sidney, Sir Philip. *A Defence of Poetry*. Ed. Jan Van Dorsten. Oxford: Oxford University Press, 1982

Sims, James H. "The Miltonic Narrator and the Scriptural Tradition: An Afterword." *Milton and Scriptural Tradition: The Bible into Poetry*. Ed. James H. Sims and Leland Ryken. Columbia: University of Missouri Press, 1984

Snare, Gerald. "The Poetics of Vision: Patterns of Grace and Courtesy in *The Faerie Queene*, VI." *Renaissance Papers* (1974): 1–8

Spearing, A. C. *Chaucer: Troilus and Criseyde*. London: E. Arnold, 1976

Criticism and Medieval Poetry. New York: Barnes & Noble, 1964

"Narrative Closure: the End of *Troilus and Criseyde*." *Readings in Medieval Poetry*. Cambridge: Cambridge University Press, 1987. 107–33

Spenser, Edmund. *The Faerie Queene*. Ed. Thomas P. Roche, Jr. *et al.* New Haven: Yale University Press, 1981

The Yale Edition of the Shorter Poems of Edmund Spenser. Ed. William A. Oram *et al.* New Haven: Yale University Press, 1989

Steadman, John M. *Disembodied Laughter: Troilus and the Apotheosis Tradition*. Berkeley and Los Angeles: University of California Press, 1972

Epic and Tragic Structure in Paradise Lost. Chicago: University of Chicago Press, 1976

Stein, Arnold. *The Art of Presence: The Poet and Paradise Lost*. Berkeley and Los Angeles: University of California Press, 1977

Stewart, Stanley. "Sir Calidore and 'Closure.'" *SEL* 24 (1984): 69–86

Summers, Joseph H. *The Muse's Method: An Introduction to Paradise Lost*. New York: W. W. Norton and Co., 1968

Tasso, Torquato. *Discourses on the Heroic Poem*. Trans. Mariella Cavalchini and Irene Samuel. Oxford: Clarendon Press, 1973

Tayler, Edward W. *Milton's Poetry: Its Development in Time*. Pittsburgh: Duquesne University Press, 1979

Taylor, Davis. "The Terms of Love: A Study of Troilus' Style." *Chaucer's Troilus: Essays in Criticism*. Ed. Stephen A. Barney. Hamden, Ct.: Archon Books, 1980. 231–56

Taylor, Karla. *Chaucer Reads The Divine Comedy*. Stanford: Stanford University Press, 1989

"Proverbs and the Authentication of Convention in *Troilus and Criseyde*." *Chaucer's Troilus: Essays in Criticism*. Ed. Stephen A. Barney. Hamden, Ct.: Archon Books, 1980: 277–96

Teskey, Gordon. "From Allegory to Dialectic: Imagining Error in Spenser and Milton." *PMLA* 101 (1986): 9–23

Todorov, Tzvetan. *Grammaire du Décaméron*. The Hague: Mouton, 1969

The Poetics of Prose. Trans. Richard Howard. Ithaca: Cornell University Press, 1977

Toliver, Harold. *Animate Illusions: Explorations of Narrative Structure*. Lincoln, Nebraska: University of Nebraska Press, 1974

Tomashevsky, Boris. "Thematics." 1925. *Russian Formalist Criticism: Four Essays*. Ed. Lee T. Lemon and Marion J. Reis. Lincoln, Nebraska: University of Nebraska Press, 1965. 61–95

Tonkin, Humphrey. *Spenser's Courteous Pastoral: Book VI of The Faerie Queene*. Oxford: Clarendon Press, 1972

Toolan, Michael J. *Narrative: A Critical Linguistic Introduction*. London and New York: Routledge, 1988

Van, Thomas A. "Chaucer's Pandarus as an Earthly Maker." *Southern Humanities Review* 12 (1978): 89–97

Vance, Eugene. *Mervelous Signals: Poetics and Sign Theory in the Middle Ages*. Lincoln, Nebraska: University of Nebraska Press, 1986

Vinaver, Eugène. *The Rise of Romance*. Oxford: Clarendon Press, 1971

Virgil. *Eclogues, Georgics, Aeneid* I–VI. Trans. H. Rushton Fairclough. Rev. edn. The Loeb Classical Library. Cambridge, Mass.: Harvard University Press, 1974

Waller, Gary. *English Poetry of the Sixteenth Century*. London and New York: Longman, 1986

Warton, Thomas. *Observations on The Faerie Queene of Spenser*. London, 1762. Volume II

Waswo, Richard. "The Narrator of *Troilus and Criseyde*." *ELH* 50 (1983): 1–25

Webber, Joan Malory. *Milton and His Epic Tradition*. Seattle: University of Washington Press, 1979

Wellek, René and Austin Warren. *Theory of Literature*. 3rd edn. New York: Harcourt, Brace and World, Inc., 1973

Werman, Golda. "Milton's Use of Rabbinical Material." *Milton Studies* 21 (1985): 34–47

Weston, Jessie L. *From Ritual to Romance*. 1920. Garden City: Doubleday Anchor, 1957

Wetherbee, Winthrop. *Chaucer and the Poets: An Essay on Troilus and Criseyde*. Ithaca: Cornell University Press, 1984

Whaler, James. *Counterpoint and Symbol: An Inquiry into the Rhythm of Milton's Epic Style*. Copenhagen: Rosenkilde & Bagger, 1956

"The Miltonic Simile." *PMLA* 48 (1931): 1034–74

Whiting, Bartlett J. *Chaucer's Use of Proverbs*. Cambridge, Mass.: Harvard University Press, 1934

Williams, Arnold. *The Common Expositor: An Account of the Commentaries upon Genesis 1527–1633*. Chapel Hill: University of North Carolina Press, 1948

Flower on a Lowly Stalk: The Sixth Book of The Faerie Queene. East Lansing: Michigan State University Press, 1967

Williams, Helen. *T. S. Eliot: The Waste Land*. London: Edward Arnold, 1968

Wimsatt, James I. "The French Lyric Element in Chaucer's *Troilus and Criseyde*." *YES* 15 (1985): 18–32

"Guillaume de Machaut and Chaucer's *Troilus and Criseyde*." *Medium Aevum* 45 (1976): 277–93

"Realism in *Troilus and Criseyde* and the *Roman de la Rose*." *Chaucer Studies III: Essays on Troilus and Criseyde*. Ed. Mary Salu. Totowa: Rowman & Littlefield, 1979. 43–56

Wimsatt, W. K. *The Verbal Icon: Studies in the Meaning of Poetry.* Lexington: University of Kentucky Press, 1954

Wind, Edgar. *Pagan Mysteries in the Renaissance.* Revised edn. New York: W. W. Norton and Co., 1968

Windeatt, Barry. "Chaucer and the *Filostrato.*" *Chaucer and the Italian Trecento.* Ed. Piero Boitani. Cambridge: Cambridge University Press, 1983. 163–84

"Classical and Medieval Elements in Chaucer's *Troilus.*" *The European Tragedy of Troilus.* Ed. Piero Boitani. Oxford: Clarendon Press, 1989. 111–31

Wofford, Susanne Lindgren. "Britomart's Petrarchan Lament: Allegory and Narrative in *The Faerie Queene* III, iv." *Comparative Literature* 39 (1987): 28–57

Wollaeger, Mark A. "Apocryphal Narration: Milton, Raphael and the Book of Tobit." *Milton Studies* 21 (1985): 137–56

Wright, H. G. (ed.) *A Seventeeth-Century Modernization of the First Three Books of Chaucer's Troilus and Criseyde.* Bern: Francke Verlag, 1960

Yearwood, Stephenie. "The Rhetoric of Narrative Rendering in Chaucer's *Troilus.*" *ChauR* 12 (1977): 27–37

Zimbardo, Rose A. "Creator and Created: The Generic Perspective of Chaucer's *Troilus and Criseyde.*" *ChaurR* 11 (1977): 283–98

Index

Lightning Source UK Ltd.
Milton Keynes UK
UKHW010623051222
413357UK00001B/14

9 780521 107808